Poetry

2nd Edition

by John Timpane

The Poetry Center

at San Francisco State University

Marina Watts

Poetry For Dummies®, 2nd Edition

Published by: **John Wiley & Sons, Inc.**, 111 River Street, Hoboken, NJ 07030-5774, www.wiley.com

For general information on our other products and services, please contact our Customer Care Department within the U.S. at 877-762-2974, outside the U.S. at 317-572-3993, or fax 317-572-4002. For technical support, please visit https://hub.wiley.com/community/support/dummies.

Wiley publishes in a variety of print and electronic formats and by print-on-demand. Some material included with standard print versions of this book may not be included in e-books or in print-on-demand. If this book refers to media that is not included in the version you purchased, you may download this material at http://booksupport.wiley.com. For more information about Wiley products, visit www.wiley.com.

Library of Congress Control Number is available from the publisher.

ISBN 978-1-394-37555-4 (pbk); ISBN 978-1-394-37557-8 (epdf); ISBN 978-1-394-37556-1 (epub)

SKY10150597_032526

Table of Contents

Introduction

Suppose you invented a way to concentrate all the best things people ever thought and felt into a very few words. And suppose you *did* something to those words to make them pleasant, beautiful, unforgettable, and moving. Suppose this invention could get people to notice more of their own lives, sharpen their awareness, pay attention to things they'd never really considered before. Suppose it could make their lives — and them — better.

You'd really have something there.

Well, don't look now, but that invention has been around for thousands of years. Millions of people love it and make it part of their lives. They turn to it when they need a smile, a lift, or a moment of thoughtfulness. And millions of people write it, too.

What is this fantastic creation? Poetry. And it includes the work of Homer, Sappho, Kalidasa, Dante, Shakespeare, Ono no Komachi, Keats, Bashō, Byron, Whitman, Dickinson, Frost, Yeats, Plath, Ginsberg, Adrienne Rich, Gerald Stern, Lucille Clifton, Billy Collins, Mary Oliver, Joy Harjo, Martín Espada, Lena Kalaf Tuffaha, and many others. It's been a great five millennia, and we're starting the sixth in better shape than ever.

For most of the world's poetry-writing human beings, sure, the life of poetry consists of being moved to write, sitting down, and writing, drafting, working on revision, getting it right. And it may not go any further. It is an *avocation*, a beloved occupation that can be as important to them as anything else they do. But just as musicians play for hearers, painters have exhibitions, and dancers hold recitals, poets also perform.

Poetry saw a tremendous surge in popularity at the end of the 20th century — from Magnetic Poetry mania to the explosion of poetry slams across the country to an increased public appreciation of poets. And here in the 21st century, poetry continues to win more and more people over. And why not? It's great stuff. In the first quarter of that century, a new world of poets and poetry has arisen, online and off: the poetic community, where like-minded people practice the art that makes them happy, amid (if they wish) other folks who are practicing the same art. More fine poets, more fine poems, and more chances to be part of the poetry scene are open to people than ever before. Thanks to rap, hip-hop, slam poetry, and other innovations, several generations have grown up loving language and its poetic superpowers. Old anti-poetry prejudices — concerning poetry and "how it's taught," how poetry supposedly "makes people feel dumb" — are by now increasingly outdated, gripes from a former century.

As of the 21st century's third decade, poets have an unprecedented range of ways to get in touch with the poetry world — and to bring readers, in turn, *to* their work. A new upright species of biped has emerged: Entrepreneurial Poets, people who work hard in many delightful ways to let the world know what they're doing. In Chapter 17 we discuss those poets, what they do, and why you might like to try some of it yourself.

We love poetry so much that we wrote this book. Most poets write poems for anyone willing to read and listen. But sometimes between the poet's notebook and the listening public a break occurs. Our hope and vision was to offer a book that gets past the things that sometimes have divided poets and readers, things like technique, style, and school or genre, and the sometimes unaccountable, seemingly random way books, journals, and literary magazines are distributed.

Our goal in writing *Poetry For Dummies* was to bridge the literary gaps and throw open the doors of poetry — past, present, and future — to all. We hope that if you say you "don't get" poetry or "don't like" poetry, this book just may change your mind.

We do have a promise for you. If you let poetry into your life — if you read aloud and read attentively, discover how to *interpret* poetry for yourself — you'll start seeing benefits, including a broader life, a more sensitive awareness, and a more flexible spirit.

If you are a poet or want to try your hand at poetry, welcome to an ancient and ever-changing craft with many traditions, challenges, and rewards.

About This Book

Poetry For Dummies, 2nd Edition, is for everyone with an interest in reading, interpreting, or writing poetry. We hope you will discover poets you haven't heard of or read before, revisit some old favorites, and pick up some pointers on poetry that will bring you a new understanding and enjoyment of the art.

You can use this book's writing exercises to brush up on your writing skills, add structure to your writing life, or help you break out of writer's block. Have a broken heart and want to write a traditional poem to bring your loved one back?

Check out the section on writing sonnets and traditional forms (we offer no guarantees, of course).

Besides being a good introduction to the history of world poetry, *Poetry For Dummies* also offers a lot of practical information. Not sure of a literary term? Check the Index, which will lead you to places in the book where we discuss that term, or find this book's online Cheat Sheet, in one of which we define 20 or so mega-important terms. Read on for where to find advice about reading poetry, writing it, reading circles, slams, publication, and related issues.

When you start thinking about poetry, you will notice it's all around you. We give you tips on where to find it, where to find (or participate in!) poetry readings and other events, and which lit mags to read for the latest good stuff.

These are just a few of the ways you can make use of this book. The rest, as they say, is up to you.

To make the book more accessible, we divided it into five parts:

- Part 1: Reading and Understanding Poetry
- Part 2: An Intelligent Hustle Through Poetic History
- Part 3: Writing Poetry and Finding Community
- Part 4: The Part of Tens
- Part 5: Appendixes

Icons Used in This Book

Throughout the book, you will encounter *icons,* which are the pictures in the margin that alert you to a special feature, or a piece of information, advice, or instruction. They're meant to help direct you to the indispensable moments, the absolute honey of the book. We use the following seven icons:

TIP

This icon pops up whenever we encounter something truly inspiring, when you can really see the insight and invigoration of poetry happening right before your eyes. When you see this icon, you can count on finding an essential bit of advice that will make you a better reader, interpreter, or writer of poetry.

REMEMBER

Some thoughts are simply essential, such as the sentence, "Poetry is meant to be read aloud." Because such sentences appear more than once, we tag them with this icon so you remember to put them in your brain for keeps.

This icon points to historical or technical information of great value. So open up your brain and get ready to get technical. But if you're just looking for the basics on a subject, you can skip over the information flagged by this icon and come back later when you have more time.

When you see this icon, you know to avoid the idea or habit it highlights. Or at least handle the topic gently.

This is one icon you see a lot of throughout this book. Whenever you see this icon next to a passage we quote, we mean for you to read the passage aloud. Poetry is meant to be read aloud for the best and fullest effect. This is your opportunity to give your voice to poetry. And if you seize that opportunity, you'll get the most out of *Poetry For Dummies.*

Beyond the Book

The *Poetry For Dummies,* 2nd Edition, Cheat Sheet extends the reach of this book. It gives you inroads to poetry, new resources, and new ways to sharpen your poetic game. To check out this book's online Cheat Sheet, go to `www.dummies.com` and search for "Poetry For Dummies Cheat Sheet."

Where to Go from Here

Poetry is for everyone. Poets write for the world, which, last time we checked, is where you live. And knowing about poetry can make your world better.

The idea is not to know it *all;* nobody ever could. The idea is to get *started,* to discover a little about how poetry works and how writing poetry works, and then blaze your own path. Think of this book as your first step in forging your very own personal taste in poetry, or in exploring your own powers as a poet. Talk about the thrill of beginnings! So what are you waiting for? Turn the page and start.

1 Reading and Understanding Poetry

IN THIS PART . . .

See what poetry is, why people have been reading and writing it for thousands of years, how to live the life of a poet, and how you can bring more poetry into your life — even write a little.

Discover how crucial reading aloud is to understanding and sharing poetry, and how to give body, expressiveness, and power to your own reading.

Get to know poetry as a storytelling medium.

Become more and more sensitive to language, the material out of which poets create their art.

Lean in to interpretation, the solid gold, the practice of accounting for what the poem means and how it makes you feel.

IN THIS CHAPTER

» Knowing what sets poetry apart from other kinds of writing

» Creating your own poetry

Chapter 1
Knowing Poetry When You See It

To like poetry, you don't have to join some secret club, wear a moose hat with antlers, stand on one leg, and recite secret ritual formulas in Greek . . . although that would be fascinating, and we'd be happy to watch if you volunteer.

Poetry is something human beings have always done and always loved. Lots of people love it. A 2017 survey by the National Endowment of the Arts (not that we need a survey to say this) estimated that in the United States, about 22.4 million people had read poetry at least once in the preceding year.

Interested in the poetry world? Come along. In this chapter, we give you a working definition of poetry itself; discuss why people have been writing it for thousands of years; focus on reading poetry — especially, reading it aloud; list some great places to find more poetry; and if all this talk about poetry has inspired you (and we hope it has!), we invite you to dive right in and write a poem of your own.

Poetry as Art and Exploration

Poetry is the practice of creating artworks using language. Sculptors use marble, steel, cardboard, goose liver pâté, or whatever material they choose. Musicians use sound. Painters use paint. Furniture-makers use woods and fabrics. And poets use language.

Poetry differs from other uses of language, however. Here are five things almost all poetry has *more of*:

- **Attentiveness:** Poets are extremely careful with the way they use language. They pay extremely close, constant attention to everything from spelling to the way the words sound, what they mean, even how many letters they have. They think — and think *hard* — about punctuation and the spaces between and around words. Most people simply don't pay as much attention to these details, but paying attention is the poet's job. And poets want *you* to pay that sort of attention, too — to the language you read and the life you live.
- **Concentration:** Poetry has more meaning, music, and emotion per word, syllable, and letter than other kinds of writing.
- **Experiment:** Poets try to use language in as many new, surprising, and challenging ways as they can to startle, awaken, or challenge you.
- **Originality:** Poetry says or does something new to make something new happen in the reader's mind. Here are some examples:
  - Totally fresh observations about life
  - Neat ways of saying something many other people have thought or said
  - Refreshing flourishes of sheer sound or rhythm

  REMEMBER

  You can tell something is original when it doesn't do or say things you've seen elsewhere. Poetry finds its own way.
- **Form:** Poetry very often involves *form* — the very shape or structure a particular group of words takes. And all forms carry their own worlds of meaning.

REMEMBER

Short stories and novels are language-based works of art, too. But poetry usually has a greater degree of attentiveness, concentration, experimentation, and form than you find in most other uses of language.

Poets explore the universe through the written word. That includes any experience you can have. Here are some poems that explore very particular things. *Look up one or a few of these and read them. Feel what the poet is trying to do.* Find. Read. Re-read. Ponder. Love:

- The world of dreams and fantasies, as in "dream where every black person is standing by the ocean" by Danez Smith (`https://poets.org/poem/dream-where-every-black-person-standing-ocean`)
- The taste of a cold plum, as in "This Is Just to Say" by William Carlos Williams (`www.poetryfoundation.org/poems/56159/this-is-just-to-say`)
- Leaving someone you love, as in "Leave-Taking" by Louise Bogan (`www.poetryfoundation.org/poetrymagazine/poems/15668/leave-taking`)
- Imaginary worlds with imaginary inhabitants, as in "The Man He Imagined" by Nicanor Parra (`www.nicanorparra.uchile.cl/english/antipoems/manimagined.html`)
- All the things the moon means, as in "Moon Ghazal" by Dorianne Laux (`www.poetryfoundation.org/poetrymagazine/poems/159041/moon-ghazal`)
- The relationship between human beings and God, as in "I Asked God for the Moon" by Natasha Oladokun (`https://artlitlab.org/all-review/i-asked-god-for-the-moon`)

You can find out more about these poets with a tap of your keyboard or an afternoon at the bookstore or library. If some of these poems take you unexpected places, consider how you felt when you got there. Poetry involves exploration. Happy exploring!

Why Do People Write Poetry?

TIP

No one could cover all the motivations for writing poetry. But most poets are trying to do one or both of the following:

- Create an intense emotional experience.
- Draw attention to something true, revealing, enlightening, or entertaining.

Poets often have other important motivations, too — such as telling a story or exploring language itself (read "Silent Poem" by Robert Francis, Chapter 2, or "Vermont Apollinaire" by William Corbett, Chapter 14).

Figure 1-1 shows Ada Limón, then Poet Laureate of the United States, take the mic at Great Smoky Mountains National Park in Gatlin, Tennessee, on July 20, 2024. The event was part of her signature project, You Are Here: Poetry in Parks (`https://go.nps.gov/poetryinparks`).

But to get started, let's stay with our two main, sweeping goals.

FIGURE 1-1: Ada Limón, then-Poet Laureate of the United States, takes the mic at Great Smoky Mountains National Park, Gatlinburg, Tennessee, on July 20, 2024.

Photo: NPS/Camille Bennett. Public domain

Creating an intense emotional experience

Poetry constantly presents its readers with bursts of concentrated emotion. Some poems celebrate days of joy or triumph. Others praise God, mourn the dead, or exult in the universe. The more attention you pay to poetry, the more you'll savor such surges of passion and understanding.

Ben Jonson lived at the same time as Shakespeare. Here, he writes a poem of farewell to his son Ben, who has died at just 7 years old. The poem contains a little Renaissance English (words that you may trip over initially), but only a little. Read the poem silently, and then read it aloud:

READ ALOUD

On My First Son

Farewell, thou child of my right hand, and joy;
My sin was too much hope of thee, loved boy:
Seven years thou wert leant to me, and I thee pay,
Exacted by thy fate, on the just day.
O could I lose all father now! For why,
Will man lament the state he should envy,
To have so soon 'scaped world's and flesh's rage,
And if no other misery, yet age?
Rest in soft peace, and asked, say, "Here doth lie
Ben Jonson his best piece of poetry."
For whose sake henceforth all his vows be such.
As what he loves may never like too much.

TIP

Here are some words and phrases that may be unfamiliar:

- **child of my right hand:** The name *Benjamin* means "son of the right hand" in Hebrew, so this phrase both means "son of whom I'm especially proud" and puns on the name of both father and son.
- **thou wert:** You were.
- **The just day:** The day on which payment is due on a debt. The boy was "lent" to the speaker for seven years, and then "fate" (the lender) "exacted" (required) repayment on the due date.
- **O could I lose all father now!** This passage could mean, "Now I am no longer a father," or "After such pain, I never want to be a father again."
- **'scaped:** Escaped.
- **And if no other misery, yet age:** Even if his son escaped no other misery, at least he escaped getting old.
- **Ben Jonson his:** "Ben Jonson's."
- **Whose/his:** The *whose* refers to little Ben; the *his* refers to his father, the speaker of the poem.

"On My First Son" is a quiet, dignified poem, but its concentrated emotion is unmistakable. Notice that Jonson never refers directly to his own pain. The line "O could I lose all father now!" is the closest the poem comes. But great suffering lies within the poem's tender restraint. "Rest in soft peace" is one of the saddest, most fatherly leave-takings in all poetry. The pun on the name *Benjamin* and in "best piece of poetry" (the son is the best "poem" Ben Jonson ever created) suggest, without outright statement, the father's fondness for his son. So does that closing vow — to love things in this world, but never again to become attached to them. You may be asking: "But can he, can anyone, really do that?" Well, what do you think? This Ben Jonson is good, right? He does what poets everywhere try to do: Lead you into intense encounters with reality and feeling.

Drawing attention to something real

Let's admit it: most of us are so busy living our lives that we don't pay attention to what's around us. Poets, in the meantime, are constantly inviting readers to stay alert to the things of this world — both familiar things that become invisible to you through habit, and miraculous things, right in front of you, that you're too busy to notice.

Japanese master-poet Issa captures an exquisite moment:

READ ALOUD

morning:
one deer licks
snow from the other's
coat

This delicate image suggests it's a cold morning and the deer have spent the night out in the snow. Issa doesn't have to comment; he simply lets the truth show and lets you marvel. You may find the words meaningful, or you may find no meaning beyond their beauty. Either way, making the moment into a poem was worth it.

Li Bai, a Chinese poet from the T'ang Dynasty (618–907), mistakes one thing for another and gives you a vivid experience that ends on a meditative note:

READ ALOUD

Moonlight pools at the head of my bed —
I mistook it for frost blanketing the earth!
I look up: see the moon on the mountain;
I look down: think long thoughts of home.

Imagination is led from *moonlight* to *frost* and back again. After realizing it *is* moonlight, the speaker follows it up to the source of the light itself. Neat, right? A call to be sensitive, just like the Issa poem earlier in this section — but then the speaker looks down and becomes nostalgic. Maybe it was something about seeing the moon on the mountain. Sometimes that happens: An image out of nature unlocks old memories, unexpected feelings.

Ben Jonson, Issa, and Li Bai lead us to unspoken yet still powerful emotions and meanings. They beckon us to *speculate*, make connections for ourselves.

Poetry invites you to pay attention. It's a way to expand your awareness, your understanding, your store of experience.

Bringing Poetry into Your Life

Poetry is all around us. It's in the subways in London, Chicago, New York, and elsewhere; it's also in urban graffiti. Many of us post poems on the refrigerator, next to the bed, or on office walls, just to have inspiration near. A friend of ours has Robert Frost's "A Swinger of Birches" on the fridge. Another has "Wild Geese" by Mary Oliver. (Look these up and read them. If you like them, share them on social media!)

Online, you can connect to poetry from all over the world, sampling the best of all time for the cost of logging on. Oh, yes, and of course there are books and magazines. Part 4 of this book contains twenty poems to get you started.

In the following sections, we glance at a few ways you can inject some more poetry into your life.

Online is just fine

Thousands of websites feature poetry, and they're yours for the reading. In Chapter 11, we state the monumental, obvious truth: The Digital Age just blew the roof off the poetry world. Reading poetry, writing it, getting it published, reading in public — it's all changed in a very cool way.

Consider Emily Dickinson. We asked Google Gemini (an AI chatbot) how many websites mention her. Gemini immediately rolled over on its back, belly up: a "specific count of web pages mentioning Emily Dickinson is unattainable." Gosh, thanks! So, we typed *Emily Dickinson* into a search field, and the fun began. We get a photo, birth and death dates. We get a link — this is just delicious, really — to no less than *Forbes* magazine, "10 Famous Emily Dickinson Poems Worth the Read" (`www.forbes.com/sites/entertainment/article/emily-dickinson-poems`).

Everyone wants in on the Emily thing. Wikipedia and Brittanica want to tell you all about her. The Poetry Foundation has a huge selection of Emily. Project

Gutenberg (https://gutenberg.org) offers Emily e-books. If you need a physical Emily book in your home, as we do, Amazon, Barnes & Noble, and myriad other outlets will sell you good collections costing not much. And, we know, we know, Emily is now a star of film and TV.

You can find lots and lots of Emily-adorers reading her aloud online. The Library of Congress has posted an entire Emily Dickinson Marathon Reading (https://www.youtube.com/watch?v=gtH6LU_THE0)! In Figure 1-2, Elizabeth Robinson takes the mic during the Emily Dickinson Marathon Reading at the Library of Congress, December 8, 2014.

FIGURE 1-2: Elizabeth Robinson takes the mic during the Emily Dickinson Marathon Reading at the Library of Congress, December 8, 2014.

Library of Congress. Public domain.

So how to handle all this Emily? You *could* just dive in . . . or perhaps you might follow a more patient course:

- **Start** with just a handful of poems.
- **Book up:** Learn about her fascinating, idiosyncratic poems and life. She is a personality, we'll say that.
- **Download or purchase a collection** and keep it around the house, to pick up and read when the impulse hits.
- **Listen to a podcast or watch an online discussion:** The BBC podcast *In Our Time* has a good one (www.bbc.co.uk/programmes/b08p51bp). As for video, check out *Trailblazing Women: Emily Dickinson and Poetry in America*, a PBS Books panel discussion (www.youtube.com/watch?v=pHyJayP9pac&t=1s).

» **Do the bounce-bounce:** Poems-Wiki-poems-experts-podcasts-videos-poems! Whenever you want to know more, return to your online or analog reference sources and book up. And always, back to the poems!

Emily Dickinson is only one of many poets, including Walt Whitman, C.P. Cavafy, Rainer Maria Rilke, Federico García Lorca, Lucille Clifton, and Anne Sexton, whose work has a big online presence. Online is definitely the most immediate pathway to poetry. Start with moderate steps, as we suggest in the preceding list. You're building your personal tastes: No one is looking over your shoulder (least of all *us*).

Checking out libraries

Your local library is a great source for poetry — and best of all, it's free. Libraries are wonderful, supportive places where reading (silently) is celebrated and encouraged. Ask the reference librarian where the poetry section is (or look up a favorite poet), go there, and read. You could also pull a book out at random. We did, and we came upon these lines:

> Summer swallows spring and goes into September
> Like long division it is always there
> Autumn, fall we say, fruit releases itself
> You are new enough so the old catches up
> Cross this bridge come to that one
> You grow up and ancient history snaps back
> Rubber band and rake handle

The poem turns out to be "Vermont Apollinaire" by William Corbett. Not bad for a stab in the dark at a random shelf in a library.

That first line tells you about the subject is autumn. Corbett writes about summer "go[ing] into" September, an echo of long division, in which things "go into" other things. The poem explores how the past comes back to you, snapping back like a rubber band, or a handle when you step on a rake.

Note: Corbett compares the past with the rubber band and rake handle in an implicit, unspoken way. That's a *metaphor.* Had Corbett said, "ancient history snaps back *like* a rubber band or a rake handle," he would have been using a *simile.* Welcome, metaphors and similes! Our first glimpse of two of the most important techniques in a poet's repertoire! (To read more about metaphor and simile, see Chapter 4.)

TIP

Try selecting a poetry book off a library shelf yourself, and if you like what you read, check out the book and sample more. Note that libraries often host poetry readings or reading circles. Get online, see what's up, take part.

In Figure 1-3, Joseph Chelius (back, center) discusses his new poetry book, *Playing Fields*, at a July 2025 reading at the Indian Valley Public Library, Telford, Pennsylvania.

FIGURE 1-3: Joseph Chelius (back, center) discusses his new poetry book, *Playing Fields*, at a July 2025 reading at the Indian Valley Public Library, Telford, Pennsylvania.

© Joanne Leva

Browsing through bookstores

Maybe checking out library books terrifies you, or you'd rather own your own. Well, then, go to your local bookstores, or their online catalogues, or just call them up and order a book.

Peruse the following list of inexpensive books of poetry. Select two or three and see what you think. All these are paperbacks. (You can buy e-books, but they tend not to be as easy or as good to read with poetry. Decide for yourself, though.)

COLLECTING FLOWERS: ANTHOLOGIES

Anthologies are collections of work by a number of poets. (The word *anthology* is descended from a Greek word for "collection of flowers.") Anthologies are fine starting-points for anyone interested in poetry. Check online or browse in your local library or bookstore(s).

Thousands of poetry anthologies are in existence — many with specific themes — and many display the best a particular culture or group has to offer. Start your personal flower collection today!

TIP

» *Inferno,* by Dante Alighieri. Translation: Mary Jo Bang. Drawings: Henrik Drescher. (Graywolf Press, 2013).

  If you like *Inferno*, keep going with Bang's translations of *Purgatorio* and *Paradiso*!

» *The Kingdom of Surfaces,* by Sally Wen Mao (Graywolf Press, 2023).

» *The Penguin Book of Modern African Poetry* (Penguin, 2007).

» *With My Back to the World,* by Victoria Chang. (Farrar, Straus and Giroux, 2024).

» *Twenty Love Poems: And a Song of Despair,* by Pablo Neruda. Translated by W.S. Merwin. (Penguin, 2006).

» *When the Light of the World Was Subdued, Our Songs Came Through: A Norton Anthology of Native Nations Poetry.* Edited by Joy Harjo. (W.W. Norton, 2020).

» *In the Lateness of the World,* by Carolyn Forché. (Penguin, 2021).

Attending readings

It's likely you can find a number of places near you where poetry readings, like the one shown in Figure 1-4, happen. Try local colleges, universities, libraries, coffee shops, and bookstores. There may even be poetry-reading groups in your town. (If not, you could always start one.)

You can find these events on the device of your choice. Tell your browser to find either *poetry readings near me* or *poetry readings near* [local town or Zip Code]. You can also check EventBrite (`www.eventbrite.com`) or AllEvents (`https://allevents.in/`[*input your town's name*]), sites that often list poetry readings or related gatherings. Also hit the websites of your local bookstores, coffee shops, colleges, or universities.

TIP

Most papers — local weeklies, especially — have entertainment sections that list things to do; poetry readings often make such lists. Also, if your town has its own website, check to see what's available.

However you find it, poetry is often a pleasant surprise.

FIGURE 1-4: A 1995 poetry reading at City Lights Bookstore in San Francisco, California, featuring poet Lawrence Ferlinghetti.

© Christopher Felver

Writing Poetry

Millions of people have tried. And you could be one of them. Many turn to writing verse at times of great emotion, insight, or need. And many who always loved poetry have thought about writing it.

The nice thing is this: *There's no one to ask for permission!* We could never cover everything about writing poetry in just one chapter (we devote a all of Part 3 to it). But here are some guidelines to consider right now, if you just can't wait.

Becoming a poet

Writing poetry involves more than scribbling in a notebook; it involves undertaking a way of life, one in which you value being creative and sensitive. Poets often do the following:

- **Discover as much as you can about the poetic craft.** Read lots of poetry. Meet other poets. Become part of a poetic community. Find a mentor. Attend readings and workshops. Take writing classes.
- **Become as sensitive as you can to life and to language.** Figure out your personal sense of what is beautiful, emotionally moving, startling, worthwhile — in life *and* in poetry.
- **Think *divergently* (that is, keep your mind open and nimble, and be willing to think in different ways and new directions).** You never know when, where, or how the creative urge will come to you, but you can prepare the way for it.
- **Make time for write.** After all, if you don't write, you're not a writer.
- **Be disciplined. Revise. Revise again.** Don't settle for clichés or what others say. Find out what kind of poetry only *you* can write.

Keeping a poetry journal

Many poets keep journals: repositories of ideas, images, topics, drafts of poems, other people's poetry, *found objects* (things you pick up that inspire you or that could become the basis for poems, such as someone else's grocery list). You can keep a journal in a notebook or on a laptop, tablet, smartphone, or micro recorder of your choice.

TIP

Many poets commit to writing in their journals each day. Their journals are, essentially, the "office" where their poetry work takes place. Keeping a daily journal is a good idea, so we heartily recommend you go out and get a journal for your own use.

What do you put in your journal? It's blissfully, beautifully up to you. Some poets keep a diary. Some write down dreams, meals, scraps of personal or overheard conversation. Only you can decide the exact way in which you'll fill your journal. Chapter 15 provides some journal exercises you may want to try.

IN THIS CHAPTER

» Embracing the benefits of reading poetry aloud

» Developing good reading habits

Chapter 2

Reading Poetry Aloud

Poetry is *meant* to be read aloud. That's right, aloud — as though you were delivering the poem to an attentive audience. In this chapter, you'll find out why reading aloud is so important, and how you can develop excellent reading habits.

Why You Should Read Poems Aloud

Here's why you should read poems aloud:

- **Almost all poetry has an ancient, built-in oral aspect.** The earliest poetry was *oral.* People chanted it, sang it, recited it — and they still do. The *music* of poetry — its sounds and rhythms — is not just for the eye and the mind. It's meant to be given voice. Poetry is supposed to be a living thing, and poets write accordingly, with an audience in mind.
- **You experience the whole poem when you read it aloud.** Poems read aloud are different animals from poems read silently. A big part of poetry is sound and rhythm — and the best way to give them full impact is to put them into action, pronouncing them with lips, teeth, tongue, throat, and lungs. Sound and rhythm don't exist just for their own sakes, either; they exist to give you pleasure (because people naturally like music and rhythm) and lead you to the poem's meanings. And don't forget *pauses*! Commas, line endings,

spaces between words and lines, and other pauses may suggest a range of emotions — melancholy, thoughtfulness, reluctance, or passion. Punctuation has its traditional functions (exclamations! questions? wistfulness . . .), and it often also is used in unexpected ways — or not used at all. You may miss all these signals if you don't read aloud.

» **You understand and remember more.** Memory and understanding are everything. If you remember something *and* understand it, it takes up long-term residence inside your brain. With that knowledge, you can go on to discover more and more about the world of poetry.

To see all this in action, read these four lines (Sappho!) silently:

The moon has set
and the Pleiades. Middle of the
night. Time passes
and I lie here alone.

Reading silently is a great way to make a poem's (or a song's, in this case) acquaintance. The speaker lies alone and can feel time crawling by. Now read the lines aloud. Pause a little at the end of each line. Notice how each pause carries a little information, a little jolt of feeling.

READ ALOUD

The moon has set
and the Pleiades

Look up *Pleiades*, and you'll find they're that familiar cluster of stars near Orion. The moon sets and so do the Pleiades, which could make the hour very late (depending on the time of year). The speaker seems to be painfully marking time. So, the word *and* might deserve an extra stress: "*and* the Pleiades." As in *and even the Pleiades!*

Now you come to another pause:

Middle of the [pause]
Night

You can almost *hear* the speaker groan. Pausing helps emphasize how weary and restless she is. Is she waiting for someone? You may spot an answer in the last two lines:

Time passes [pause]
And I lie here alone.

This insomniac speaker is alone. You get a feeling (without being told) that she wishes she weren't. That last word, *alone*, followed by silence, resounds with regret and sadness.

REMEMBER

Keep your online or print reference works handy when reading poetry!

Chances are, you understand Sappho's lines better for having read them aloud. And that's the way she would have wanted it.

How great is it that you just connected with something 2600 years old? This Sappho is good, right?

Good Habits for Good Reading

We hope we've persuaded you of the importance of reading poetry aloud. Now for the best ways to do it. Note: You don't have to take the suggestions below one by one. Think of them as components of good poetry reading.

Having the right tools handy

A firefighter who charged into flames without a hose wouldn't be very well prepared. And you wouldn't start painting your house or shampooing your dog without the right tools, would you? Reading poetry isn't any different.

TIP

When it comes to poetry, the right tools include the following:

- **A dictionary.** Whether online or in print, a dictionary is a great help when you come across words you don't know. Don't be ashamed — they happen, such words. Looking them up can help you understand more of the poem — and of the poet who wrote it (see the discussion of the word *Pleiades* in "Why You Should Read Poems Aloud").
- **A book about the history and forms of poetry.** Such a book can help answer questions that arise as you read — questions about kinds of poems, traditions, histories of poetry in different languages, and so on. We recommend *The New Princeton Encyclopedia of Poetry and Poetics,* edited by Alex Preminger and T.V.F. Brogan (Princeton University Press) as a great reference of this kind.
- ***Poetry For Dummies.*** This, of course, is a fine book providing much good information on poetry. And we're not at all biased. Nope. Not one bit.

Reading silently first

When you first look at a painting, you might step back to take in the whole thing before you move closer to see the details. Follow the same approach with poetry:

1. **Scope out the poem.**

   Skim over it, noting its title, length, and overall structure. Do you see one big flow of words on the page? Or is the poem broken into groups of lines (often called *stanzas*)? Does the poem rhyme? Who wrote the poem? If you can, find out when the poet lived. Such background information could come in handy.

2. **Read the poem silently.**

   Enjoy yourself. Stay relaxed and open. No one's timing you. In fact, the slower you read, the better — because you can absorb more.

3. **Take notes as you read silently, if you want.**

   Taking notes while you read a poem isn't required, but it's a good idea — especially if the poem includes unfamiliar words, *allusions* (references to persons, places, things, or history, for example), or concepts you don't understand. If it's in a book you own, you may even want to make notes in the margins, jotting down the meaning of this or that line. The notes some people make in their poetry books become a sort of journal for them, a history of their reading and thoughts.

Noting surprises and unfamiliar words

As you read, you're likely to run across some words you're not familiar with or words whose impact (in the context of the poem) you aren't ready for. Even in the shortest poems, you get them.

Take a look at this Native American song:

Song of Naquali

I wonder what
    my future life
will do to me.

The first two lines are "normal" enough — but "will do to me" is unexpected. You may expect the speaker to say, "I wonder what / my future life / will be like," or "I wonder what / my future life / has in store." Instead, we have "will do to me." That tiny word *to* is explosive: it's as if the future were aiming itself, weaponlike, right at "me." And it definitely feels like that sometimes. What's going to happen

is going to happen, and much of it won't be that great. The poem is wry — meaning ironic or grimly humorous — and it is also fatalistic, meaning the speaker doesn't think you can do much about fate, besides wonder what it will do to you.

REMEMBER

You don't ever have to plow top to bottom, all the way through, when you read a poem. Stop, repeat, go back, dwell. If you really like certain lines, reread and enjoy them again. If the poem is in a book you own, underline the part you like or note it in the margin. And keep a dictionary handy so that you can look up words you're not familiar with.

Finding an engaged, conversational tone

Every poem has a *speaker* — someone you imagine saying the poem. Sometimes the speaker is a disembodied voice, just saying the words. At other times, the speaker is a character you get to know in the poem. When you read aloud, you need to use the right tone of voice for that speaker. Here are some suggestions for the kind of tone you should shoot for:

- **Engaged.** Your tone of voice should show you're really interested in what you have to say. You're leaning forward to tell someone else. If you're happy, you're *really* happy. If not, you're *really* not. Give the words a slight push; project.
- **Conversational.** Don't shout and don't whisper. True, you are performing the poem, but you can still remain close to the normal way in which you speak to people in everyday conversation. You're just reading as though you're engaged in *interesting* conversation, conversation with passion behind it.

TIP

Many poets and poetry fans like to work on their reading aloud. If you want to practice your reading, record yourself (this exercise can be humbling at first, but it's always instructive). Listen to how you read. Is your reading clear? Is it attentive to the poem? Are you pausing in the right places? Are you being expressive? Are you bringing your idea of the poem across? Attend readings and observe how other people read their poetry, too.

Resisting the urge to rush

Read at a moderate, deliberate pace. Enjoy the words and phrases you're saying. *Enunciate* (pronounce the words clearly). You may come across very long sentences as you read. Just take your time, and it will be easier to understand what the sentences are saying.

Here is a reading-aloud challenge, from the play *Antony and Cleopatra*, by William Shakespeare. It's a big moment, our first description of powerful, attractive Cleopatra. Someone is describing her as she sails down the Nile in her barge.

REMEMBER

This passage will be gobbledygook unless you relax and let it go at its own pace. When you read it over, you'll find a lot of commas and periods, which means you're meant to pause quite a bit. Consider what's being described: a queen in her private barge (a stately subject). So this is a great chance to observe that ancient piece of wisdom, "No need to rush."

READ ALOUD

The barge she sat in, like a burnish'd throne,
Burnt on the water. The poop was beaten gold,
Purple the sails, and so perfumed that
The winds were love-sick with them; the oars were silver,
Which to the tune of flutes kept stroke, and made
The water which they beat to follow faster,
As amorous of their strokes. For her own person,
It beggar'd all description: she did lie
In her pavilion — cloth of gold, of tissue —
O'er-picturing that Venus where we see
The fancy outwork nature.

TECHNICAL STUFF

Shakespeare lived in the 16th and 17th centuries, so his English is a little different from yours. Here are some words or phrases that may be unfamiliar:

- **poop:** Short for *poop deck*, which is a partial, raised deck over the front half (or stern) of a boat's main deck.
- **As amorous of their strokes:** This phrase means "as though the water were longing for the oars' strokes."
- **her own person:** Her physical self.
- **beggar'd all description:** The literal meaning is "made description go begging," a creative way of saying, "You really can't describe what she was like." This William Shakespeare is good, right?
- **pavilion:** A big tent, underneath which Cleopatra is reclining.
- **O'er-picturing that Venus:** This phrase means "outdoing that famous picture of Venus." The speaker is imagining a famous portrait of Venus, the Roman goddess of love and beauty, and then he says Cleopatra was even more beautiful than *that*.
- **fancy:** Imagination.

You may not feel you "get" the entire passage at first reading. Not to worry. The idea is to read poetry again and again, feeling your way in. Try breaking the passage down into sentences. This passage has three sentences, the first of which is:

> The barge she sat in, like a burnish'd throne,
> Burnt on the water.

"Burnt" is a surprise. The speaker doesn't mean it literally. The boat is so polished, so bright, that it's brilliant, fiery, and sunlike. (You find out in the next lines that the poop deck is "beaten gold" and the oars silver.) So "Burnt" is a metaphor — without using *like* or *as*, the speaker is comparing a brilliant, golden boat to something aflame.

The word *Burnt* gives you a good opportunity to pause, to register its full impact: "The barge she sat in, like a burnish'd throne, [pause] Burnt on the water." Hear the repeated *b* sounds in *barge, burnish'd,* and *Burnt?* That's called *alliteration* (the repetition of consonant sounds), and it's a hint to you, the reader, to emphasize those three words a little more than the rest.

REMEMBER

You can't rush Shakespeare's verse. Too much is going on; too many gorgeous images come at us. The speaker's enthusiasm grows as he warms to the description of the barge — which leads to a description of its beautiful passenger. Enjoy the imaginative images: The wind is "lovesick" for the sails, and the water is in love with the oars. The speaker is overwhelmed with the "burning" barge, the gold, the silver, the colors, the perfumes, and most of all with Cleopatra. As you get to know this passage, see whether you can read it with the same loving admiration the speaker has for her.

Pausing for power

One of the reasons people read poetry over and over is to figure out how to read it aloud. The better you know a passage, the better you'll know what tone of voice to use as you read it, where to run, and where to slow down.

One of the most powerful tools in any reader's arsenal is the *pause*. Pauses come wherever you see a powerful moment. Such moments include:

- **Any punctuated pause, including dashes, commas, semicolons, or periods.** Poets use punctuation as carefully and meaningfully as they use any other part of language; it's always powerful.
- **Any surprise.** If you find yourself surprised by a word, phrase, or image, dwell on it just a little bit — as in [pause] "*Burnt* on the water" — long enough to let it register in the mind(s) of your audience (real or imagined).

» **The end of one stanza (or group of lines) and the beginning of another.**

» **The ends of lines.**

Paying attention to line-endings

When you come to a line ending, pause slightly unless doing so is unnatural. Refer to the Sappho poem in "Why You Should Read Poems Aloud," earlier in this chapter: "Middle of the [pause] night." Just a little pause bestows such power on the word *night*.

Here's a passage from "In What Manner the Body Is United with the Soule" by Jorie Graham. The speaker suddenly realizes how to listen to music, and the epiphany is magic. This poem really *needs* you to pause slightly at the ends of lines, to lend the images and feelings their full drama.

Finally I heard
    into music,
that is, heard past
    the surface tension
which is pleasure, which holds
    the self
afloat, miraculous
    waterstrider
with no other home.
    Not that I heard
very deep,
    but heard there was a depth

As you read aloud, you'll find yourself pausing at mid-sentence commas as well as at line endings: "which is pleasure [pause] which holds [pause] the self [pause] afloat." Isn't that gorgeous?

There are no hard rules about exactly how long to pause, or whether to pause longer at commas or at line endings. Experiment. See what seems to fit. You can even decide not to pause if you feel the lines run strongly together — as some readers do with the words "heard past / the surface tension." But if there is more white space (where no words exist, as between "the self" and "afloat"), pause longer. Treat white space as time and observe that time with silence. More space, more pause.

You'll find, as you reread and reread, that some words call for slightly more emphasis. For example, try emphasizing the words *into, surface, pleasure, waterstrider* (especially the *water* part), and the word *was* in the last line. Those are just suggestions; you may choose to accent other words. Although emphasizing *was* may seem trivial, it can actually lead you to a distinction the speaker finds important: She isn't claiming she was very sensitive, but she was learning there were depths to music she never dreamed of before.

TECHNICAL STUFF

A *waterstrider* is one of those long-legged bugs that walks on water (it actually walks on the surface tension of water). It's Graham's lovely metaphor for the self, just striding along, held aloft by pleasure.

This passage has a striding, loping rhythm. Many subtle pauses in these lines set up a rhythm that allows room for the quiet depth of this passage. The self, that old waterstrider, has "no other home" than pleasure. What an interesting idea — your self is most at home when you are experiencing pleasure. Could be. We may not have seen that meaning so clearly had we not paused at the ends of the lines.

Treating white space as time

Let us repeat: more space, more pause. Just as you pause a little at the ends of lines and pause more between stanzas, pause where you see *white space* (where no words exist). If you see a little break before another word, pause a little. If you see a lot of white space, pause more. It's no accident that poems look the way they do on paper, with ragged edges, margin indents, single words appearing smack-dab in the middle of lines — poets craft the pauses as carefully as the words.

This poem by Robert Francis is almost impossible to read silently. If you read it aloud, paying attention to pauses, it turns into a striking, descriptive piece, with a sense of time passing.

READ ALOUD

Silent Poem

backroad leafmold stonewall chipmunk
underbrush grapevine woodchuck shadblow

woodsmoke cowbarn honeysuckle woodpile
sawhorse bucksaw outhouse wellsweep

backdoor flagstone bulkhead buttermilk
candlestick ragrug firedog brownbread

hilltop outcrop cowbell buttercup
whetstone thunderstorm pitchfork steeplebush

gristmill millstone cornmeal waterwheel
watercress buckwheat firefly jewelweed

gravestone groundpine windbreak bedrock
weathercock snowfall starlight cockcrow

The short pauses among the words help you — perhaps even gently *force* you — to visualize each hard, concrete thing as you come to it, until, as the reader, you are in the midst of life in the world.

One poet known for his unusual punctuation (and lowercase letters) is e.e. cummings. Here is one of his best poems. Try observing the white space as time. If words run together, run them together.

READ ALOUD

in Just-
spring when the world is mud-
luscious the little
lame balloonman

whistles far and wee

and eddieandbill come
running from marbles and
piracies and it's
spring

when the world is puddle-wonderful

the queer
old balloonman whistles
far and wee
and bettyandisbel come dancing
from hop-scotch and jump-rope and

it's
spring
and
    the
            goat-footed

balloonMan whistles
far
and
wee

TIP

"eddieandbill" and "bettyandisbel" (note how those two pairs of names kind-of rhyme! This e.e. cummings is good, right?) should come running fast. Those last three words, though — read *them* with great pauses between.

Doing it more than once

Ask anyone who likes poetry: When you find a poem you like, you keep reading it your whole life. As you change, it changes. And that changes you some more.

So whenever you read a poem aloud, read it aloud several times. Each time, you may see different things. (Use pauses differently each time, vary your tone of voice, or add more or less drama to your reading.) You wouldn't date someone you like only once, would you? One reading deserves another.

IN THIS CHAPTER

» Understanding the importance of subject in poetry

» Determining the speaker's attitude to the subject and the audience

» Paying attention to speaker, setting, situation, plot, and character

Chapter 3

Identifying Subject, Tone, and Narrative

The more you know about poetry, the more you find to like. A few simple tools — including a sharpened awareness of some of the basics, like subject, tone, and narrative — can enhance the way you read. Paying attention to details makes life, and the person living it (you, for example), better and richer. It's simply good for you, in the same way poetry is.

In this chapter, we look at three things you should always try to determine when you approach a new poem — subject, tone, and narrative — and show you how to identify them.

TIP

GETTING IN A POETRY FRAME OF MIND

When you read poetry, make sure you're open to what the poem is about and what the poet is communicating to you. Your frame of mind is best when you're:

- **Alert.** Pay close attention to the poem. Look for meaning — all the time, everywhere. Poems have meaning in every rhythm, every phrase.
- **Analytical.** Take poems apart and look at their different elements — this image, that sound, this suggestion.
- **Comfortable with ambiguities and difficulties.** Be open to *enjoying,* actually enjoying, as the English poet John Keats once wrote, "being in uncertainties, mysteries, doubts," without trying to solve them immediately. Whoever "solved" *Hamlet?* Who can claim they "understand" the *Mahabharata?* Probably very few. But many people just *love* to be in the midst of that poetry, to keep experiencing what's perplexing, what's beautiful, what's true.
- **Sensual.** Look for *pleasure.* Poetry pleases the mind (in the things it says and means) and the body (in its rhythms, music, and appeals to experience and the senses). Pleasure can exist for its own sake, or it may lock into the poem's larger meaning.

Understanding Subject and Tone

Two things you want to know right away when you're reading a poem are:

- What's being discussed.
- The poet or speaker's attitude toward it.

Those two concerns translate to *subject* (the center of discussion; the thing being regarded or portrayed) and *tone* (the author's attitude toward the subject . . . or, sometimes, the audience). In a poem of praise, you feel approval. In a satire, you feel irony. In an antiwar poem, you may feel protest or moral indignation. Tone can be playful, humorous, regretful, dismissive (see Dorothy Parker's "Résumé," in the section "Tone: It's got attitude") — and it can change as the poem goes along.

Subject: A natural starting point

Looking for the poem's subject is natural. Almost all poetry involves meanings and messages — lots of them, profound and diverse as stars. But these meanings and messages are sometimes disguised or hidden, and you have to read attentively to make them out.

WARNING

Notice that we specifically avoid saying, "The subject is what a poem's *about*" — because that implies that what a poem *says* is all there is to a poem. It's not, of course: Poetry includes sound and rhythm, visual sculpture, *and* how all these things accompany and transcend the meaning. (Chapters 4 and 5 tackle language and interpretation in more detail.)

Not all poems have a single subject. Some poems have many, and some have subjects that aren't clear. Sometimes a poem's subject is simply *itself* — the words in it and their relationships to one another. The point is to be alert for the subject or subjects of any poem as you read.

Tone: It's got attitude

When you speak, your tone of voice suggests your attitude. In fact, it suggests two attitudes: one concerning the thing you're talking about (your subject), and one concerning the people you're addressing (your audience). Same for tone in poetry. *Tone* can also mean the general emotional weather (joyous, dark, fearful, and so on) of the poem.

Sometimes you can pick up tone directly from the literal language of the poem, as in this lovely piece from the T'ang Dynasty Chinese poet Liu Zongyuan:

READ ALOUD

> From one thousand mountains the birds' flights are gone;
> From ten thousand byways the human track has vanished.
> In a single boat, an aged man, straw cloak and hat,
> Fishes alone. Snow falls, river cold.

Let's look for clues to tone.

- The birds have abandoned the mountains.
- Human footprints (signs of human presence) have "vanished" from thousands of roads.
- The old fisherman is all alone, as is his "single" boat.
- The last image is wintry indeed, with snow falling all around. The solitary man and boat are dwarfed by the vast abandonment all around them.

IF POEMS COULD SPIT

What was the *angriest* poem ever written? One contender may be the poem below, by the Victorian poet Robert Browning. Edward FitzGerald (like Browning, a fine poet) had died in 1883, and when some of his unpublished papers were published six years later, Browning read a passage in which FitzGerald spoke of the death of Browning's beloved wife, Elizabeth Barrett Browning (1806–1861), as "rather a relief to me."

In one of the strangest of poems, Browning wrote in white-hot anger to the dead poet about Browning's dead wife. "How to return you thanks would task my wits," Browning wrote (with heavy irony on *thanks*). He concluded with four lines that illustrate both the concept of tone and how you determine what a poem's tone is:

To Edward FitzGerald

Kicking you seems the common lot of curs—
While more appropriate greeting lends you grace,
Surely to spit there glorifies your face —
Spitting from lips once sanctified by hers.

So where is tone in this poem? Well, the poet first wants to kick FitzGerald — but that's "the common lot of curs," a punishment that's too ordinary. FitzGerald is so low he isn't *worth kicking*. He's not even a "cur" (a mongrel or a worthless dog).

Browning can't even spit in FitzGerald's face. Why? Because Browning's lips once kissed his wife's and therefore were "sanctified," or made holy. FitzGerald doesn't deserve the exalted blessing of being spat on by lips that once kissed hers.

Kicking is too ordinary; spitting on him would make him holy. There's no way to thank such a man (by which Browning really means "punish"). That's *irony* — saying one thing ("thank") when you really mean another ("punish"). All these clues lead you to the tone of outrage in this poem. And if Browning is so outraged at FitzGerald, he must *really* have loved his wife, as the word *sanctified* implies.

Taken together, these elements – images, setting, action, language – create an atmosphere of melancholy. If you're feeling that, you're feeling tone.

Often, poets simply allow their speakers, or the stories they tell, to *imply* their attitude. In this poem by American writer Dorothy Parker, you can determine tone from the speaker's attitude toward the subject addressed.

READ ALOUD

Résumé

Razors pain you;
Rivers are damp;
Acids stain you;
And drugs cause cramp.
Guns aren't lawful;
Nooses give;
Gas smells awful;
You might as well live.

What is this a résumé *of*? The poem doesn't tell you, but you can figure it out. Razors, acid, nooses, guns, drugs, gas — all of these are means of suicide. But is the speaker tortured, fearful, depressed? Not really. "Comically shallow" would be closer to it. Each "option" is rejected for fairly trivial reasons. And the conclusion, "You might as well live," is almost jokey, offhand. The implication: Suicide isn't worth doing unless it's easy, painless, and neat. The speaker seems to think *both* living and suicide are trivial pursuits — and that is ironic.

Irony is a common tone in poetry. *Verbal irony* is the practice of saying one thing when you mean another ("thanks" when you mean "punish," as in "To Edward FitzGerald"; see the sidebar, "If poems could spit"). Such forms of irony include *understatement*, in which the speaker says less than they mean, as in these lines from "Mr. Brodsky" by Charles Tomlinson. Tomlinson meets a man who brings him home to have supper — and afterward plays the bagpipe in the living room. Tomlinson writes,

A bagpipe in a dwelling is
a resonant instrument

Bagpipes are loud — and bagpipes indoors are *really* loud. Tomlinson says only "resonant" — which tells the truth with so much restraint that you can guess just *how* loud Mr. Brodsky's bagpipes really are. Tomlinson is *understating* the case — yet still leading his readers to the humorous truth. You could well imagine Tomlinson reading the word *resonant* with an ironic smile.

Verbal irony also includes *overstatement* (as in telling someone "Oh, you're the *best* poet who ever existed on the face of the earth," when it's clear you don't mean it).

The term *situational irony* refers to events that happen contrary to your expectations, often with a fatal overtone, as when in *Oedipus the King* by Sophocles, Oedipus declares he will find out who killed his father — only to discover it must have been himself. Sharpen your awareness of tone. You'll see it in direct statement, to be sure, but tone can also reside in:

- Images and how they are presented, as in Liu Zongyuan's poem.
- Implication, as in Dorothy Parker's "Résumé."
- The very form of a poem, its music and rhythms. Think of the singsong rhythms of "Résumé" grating against the dark topic.

Reading for subject and tone

Paying attention to subject and tone helps familiarize you with the poem in front of you and suggests new ways to explore it.

This poem by Randall Jarrell is based on the poet's time spent as a control tower operator for the Army Air Corps in World War II. It contains some shocks, but therein lies its beauty.

READ ALOUD

The Death of the Ball Turret Gunner

From my mother's sleep I fell into the State,
And I hunched in its belly till my wet fur froze.
Six miles from earth, loosed from its dream of life,
I woke to black flak and the nightmare fighters.
When I died they washed me out of the turret with a hose.

TIP

You can find plenty of metaphors here:

- The "sleep" of the mother (possibly a metaphor for her contented ignorance of the horrors of war).
- The "belly" of the State (possibly a metaphor for the way society protects young men, who stay "hunched in its belly" like growing fetuses, until it sends them off to war).
- The "wet fur" of the young gunner (young mammals have wet fur when they are born, so this may be a metaphor for the youthful vulnerability and naiveté of the speaker).
- The "dream of life" on earth (a peaceful delusion for civilians far away from the horrors of war).
- You may also sense an implicit metaphor between the ball turret in which the gunner hunches and his mother's womb (not directly referred to, but implicit in his birth). He hunches in the turret, fetus-like, and suffers a horrible "birth" when his remains are washed out later.

These lines represent a series of births and awakenings, transitions between dreams of safety and the perils of reality. The shocks of each line lead us to the devastating horror of the last.

The subject of the poem is probably pretty clear to you: war and its terrible consequences. But what separates this poem from other war poems is its *tone*. Much about it may make you feel uneasy (after all, how often do you encounter dead people narrating their own deaths?), fearful, aware of the inevitability of fate. You're feeling the penetrating irony for which this poem is famous. What makes you feel the irony? The story the poem tells. The metaphors and their implications. The matter-of-fact language of the last line.

Figuring Out a Poem's Narrative

Many poets are also storytellers, and they use all the elements of narration, including:

- **Speaker (also known as *persona*):** The imaginary person who "speaks" the words in a poem. Some poems feature speakers as full-fledged characters with names and histories. But for the sake of discussion, imagine *all* poems as having speakers.
- **Setting:** The time, location, and physical environment in which a story happens.
- **Situation:** The circumstances or state of affairs at a given moment in a poem or story. Situation also can refer to the circumstances in which characters find themselves at a given moment.
- **Plot:** The deeds and events in the story, and the shape or *arc* of those deeds and events as the poem converges on its conclusion.
- **Character:** The fictional representation of an imaginary person. A character is really a bunch of words that spurs us to have a mental image of a person.

We cover each of these narrative elements in the following sections, and throughout our discussion we refer to "The Death of the Ball Turret Gunner" (see the preceding section), so you can see how to identify all these elements in one poem.

Speaker: The person we're listening to

In "The Death of the Ball Turret Gunner," the *speaker* (the imaginary person who "speaks" the words in the poem) is the gunner himself. He's also the main *character*. Another word for the main character's role is that of the *protagonist*, the character to whom most or all the events in a story happen. "Who is the speaker and what is that speaker like?" is a pretty central question. Speakers have personalities. They also have a *point of view*, the perspective from which they tell the events they narrate. They choose what we see and when — a really good reason to keep your eye on what they let us see, what they withhold, and when they reveal things.

WARNING

Some readers just assume that, unless we're told otherwise, the poet is the speaker of a poem. That's an understandable assumption, but it often isn't correct. The speaker is very often different from the poet. In "The Death of the Ball Turret Gunner," the poet (Randall Jarrell, obviously a living human being when he wrote the poem) and the speaker (a young man who dies in an air war) are two very different entities. The speaker (even if that speaker has the poet's name) is always a fictional creation of the poet.

Think of the many times poets have used nonhuman or even inanimate speakers. In the *Crow* poems by Ted Hughes, the speaker is a big, black, voluble bird. In Diane DiPrima's *Poems of Loba*, the speaker is a wolf. And in his poem "Lightning Rod to Storm," Adam Cornford depicts a truly electric conversation between a thunderstorm and a lightning rod. Enjoy these variations — they're never there without function and meaning.

REMEMBER

Speakers are not always perfect. In fact, they're quite often flawed in interesting ways. They may not know the whole truth, may be mistaken, or may have prejudices that color what they tell you. Be sure always to evaluate what speakers are telling you. Consider what the poem tells you about the speaker's life or background, and what you observe in what speakers do and say (hints about their psychology and motivation). Consider the atmosphere the poet weaves around the speaker.

And remember: Speakers are like people — many are reliable, but some aren't. Good reason to pay close attention to what you know about any speaker you encounter.

In "The Death of the Ball Turret Gunner," you can see that:

- **The speaker is not the poet, Randall Jarrell.**
- **The speaker is narrating his death and events beyond that death.** That may strike readers with irony and horror. Such a narration literally could never happen. The speaker's voice has the calm, detached quality of a voice of the dead. Even though he speaks of harrowing things, the things he himself does

are passive. He falls, hunches, wakes, and dies — which lends his character a submissive quality. And he never raises his voice, never protests — anger or pain are absent from his language. The speaker may not feel them, but readers do.

» **The speaker's personality has an innocence you may associate with young men caught in the terrifying machinery of war.** His "wet fur" is an image usually used to describe a newborn animal. The way he wakes up implies he hasn't understood (until it's too late) what's actually happening to him.

Setting: Knowing where you are

Setting (the time, location, or physical environment in which a story takes place) can involve history and locale. Knowing the setting of a poem is important because poets and their characters alike are creatures of their settings. Read carefully to learn the time, place, and situation the poem presents. Most of the time, poems give you this information straightforwardly. Some poems may mention the time of year ("It was the merry month of May"), describe part of an exterior scene ("the humming forest," "crawling traffic," and so on), or name a place ("welcome to Miami"). But sometimes you may need to do some research — another good reason to have your reference books always near at hand.

When poets describe a scene for you, or mention one in passing, stop and imagine the scene in detail. In his poem "La Belle Dame Sans Merci," the English poet John Keats writes:

> The sedge has withered from the lake,
>   And no birds sing.

Stop and imagine it. *Sedge* is a marsh plant that often grows thickly around the margins of lakes and rivers. But here, all the sedge has withered — ominous, especially when combined with songless birds. Now perhaps you start wondering why these worrisome things have happened. Imagining setting in full will bring you forcefully into the poem.

In "The Death of the Ball Turret Gunner," the setting is the 1940s, during the Second World War, in the skies above Europe (at least, that's where the planes of the Eighth Air Force, planes Randall Jarrell helped guide, were going). Thousands of airmen and civilians died in the air war. It was a theater of terror, with new technologies, including radar, long-range *flak* (anti-aircraft) guns, and fighter planes, increasing the death and destruction.

Situation: Circumstances and their victims

Situation is the circumstances or state of affairs at a given moment in a poem or story. Most poems begin telling the story with the first words. So pay close attention to clues about the circumstances of the poem, the speaker, and the main characters as a poem opens. What characters do or say usually relates directly to the situation they're in.

The speaker-protagonist of "The Death of the Ball Turret Gunner" goes through a series of situations, from birth to the nightmare of war and death, all in this one poem.

Plot: What goes on

The term *plot* refers to the deeds and events in the story, as organized by the speaker, usually, toward a particular effect or purpose. Poems tell stories, but they may not always tell them straight. They may tell events out of sequence, imply important events, or leave out whole steps in a story (to be supplied by you, the attentive reader). Keep track of the plot as you read — ask yourself what you know and what you don't.

Sometimes, the speaker may want to hide something from you or right-out lie. Stay alert. Compare what you're being told happened to what you think *actually* happened.

The plot of "The Death of the Ball Turret Gunner" is straightforward enough — but it has a slight and all-important twist. One thing the speaker of the poem does not narrate is the death itself. One moment he is waking up from the "dream of life," and the next he is being washed out of the turret. You are, therefore, forced to imagine what happened in between, which involves you more deeply.

Character: What kind of person would do a thing like that?

The word *character*, as in "the character of King Arthur," refers to the fictional representation of an imaginary person. Character is important to poetry. Every character in a poem has a different point of view, a different motive, a different goal. When you put characters together, you get tension and drama.

Consider the people in "The Death of the Ball Turret Gunner" other than the protagonist: the mother, the men who operate the enemy guns and planes, and the faceless "they" who have to hose out the turret at the end. Think of how different they are from the gunner and from one another. You're told that the mother was in a "sleep," a metaphor for many things, including the civilian unawareness of the loss and pain of war. The enemy guns and planes are part of a "nightmare," however — the nightmare, real and unrelenting, of human savagery. The scrubs who do the hosing belong to the obedient young who, like the speaker, have to do what they're told.

You may also think of the "State" as a character. Because the fur freezes in the belly of the State, you presume that it's cold. The shocking last image, the hosing-out, is also cold and wet, unceremonious and without feeling.

One more trenchant irony: If the ball turret is a kind of womb, what is the hose? After the gunner's death comes a sickening reenactment of the sexual act that led to his conception.

The speaker is also a character, which brings up a neat trick Jarrell turns with the *point of view* here: The speaker never pities himself — yet *you* feel the pity. The speaker never says a word against war — yet *you* get the fury and *pathos* (the evocation of pity or compassion). How? From the poem-as-written, not from any outright protest from the speaker.

Although the poem is ironic, the speaker is *not* ironic about what happens to him. As a gunner, he is definitely a warrior, a dispenser of death, yet he seems nevertheless innocent. Perhaps the mother should have known better; perhaps the State is at fault, in its cold impersonality, its unleashing of the nightmare. But one person remains beyond blame: the gunner himself.

"The Death of the Ball Turret Gunner" operates through both language (metaphors and irony) and storytelling (plot, character, speaker, situation, and setting). In this chapter, we've run this little poem through the machinery of narration to show you how a little attention can discover worlds in even the shortest poem.

REMEMBER

Considering subject, tone, and narrative — following them in detail, keeping track of them — can reveal not only the poem's possible meanings but also the poet's craftsmanship. If you want to be a poet, reading with such attention can help you see what's possible, if you work at it.

IN THIS CHAPTER

» Becoming more sensitive to language, the material of the poet's art

» Knowing the tools poets use to expand meaning: images, symbols, similes, and metaphors

» Understanding what allusions are and why poets use them

» Appreciating the role of music in poetry

» Tracking the way poets use the shape of lines and stanzas

Chapter 4
Tuning in to Language

Sometimes, language seems spiritual, as insubstantial as breath on a winter's day. Yet language is also a *physical* thing, something the body produces and *does*, with a "feel" (think of the terms "smooth-talking" or "rough language"), an impact on ear, body, mind, plus characteristics and oddities in sound and shape. To get closer to poetry, we can fine-tune our sensitivity to language and its histories, sounds, rhythms, undertones, overtones, meanings, and suggestions.

In this chapter, we take a short tour of ways poets mine this mother lode of human expression. We divide our tour of language into *figures of speech* (including symbols, similes, and metaphors) that help expand meaning and suggestion; *music* (sounds and rhythms); and *visual rhythm* (the shape and flow of lines, stanzas, and sections of poems).

Understanding Figurative Language

As of the 2020s, many poets in English write in a fairly direct, seemingly (but only seemingly!) "normal" way. But very often, poets also use what's known as *figurative language*: ways with words that evoke new meanings and new readerly emotions.

When people speak vividly or imaginatively, they may use language creatively. When you're hungry, you may say, "I could eat a horse." Of course, you and your audience recognize that you're being imaginative (not literal) in your language. Your audience switches with you into that imaginative gear and knows that you're really just saying you're very, very hungry. In saying you could eat a horse, you're using a *figure of speech* (any turn of phrase that is not to be taken literally yet has a meaning you and your audience can recognize).

REMEMBER

Poetry is *language under pressure.* Poets are trying to pack in more meaning per word than people pack into ordinary language. They supercharge language with significance, thought, feeling. They're looking for what's new, what's fresh, what connects. So should you as a reader of poetry! As you read, stay open to the possibilities: try to make sense of the images, the tone, all the signals, to get as much of that extra flavor, energy, or emotion as you can. This way of reading is called *interpretation.* We discuss it in Chapter 5.

TIP

Approach poems with an open, alert mind. Look for different possibilities in the words and phrases you're reading. If you find an *implication* (that is, something the poem *suggests* without coming out and saying it), great.

Try reading this poem by Fanny Howe. At first glance, it may seem close to nonsense, but stay with it, and you'll see that its unusual uses of language pack more possibilities of meaning per word than normal uses do. Her words are pretty simple, but with a little attention paid — to where the words *come from,* the worlds (like anatomy, math, horse-racing, even physics) they normally inhabit — you'll see they bring into play new meanings, new power, including humor, and a fresh point of view. That power comes partly from the fact that these words and phrases have been taken *out of* those worlds and plunked into the poem. You *could* say that the apparent "nonsense" ends up being *super*-sense.

READ ALOUD

About Face

I wrap my bones around my head
Speak through the holes

It sounds like math
is rounding the curves

or a mouth is light years
ahead of words.

We usually speak literally, trying to limit our words to a single meaning. So much of this poem, on the other hand, has more than one possible meaning. Look at the title: "About Face." It *could* mean "a turnaround or reversal." Or it could indicate that this poem concerns . . . having a face!

None of Howe's words is difficult or unusual. But everything that happens is *very* unusual, starting with the startling first line: "I wrap my bones around my head." The poet *can't* mean it literally — so you know you're in the presence of a *metaphor*. Let's see what the metaphor might be.

Think about *speaking* for a moment — just the act of using your mouth to make words. (***Remember:*** This is just our guess, not a certain statement.) People are always speaking through the bones around their heads — teeth, jaws, and facial bones (even sinuses, which are, yes, organized around bones).

And the second line? Well, if our subject is having a face, "Speak through the holes" makes sense, because holes (eyes, noses, and mouths) are what people speak through.

So "About Face" may be exploring what the act of speaking *involves*.

Next stanza: When I speak, "It sounds like math / is rounding the curves" — two more simple but initially puzzling lines. In math, you round off numbers a lot, to the nearest tenth and so on. But instead of rounding off *numbers*, Howe gives you "rounding the curves." Whoa — with a flick of her mind, she has switched her metaphor worlds, *like that*, from math to . . . horse racing! Expressing ourselves is a kind of race: we're always trying to get somewhere, *say* something. In "About Face," though, we're "rounding the curves," getting close to the finish line.

So . . . speaking can "sound like math" (our guess) because it's always *approximating* the things people want to say or the things they want to indicate in the world. We are always rounding things off — we may seldom say the exact thing we want, but we get close.

"About Face" *seems* to point out how speaking doesn't quite do everything people assume it does. Language does a good job, but it's approximate. So maybe that's how "a mouth is light years / ahead of words" — a mouth is something real, and words are only a rough-and-ready attempt to get at reality. No word could ever get all the way. All the word *mouth* can do is *refer to* a real mouth — it can't *be* a mouth or *give* you one. So an actual mouth always will remain "light years / ahead of words." (Yet another possibility: We all are "ahead of words," because we *are* "a head of words" — we're thinking words all the time.)

This Fanny Howe is good, right? She's got us thinking about having bones in our faces, about mouths, and about words and what they can and can't do. This witty poet has created figures of speech to release all kinds of unexpected meanings. All in 29 words!

We hope we've sold you on the value of snuggling up to language. In the rest of this chapter, we turn to some basic tools of the poet's art.

Opening the Poet's Figurative Toolbox

Figurative language is different from literal language. When you say, "I'd like a hamburger and a vanilla milkshake," you usually have one meaning and that's it. You want to be taken *literally*. But, in both nonpoetic life and poetry, we often use *figurative language*, including symbols, similes, metaphors, and allusions to deliver meaning. People use symbols to *stand for* things, they use similes and metaphors to *compare* things, and they use other figures of speech to make their words powerful and moving. Good poets are masters of these tools.

In the following sections, we look at the heavy hitters of figurative language: symbols, similes, metaphors, and allusion.

Symbols: When A stands for B, which brings in C

People use symbols all the time. Symbols are central to the way our minds and worlds function. Think of all the symbols you see every day: Stop signs, for example, which *stand* for your legal obligation to stop. No police force, judge, or jury waits for you at a stop sign; the sign itself stands for the whole machinery of safety, social duty, and law.

Words themselves are symbols: They *stand* for the things they refer to. Instead of lugging a horse into the room each time I want to discuss a horse, I can say a word — *horse* — that *stands* for that animal. Even the letters in words are symbols: They *stand* for the sounds you'd make if you spoke the word aloud. We just couldn't function as human beings without symbols.

A symbol stands for something else — which in turn brings with it an intense world of meaning. It's an A that stands for a B, which results in a C (a greater meaning). Symbols unite a concrete thing with an idea or concept greater than that thing. Here are a couple of symbols and how this pattern works with each one:

- **Money:** Physical currency (a dollar, pound, or ruble) is really just a piece of paper or metal, or a digital sign. That paper, metal, or sign is the A (the real element). But it *symbolizes* (or stands for) a certain economic value, which is the B. So, what's the C? Buying power. Everyone agrees to abide by that symbolism. If they didn't, you wouldn't be so reluctant to part with your money, or so pleased to discover some in your jeans pocket.
- **A wedding ring:** Many wedding rings are just pieces of metal, molded into a certain shape. That metal is the A. But it symbolizes (stands for) a marriage, which is the B. And what's the C? Lifelong commitment and unending love, all symbolized by that never-ending circle of the wedding ring.

Identifying symbols in poems

So how can you tell whether something is a symbol? You can be relatively sure something is a symbol if:

- **You already recognize the symbol as a symbol.** Money or wedding rings, for example. A lot of literature and other art contains common symbols you probably recognize: roses, storms, sunrises, skulls, knives, and more. These symbols come ready-made with their own meanings (storms, for example, usually symbolize trouble, but sunrises often symbolize hope). If you see such things in a poem, try looking at them as symbols and see what that does for your understanding.
- **The poet leaves indicators that the poem represents a larger world than its images normally would by themselves.** For example, in Robert Frost's poem "The Road Not Taken" (`poetryfoundation.org/poems/44272/the-road-not-taken`), a hiker comes to a crossroads and must decide which road to take. That event is not, in and of itself, too meaningful. But later, the speaker says his choice of road has made "all the difference." That statement invests the choice of road with a big (and unexplained) importance, leading you to wonder about all such choices, all such crossroads. And that makes it a symbol.
- **The poet has created a highly-charged *setting* around these objects or events — a place or time or circumstance in which everything takes on a heightened meaning.** A familiar kind of heightened setting is the horror movie, in which almost everything symbolizes good, evil, devils, spirits, and so forth. Dreams are another heightened or supercharged setting.

» **The possible symbol takes on a great deal of importance within the poem itself.** Think of the sword in the stone in many King Arthur tales. Swords are symbolic already, of course: They often stand for war or political power (such as in kingship). But when the little boy draws the sword out of the stone, something none of the great warriors of the world can do, the sword comes to *stand for* the child's glittering future as the king of Camelot, as well as his close alliance with magic.

» **You think it's a symbol.** If something strikes you as symbolic, go with that feeling. Apply it to the rest of the poem and see how it works. Trust your powers of reading.

Figuring out what symbols stand for

You can find symbols everywhere in poetry, as in this poem by English poet William Blake:

READ ALOUD

The Sick Rose

O rose, thou art sick.
The invisible worm
That flies in the night
In the howling storm

Has found out thy bed
Of crimson joy,
And his dark secret love
Does thy life destroy.

TIP

We *could* read this poem literally (a flying worm destroys a flower). But we can appreciate the poem more — and understand it better — if we slow down and try to figure out what the symbols mean. Here are some guidelines:

» **You get a sense that the events in the poem *transcend* themselves.** These events don't stand only for themselves, a *particular* rose being savaged by a *particular* worm. If that were all, you could easily say, "Who cares? Worms eat plants. Big deal." But these events suggest a larger world of meaning. How do you know? In this case, both the rose and the worm are well-established symbols: Roses often signify love or beauty, and the worm is often used to signify death and decay. So here, you see one famous symbol (which you know as a symbol for death) destroy another famous symbol (which you're familiar with as a symbol for beauty). Although literally all you read about is a worm destroying a flower, you *feel* a great weight of significance, pulling you to think of *other* kinds of destruction, other losses of beauty, innocence, or life.

» **The *setting* of the poem is gruesome and frightening.** You feel the setting in the words the "howling storm," the night, and the invisible, flying worm that with its "dark, secret love" destroys the rose — all scary notions. These words invest everything that happens with a heightened feeling, as in a melodrama or frightening story. That heightened character helps suggest that the action is symbolic.

» **This poem seems to create its own universe, in which the death of a rose involves sickness and sorrow.** The worm is "invisible" and its love "secret." Secrecy and invisibility imply stealth and furtiveness, as though fate or some evil entity were attacking the rose.

» **The speaker addresses the rose as "thou," an unfamiliar way to talk to a plant.** Blake is using *personification*, a figure of speech in which a poet gives human attributes to something not human. The rose had a prior life of "crimson joy" that it is now losing; in addressing the rose directly, the speaker prompts in us a more intimate sense of pity. In the worm's insidious sneakiness, we may also feel more personification.

Shall we agree that the rose and the worm are symbols? Excellent. So what do they stand for? The poem doesn't explicitly say, so it's time for some intelligent guesswork.

Traditionally, roses symbolize beauty and love, and worms symbolize death. So does this poem depict death destroying beauty? Definitely a possibility. The rose also seems innocent and vulnerable; it doesn't stand much of a chance, what with a howling storm carrying lethal worms. The rose is "crimson," a bright red, while the worm is invisible and emerges from the darkness. As a reader, you may feel not only the death of innocence (symbolized by the death of the rose) but also the inescapability of that death. Many readers see the rose's "bed / Of crimson joy" as a symbol for sexual innocence, which imparts a whole other world.

TIP

Watch for indicators (including your own feelings) that the poem represents a larger world than its images normally would by themselves. In "The Sick Rose," we enter such a universe, the play of love, life, joy, sickness, and chaos. Many poems, possibly most, include a moment when you feel the poem's universe enlarge or radiate into a larger one, a wider network of meaning. That's when you know you're in the presence of symbols.

Discovering private symbols

With some symbols, the poet gives you an obvious A, but you get few clues as to B or C — that is, what the symbol stands for and what it means. These are known as *private symbols*. Indicators in the poem — sometimes just the emotion with which the poem is written — tell you they *are* symbols, but you just don't know what they stand for. The French poets called the *Symbolists* created an entire poetic technique from this kind of symbolism, and it dominates much poetry written today.

One of the most famous of private symbols is from Arthur Rimbaud's "Bateau Ivre" ("The Drunken Boat"):

READ ALOUD

If I desire one water in Europe, it's the pond,
Black and cold, where, against the perfumed twilight,
A crouching child, full of sadness, launches,
A boat, frail as a May butterfly.

Here, the A is clear and detailed: cold pond, sad child, boat, butterfly. Our guess is that this image is packed with the sadness, loneliness, and fragility of childhood. Maybe this symbol is from Rimbaud's childhood, maybe not. Either way, the setting is definitely emotionally charged. Everything seems to take on a larger meaning than you'd expect in the simple image of a child playing with a boat on a pond. That heightened setting, suggesting a larger meaning, is why many readers think this seemingly private moment stands for all childhoods, not just Rimbaud's.

TIP

How do you know when a symbol *is* a symbol? In general, whenever an image seems to evoke meanings that extend far beyond itself, you can call it a symbol — even when you can't work out the B and C for sure.

Similes: My love is like a can of tuna

A *simile* is an explicit comparison — it is directly stated, often using the words *like* or *as*. If a poet writes, "My love is like a can of tuna," that silly poet would be coming right out and saying, "He resembles that can of tuna in many ways." (Cold and hard on the outside, soft and nourishing and a bit fishy on the inside?)

You can find similes everywhere. In Homer's *The Iliad*, the great warrior Achilles changes a battle simply by letting loose a great shout:

READ ALOUD

Infinite terror wracked the foe:
Like the piercing shrill of a trumpet
The lucid voice of Achilles rang
And when the Trojans heard his brassy cry
Their hearts hurt, their thick-maned horses
Bucked, sensing agony near

The shout was *like* "the piercing shrill of a trumpet," which is a simile.

Notice how the word *brassy* continues the comparison of Achilles's voice to a trumpet. This Homer is pretty good, right?

When the English poet Lord Byron wants to describe the savage attack of the Assyrian army in "The Destruction of Sennacherib," he compares it to a wolf attacking a flock or "fold" of sheep:

> The Assyrian came down like a wolf on the fold

Byron says the Assyrian was *like* "a wolf on the fold."

REMEMBER

Similes help make an image or state of feeling more precise. The two similes above help us feel the reverberant shout of Achilles and the Assyrian attack.

Metaphors: My love *is* a can of tuna

Metaphor makes a comparison *without* using *like* or *as.* Instead, the poet talks *as though* thing A really *were* thing B. (My love isn't *like* a can of tuna; he *is* a can of tuna.)

Where simile works with similarity, *metaphor* is an apparent claim of exact equivalence or identity. It's far more intimate than simile, and it packs a greater emotional punch. When in "The Search" Ghanaian poet Kwesi Brew writes that "The past / Is but the cinders / Of the present," the unspoken comparison between the passage of time and the destructiveness of fire drives home the way time erases what used to be (much stronger than if he had written, "The past / Is *like* the cinders / Of the present").

Metaphor invokes a kind of psychological magic. Unspoken comparisons challenge *you* to think of all the ways two things are alike — for example, the passage of time and the destructiveness of fire.

TIP

How do you know when you're seeing metaphors? When poets speak of one thing as being another, even though literally those two things *aren't the same.* My love is not *literally* a can of tuna, but I *call* him one to bring out the similarities between him and that foodstuff. In *The Iliad,* Homer writes of war-spears "stuck in the ground, longing for their fill of flesh." Spears can't long for gore; only warriors can. But Homer speaks as if the spears *can* thirst for blood, as if the spears were *literally* warriors. This is definitely a metaphor (*personification* again, as in "The Sick Rose"; see the section "Figuring out what symbols stand for"); it rams home the all-penetrating rage of war.

Shakespeare seems to *think* in metaphors. When Hamlet feels he has done something wrong, he cries, "O, my offense is rank; it smells to heaven," implicitly comparing his misdeed to the smell of something rotten. When a servant in *Timon of Athens* wants to say Timon has no money, he declares, "'Tis deepest winter in Lord Timon's purse," comparing the emptiness of winter to the emptiness of Timon's wallet. These images have greater power for *not* using *like* or *as*.

TECHNICAL STUFF

It helps to lay out metaphors into three aspects: *vehicle*, *tenor*, and *grounds*. The vehicle is the thing being compared, the tenor is the thing to which it is being compared, and the grounds are the specific point(s) of comparison or connection:

Source	Vehicle	Tenor	Grounds
Brew's "The Search"	Fire	Time	Destructiveness
Homer's *The Iliad*	Spears	Warriors	Bloodthirstiness
Shakespeare's *Hamlet*	Hamlet's offense	Something rotten	Smell; corruption
Shakespeare's *Timon of Athens*	Timon's finances	Winter	Emptiness

Sometimes you get only the vehicle, and the tenor is left strongly implied. That happens in Christopher Marlowe's *Doctor Faustus*, when Faustus cries, "Fair Nature's eye, rise, rise again, and make / Perpetual day." The vehicle is "Fair Nature's eye," and Marlowe doesn't tell you that the tenor is "the sun," but it's pretty clear that's what is rising and making day.

Metaphors come in different varieties. Here are two common flavors:

- **Metonymy:** The poet replaces the name of a thing with the name of something *closely associated with* that thing. People do this all the time, as when they speak of the *White House* when they mean the *President, Silicon Valley* when they mean *the U.S. tech industry,* or *suits* when they mean *bosses.* In the table above, we saw Homer doing it with those bloodthirsty spears, a metonymy for warlike warriors.
- **Synecdoche:** The poet uses a part of a thing to stand for the whole thing, as when people say, "Nice wheels!" when they mean "Nice car!" or "Sweet threads!" to mean "Nice clothes!" In *Macbeth,* a servant is told, "Take thy face hence," when Macbeth, of course, wants *all* of him, not just his face, to get out.

REMEMBER

Knowing the names of these tools is not as important as staying alert for them. When you come upon a metaphor, try to sort out *vehicle* and *tenor*, and think about the *grounds*. The poet's art, and much of the poem's psychological magic, will become a little clearer and all the more powerful.

Allusions: If you know, you know

An *allusion* is a reference to something — a person, place, story, historical event — outside the poem. Poets allude to these things to create metaphors and intensify the message of their poetry.

Renaissance poet Edmund Spenser's "Epithalamion" concerns his wedding day. The speaker describes his bride-to-be, who approaches "Like Phoebe from her chamber in the east." Who's Phoebe? AI, search engine, or reference books will tell you Spenser is *alluding* to Phoebe, the Greek goddess of the moon, a virgin goddess. The moon rises in the east. So, his bride is coming like the rising moon, a virgin goddess. His allusion creates a simile: he's praising his fiancée for her beauty and chastity. If you know about Phoebe, you're off to a great start; if not, you owe it to yourself to find out who she is and why the poet alludes to her.

Writers of all eras make allusions — none more than contemporary writers. The lyrics of hip-hop, rap, and metal music are full of allusions. In his track "m.A.A.d city," Kendrick Lamar alludes to BG's, Crips, Piru's, Rosecrans, AKs, ARs, choppers, nines, YG Lucky, Conans, L Boggs, Yan Yan, TEC, slave ships, pyramids, hieroglyphics, Compton, Halle Berry, Angelina Jolie, the Bible, and much, much else. These allusions are familiar to many readers. If you're one of them, you have a deep appreciation of his art. Anyone else will have to get busy with the research.

Here is distinguished chemist and poet Roald Hoffman, in a passage from his poem "Deceptively Like a Solid," which concerns glass (a liquid deceptively like a solid). The poem ends in a spasm of allusions, all having to do with glass:

READ ALOUD

Optical fibers   Crystal Palace
The Worshipful Company of Glass Sellers
Recycled   Millefiori
prone to shattering   Prince Rupert's drops
Chartres, Rouen, Amiens   Float
Pyrex   Vycor   glass wool
network modifiers   the Palomar mirror

TIP

As with Lamar's "m.A.A.d city," if you really want to know "Deceptively Like a Solid," you'll track down these allusions. "Chartres, Rouen, Amiens," for example, alludes to three great Gothic cathedrals in France; each one has a magnificent stained-glass window. And "the Palomar mirror" refers to a huge reflecting surface created for a giant telescope at Hale Observatory on Mt. Palomar in California. Like the cathedrals' windows, the Palomar mirror is an astonishing thing done with glass.

REMEMBER

Tracking down allusions enriches your understanding of poetry. With both Lamar and Hoffman, as with any poem, if you do the legwork, you'll be able to embrace much more of the poem — and the world.

Music: What You Hear, Feel, and See

When people talk about poetry, they use some of the same terminology that they use when they talk about music. For example, a *line* of poetry is a group of words printed as a unit on the page — usually on the same physical level. Here's one line from Shakespeare:

> Farewell — thou art too dear for my possessing

And two lines from Jack Spicer:

> Poet,
> Be like God.

People also speak of numbers of lines as units. Two lines are a *couplet;* usually we use this word to refer to two lines in the same form, like these two from John Milton's "L'Allegro":

> Come and trip it as ye go
> On the light fantastic toe

They also speak of *tercets* (three lines), *quatrains* (four), *cinquains* (five), *sestets* (six), *septets* (seven), and *octaves* (eight).

Just as in music, a *stanza* is a group of lines arranged as a unit. The most familiar kinds of stanzas are those the poet repeats in exactly the same form again and again, as in the poem by Robert Herrick's:

READ ALOUD

To the Virgins, to Make Much of Time

Gather ye rosebuds while ye may,
  Old time is still a-flying;
And this same flower that smiles today
  Tomorrow will be dying.

The glorious lamp of heaven, the sun,
  The higher he's a-getting,
The sooner will his race be run,
  And nearer he's to setting.

But the word *stanza* can also refer to any group of lines considered as a unit — not just those that have a repeated form.

Finally, the word *music* is used to denote the sounds and rhythms in a poem. In the following sections, we separate music into these elements:

- The sounds of words
- **Rhyme** (the echoing or repetition of sounds)
- The rhythms of lines

Orchestrating sound

Poets are supremely conscious of the following physical properties of words:

- **Length** in letters and syllables
- **Length** in time (how long it takes to say them)
- **Vowels** (long, short, double vowels, diphthongs)
- **Consonants** (soft, hard, liquid, rough, and so on)
- **Physical properties** of words and letters (their actual appearance; how they sound, alone and in combinations; where sounds come within words and across lines or sections of poetry)
- **Ease or difficulty of pronunciation**

Poets know what sorts of sounds are smooth and sweet, and which are clotted and ugly. When sounds are pleasant together, it is referred to as *euphony;* when they are uncomfortable, rough, or ugly, it is called *dissonance.* Whenever a line sounds sweet and smooth, there's a reason; same thing when a line sounds cramped, crude, or guttural.

Poets are famous for writing beautiful, sweet-sounding verse — and they should be. Here are four lines of pleasing sounds from "The Garden" by the 17th-century English poet Andrew Marvell. The speaker finds himself in a beautiful place:

READ ALOUD

What wondrous life is this I lead!
Ripe apples drop about my head;
The luscious clusters of the vine;
Upon my mouth do crush their wine;

Listen for the vowels in the first line: "Wh*a*t wondr*ou*s l*i*fe *i*s th*i*s *I* l*ea*d!" Many readers find these vowels light and delightful. This line is a good example of euphony. Marvell chose the vowels on purpose to create this scene of a rich garden offering itself to the inhabitant. Read aloud the phrase "luscious clusters of the vine," with its *u* and *s* and *sh* sounds! Truly luscious.

Here are three lines of very ugly sounds from Jonathan Swift's "Description of a City Shower." Swift is describing a flood that washes through London, sweeping before it a sickening tide of garbage:

READ ALOUD

Sweepings from butchers' stalls, dung, guts, and blood,
Drowned puppies, stinking sprats, all drenched in mud,
Dead cats, and turnip tops, come tumbling down the flood.

Can you hear the nasty, revolting upwelling of consonants *(ng, g, bl)* in phrases such as "dung, guts, and blood"? Swift arranged these sounds to disgust you. Poets *want* poems to sound ugly when ugliness is appropriate — as, for example, in describing war, suffering . . . or city trash. These three lines are a resounding, nauseating example of dissonance.

The poet's challenge is to orchestrate the sonic properties of words. So, in a poem, you'll find patterns of sounds, repetitions, or combinations — all of which are there because the poet brought them together in that specific way.

Alliteration

When a particular consonant sound is repeated in a passage of verse, it's called *alliteration*. (Some people use this word to mean repetition of the same sound at the *beginnings* of neighboring words, but we use it more generally.)

Read the following lines from Jackson Mac Low's poem "Antic Quatrains":

READ ALOUD

Granados labeled a gateleg table stable
As droll goaltenders tensed at tenebrist rites

See and hear all the *l* and *t* sounds in this passage? That's alliteration (the repetition of the same sounds).

Assonance

When the same *vowel* sound is repeated in a group of neighboring words, it's called *assonance*. Listen for the assonance in Barbara Guest's poem "Red Lilies":

READ ALOUD

> snow erupts from thistle
> to toe; the snow pours out of you.

Repeat Guest's lines and feel and hear — especially in the second line — the deep vowels roll slowly over and over.

How alliteration and assonance work together

Just *seeing* alliteration and assonance is one step; the next is seeing how these patterns connect to the poem's meaning and its impact on you. The English Romantic poet Percy Bysshe Shelley's poem "Ode to the West Wind" portrays the wildness of the spring wind, largely through its use of sound. Listen to these lines, in which he addresses the wind:

READ ALOUD

> Thou, on whose stream, 'mid the steep sky's commotion,
> Loose clouds like earth's decaying leaves are shed,
> Shook from the tangled boughs of heaven and ocean.

This poem is famous for its spectacular depictions of the clouds, sky, and winds. But what makes those images *physical* are the alliteration and assonance. Hear all those *s* and *sh* sounds, rushing like the wind? A variety of *o* sounds swirls throughout, and the second line is rich with long *e* sounds. Shelley adores this wind as a worshiper would adore a wild god, and the wildness and divinity come through in the *sound palette* (collection of sounds) he chooses to embody his ecstatic images.

TIP

You can find Percy Bysshe Shelley's poem, "Ode to the West Wind," in hundreds of print anthologies of poetry and from online sources, including the Poetry Foundation: `www.poetryfoundation.org/poems/45134/ode-to-the-west-wind`.

Recognizing the varieties of rhyme

Rhyme is the repetition of a sound; it's an echo. In English, the most familiar kind of rhyme is called *perfect rhyme*, in which the echo is fairly exact, as in *moose* and *noose*, *floss* and *moss*, and *sting* and *ring*. The most familiar place for rhyme is at the ends of lines, which is called *end rhyme*.

End rhyme is what you hear in the Elizabethan poet Thomas Campion's "When to Her Lute Corinna Sings":

When to her lute Corinna sings,
Her voice revives the leaden strings,
And doth in highest notes appear,
As any challenged echo clear,

End rhyme helps organize poetry, helps make it musical, songlike, and memorable. But there's more: Rhyme very often *helps carry out what the verse is doing.* Corinna sings; we hear the strings revive. The *ing* sound that was in *sings* comes back around in the *ing* sound of *strings,* so the poem is doing exactly what it's describing: Corinna's voice really *is* reviving the strings. In the last two lines, her voice is made to *appear,* and it is like an echo, *clear,* just like the rhyme. Was Campion just lucky? No, he built these effects into his poem to body forth the meaning.

Rhyme isn't just an echo. Often it's how poets impart a physical impact to the pictures they are trying to create in your mind.

Many kinds of rhyme are not as exact as perfect rhyme. They tease and tickle the ear with almost-likeness. Many varieties of rhymes almost echo, but not quite.

- In **slant, near,** or **partial rhyme,** poets can rhyme only the final consonant sounds in the accented syllable of two words, as in *amaze* and *freeze.*
- In **vowel** rhyme, poets may rhyme *only* the vowel of two words, as in *nose* and *mope.*
- In **sight rhyme**, poets can rhyme words that *look* as if they rhyme even though they don't. English, which has wacky spelling, is full of such sight-rhyming pairs, like *bough* and *tough, or* lead and head in Marvell's "The Garden" (see the earlier section, "Orchestrating sound").

The names of these techniques are less important than what poets use them to achieve. Good readers look for those effects and watch how poets achieve them.

Emily Dickinson was quite an experimenter with rhyme:

I taste a liquor never brewed —
From Tankards scooped in Pearl —
Not all the Frankfort Berries
Yield such an Alcohol!

Alcohol and *pearl* share that final *l* sound, and their final vowel sounds, although not the *same*, are close enough for a very interesting effect.

Rhymes can come anywhere in a line of poetry; they don't have to come only at the end of the line. Edgar Allen Poe's poem "The Raven" features several lines in which there is internal rhyme — that is, rhyme occurring within lines, as well as at the ends: "Once upon a midnight dreary, while I pondered, weak and weary . . ."

REMEMBER

When reading poetry, watch for the poet's use of echoing sounds. In Poe's line, the rhyme is there for more than just pretty noise. The adjective modifying *midnight* rhymes with the adjective modifying *I*, which links the dreary night with the weary speaker.

Internal rhymes can cut across line endings! Rhymes in one line can chime with rhymes in the previous one, or the next. When you read Elizabeth Barrett Browning's Sonnet 43 (see the next section, "Feeling rhythm and measuring meter"), follow the long and short *e* sounds from line to line. Read aloud, dwelling on the long *e* sounds. It's a thrilling performance by a poet with a sharp ear for music.

Feeling rhythm and measuring meter

The general term *rhythm* denotes the natural occurrences of stressed and unstressed syllables in spoken or written language. When you speak, you *stress* some syllables and leave others *unstressed.* When you string a lot of words together, you start seeing patterns. Even in that last sentence, you can hear them:

> When you *string* a *lot* of *words* to*geth*er, you *start see*ing *pat*terns.

Rhythm is a natural thing. It's in everything you say and write. But these are *natural* rhythms; there's no pre-established pattern, just the rhythms this string of words happens to have.

Traditional forms of verse, however, use pre-established rhythmic patterns called *meters.* That's an important distinction: the language we use every day has natural, unmetered *rhythms.* Poetry, though, often uses *meter*, those pre-established patterns used for millennia in traditional poetry.

TECHNICAL STUFF

The word *meter* means *measure* in Greek, and that's what meters are — premeasured patterns of stressed and unstressed syllables.

Much of English poetry is written in lines that string together one or more *feet* (individual rhythmical units). Feet are the individual building blocks of meter.

Here are the most common feet, the rhythms they represent, and an example of that rhythm:

- **Anapest:** duh-duh-DUH, as in *but of course!*
- **Dactyl:** DUH-duh-duh, as in *honestly*
- **Iamb:** duh-DUH, as in *collapse*
- **Trochee:** DUH-duh, as in *pizza*

To build a line of verse, poets can string together repetitions of one of these feet. Such repetitions are named as follows:

- 1 foot: monometer
- 2 feet: dimeter
- 3 feet: trimeter
- 4 feet: tetrameter
- 5 feet: pentameter
- 6 feet: hexameter

So the famous *iambic pentameter* is a string of five iambs, as in Christopher Marlowe's line from *Dr. Faustus* below. We've indicated the syllables that are *stressed* (in italics) or unstressed (regular typeface), and below the line we show the regular iambic pentameter meter in alternating patterns of unstressed (duh) and stressed (DUH).

> Was *this* the *face* that *launched* a *thou*sand *ships*
> Duh-DUH-duh-DUH-duh-DUH-duh-DUH-duh-DUH

In this case, the line is very regular — that is, it conforms closely to the rhythm, all stresses in place. There are five unstressed syllables alternating with five stressed — in other words, five duh-DUHs. For the 2016 Tony Awards, composer and playwright Lin-Manuel Miranda read a sonnet (a Shakespearean sonnet, actually) that included this memorable moment:

> And love is love is love is love is love
> Is love; cannot be moved or swept aside

That first line falls into the same pattern as Christopher Marlowe's line from *Dr. Faustus:* And LOVE is LOVE is LOVE is LOVE is LOVE. In both rhythm (the natural way of reading it) and meter (the ideal, premeasured pattern), it's in iambic pentameter. (And we *do* love how the *loves* cascade around the end of the line, as if they, indeed, cannot be swept aside.)

As you read more poetry, you'll start to recognize feet and meters.

REMEMBER

Rhythm is not the same as meter. The difference between rhythm and meter is the difference between the beat of a song (which, like poetic meter, is always predetermined and usually fixed) and the rhythms played over that beat (which can be spontaneous and very various). In poetry, natural rhythms occur all over the place and help get meaning and feeling across. But so can *meter*, and that's why poets have used it for thousands of years.

To explore the difference between rhythm and meter, take a look at Sonnet 43 from *Sonnets from the Portuguese* by Elizabeth Barrett Browning:

READ ALOUD

How do I love thee? Let me count the ways. (A)
I love thee to the depth and breadth and height (B)
My soul can reach, when feeling out of sight (B)
For the ends of Being and ideal Grace. (A)
I love thee to the level of every day's (A)
Most quiet need, by sun and candle-light. (B)
I love thee freely, as men strive for Right; (B)
I love thee purely, as they turn from Praise. (A)
I love thee with the passion put to use (C)
In my old griefs, and with my childhood's faith. (D)
I love thee with a love I seemed to lose (C)
With my lost saints — I love thee with the breath, (D)
Smiles, tears, of all my life! — and, if God choose, (C)
I shall but love thee better after death. (D)

This is a *sonnet* — a songlike poem of 14 lines. This sonnet is written in iambic pentameter (count the duh-DUHs in each line; you should find five duh-DUHs, five iambs). It also has an interesting *rhyme scheme*. We've marked out the rhymes at the end of every line; each A rhymes with each other A, and so forth. The poem has two *quatrains* rhyming ABBA ABBA, and a *sestet* rhyming CDCDCD.

A form like this is challenging to write because the poet has to come up with four rhymes for two of her chosen sounds. A couple of the rhymes — *grace* and *ways*; *faith* and *breath* — are beautifully slanted or partial. Browning is playing with your ear, inviting you to delight in the difference between what you expect (perfect rhyme) and what she gives you (just this side of perfect). And as we mentioned above, long *e* sounds course through this poem, beginning to end.

Now take a look at the *meter* and how it compares to the *rhythm*. Iambic pentameter, as mentioned, goes like this:

> Duh-DUH, duh-DUH, duh-DUH, duh-DUH, duh-DUH

Apply that to the very first line of the poem:

> How *do* I *love* thee *let* me *count* the *ways*

A robot might say it that way. But reading it like this is more natural:

> *How* do I *love* thee? *Let* me *count* the *ways*

The first foot, which we expect to be duh-DUH, gets *reversed* into DUH-duh. You can do that; no rule against it. In fact, poets make *substitutions* like that throughout a metered line. What Browning is doing is *varying the rhythm*. In fact, it's pretty much a rule that any metered poem of appreciable length *has to* vary the rhythm; otherwise, it could get old fast. Iambic pentameter is in the background, as steady as the beat in a song, but Browning is playing natural rhythms over the meter, just as a jazz soloist might play all sorts of riffs and rhythms over a steady beat.

Certainly, this poem has lines that adhere closely to iambic pentameter, such as this one:

> I *love* thee *to* the *depth* and *breadth* and *height*

although you *could* read that line like this:

> *I love thee* to the *depth* and *breadth* and *height*

Can you feel the emotional difference between the two? Those three strong stresses in *I love thee* truly sell the notion that the speaker loves the beloved.

Consider this way of reading line 4:

> For the *ends* of *being* *and* *ideal* *grace*

It's still an iambic pentameter line. You can't read it:

> For *the* ends *of* be*ing* and *i*deal *grace*

The first way is more natural. That first foot is actually an *anapest* (duh-duh-DUH) substituted for the iamb. You don't necessarily need to know that — only *hear the beat of the iambic pentameter meter behind the spoken rhythms of the poem.*

Browning ends some of her lines with commas or periods, which we call *end-stopped lines*, but she also runs some sentences right over into the next line without intervening punctuation, as in:

> I love thee with a love I seemed to lose
> With my lost saints

That is called *enjambment* — the practice of continuing a phrase or clause from one line to the next without intervening punctuation. You expect to pause at the end of each line, but Browning tugs you irresistibly into the next.

Poets use enjambment to pull you into all manner of surprises — for example, the poignant echo of *lose* with *lost*. Enjambment is a way to emphasize words and phrases, create tension, or lead the reader around the end of one line to a realization or discovery in the next one — as in "With my lost saints." Lin-Manuel Miranda does it, too! Love is love . . .

Browning is working with rhyme and rhythm *along with* the words and images she's orchestrating. The music is part of the words but also a world, so to speak, *underneath* the words, a physical world of sound and stress. Browning knows what rhythm and music do to you, and she knows how to use them. This Elizabeth Barrett Browning is good, right?

As a reader, sharpen your sensitivity to music and rhythm. Watch how poets use them. With poems in regular meters, stay alert to how natural rhythms and meter play against each other — and enjoy the world under the words.

Shape and flow: Visual rhythm

Visual rhythm is a poem's shape and the physical length of its lines. Much of the way you *feel* about a poem has to do with that shape, the ins and outs of its lines. So in reading a poem, you're not only trying to figure out its *sense* (what it's saying), and not only taking account the music and rhythm and how they contribute to the meaning. You're also taking into account the *visual aspects* of the poem — the way it looks, its shape, the way lines and words are arranged on the page, flow from here to there across line breaks, spaces, and stanzas. That, too, has a lot to contribute to the poem's impact.

Consider these lines from "Death" by George Herbert:

> Death, thou wast once an uncouth, hideous thing,
> Nothing but bones,
> The sad effect of sadder groans:
> Thy mouth was open, but thou couldst not sing.

That first long line contracts to a shorter line, which opens to a somewhat longer line, a little less indented, and then back to a long line. The two shorter lines seem enclosed (coffinlike?!) in the longer ones, and you're invited to expand and contract your attention along with the lines.

See how the first line, containing the "uncouth, hideous thing," contracts to "Nothing but bones," as though it were a body decomposing? This George Herbert is good, right?

Visual rhythm is *supremely* important in *open-form verse*, in which there is no preplanned meter, no regular line lengths, meaning the poet sculpts each line to its perfect length. George Oppen, one of the finest of the Objectivist poets, handles the visual rhythms of these lines from "Psalm" with almost unbearable sensitivity. His theme is deer and the natural world:

Their paths

Nibbled thru the fields, the leaves that shade them
Hang in the distances
Of sun

The small nouns

Crying faith
In this in which the wild deer
Startle, and stare out.

Oppen, a master of white space, goes from a very short line, much indented, to a much longer one, perhaps giving the sense of how deer paths wander through the fields. (Note the enjambment in "Their paths / Nibbled thru the fields," which makes you follow the clause around the end of the line all the way back to the word *Nibbled*, as if *you* were following a path, too . . . because you are!) The stanza contracts to "Of sun," concentrating your imagination on the sun (he actually makes you look right at it) and how it illuminates distance. *The small nouns*, three small words, are isolated away from the other lines, again redirecting your attention to the words of which this poem is made. Some readers may feel that the deer are also "nouns," living souls that cry to one another and have a kind of faith in the world in which they live — and then startle and stare. Again and again, the shape of the poem guides your understanding and experience, both of what the words are saying, and of the very words as objects in and of themselves.

Oppen uses enjambment to keep you unraveling the sentence all the way to the end and the final image. Constantly, he moves you in and out, left and right. That *visual rhythm* lends drama and wonder to the poem.

IN THIS CHAPTER

» Understanding the elements of interpretation

» Getting comfortable with speculating (as opposed to knowing for sure) about a poem's meaning

» Determining what is explicit in a poem and what is implied

» Practicing informed speculation

» Using subject, tone, language, music, and narrative elements to help you interpret

Chapter 5
Practicing the Art of Interpretation

Poetry is often said to *burst* with meaning. So, here's the poem, and here's you, the reader. Your job, should you decide to accept it, is to pay close attention to (a) what's happening in the poem and (b) what's happening to you as you read, which may get you to (c) the meanings, sensations, and emotions evoked in the poem.

There are strategies to doing all that, ways of thinking, ways of feeling, ways of breaking things apart and putting them back together, ways of discovering meaning. These are the kinds of things you get better at — for a lifetime, if you want to — the more you do them.

Reading for Discovery

Interpretation is the act of accounting for the ideas and feelings the poem gives you when you read it. You start by investigating what a poem is doing and how it does it. Then you can begin to unlock what all that poetic energy *means*, how it feels to you, how it spurs your thoughts and emotions. In this chapter, we give you guidelines and pointers to become a good interpreter.

Pay close attention to poetry. When you do, often you're rewarded with an understanding that goes much further, much deeper — and lasts much longer — than a quick read gives you. In fact, poetry itself, as the poet Robert Creeley once said, is "an act of attention"! Reading (and writing) poetry is a great way to learn how to pay attention to the world. (Robert Creeley's love poem, "The Business," appears in Chapter 19.)

Pay attention to at least two things at once: *what* a poem is doing and *how* the poem accomplishes it. A tricky assignment — kind of like making bread while riding a unicycle — but it's worth it. The question is, what do you pay attention *to*?

Start by paying attention to two general aspects of poetry: *sense* and *music*, as covered in the following sections.

Sense: Getting direct and literal

Many people think of poetry as being full of profound statements and insights. And it is. Pay attention to them when you find them. But not *all* poems make statements outright. Some poems simply present a picture, ask a question, or plunge the reader into an experience. Almost all poems have a *sense*, something they mean to express, to do, or to call to your attention.

REMEMBER

Sense is what the poem is saying or appears to be exploring; its explicit meaning, without considering metaphor, symbols, or other figures of speech or poetic aspects. This aspect is often called the *literal interpretation* of a poem.

Poems with an explicit point to make

Many poems *do* make outright statements. The poet has something to say about life, a judgment to make, a truth to reveal.

Here's an example, by the Arabian poet Abû-l-`Alâ' al-Ma'arrî:

READ ALOUD

Friend, this world is like an unburied corpse,
And we're the dogs barking round it.
If you go in and eat, you're a loser;
If you stay out, and hunger, you gain.
Anyone the night doesn't mug,
Gets rolled: Time's disasters at dawn.

You can pay attention to a poem in several different ways. Here are three different kinds of attention you can pay to the poem by Abû-l-`Alâ' al-Ma'arrî. You can apply this to any other poem as well:

- **First-glance attention:** Here, you're reading for (1) basic facts and background and (2) literal meaning. In (1) you note the poem's length, the name of the poet, the title, and the structure. This poem, for example, is untitled, short, and doesn't rhyme; it doesn't seem to fall into any particular form.

  First-glance attention includes a little research. Hop online — or consult a print encyclopedia — and discover more about the poet's life and times. Here, we find that the poem is written by an Arabian poet of the 10th and 11th centuries AD. Reading a poem without such research is like buying a car without knowing the make, model or date. It also denies you the added pleasure of *learning new stuff.*

  First-glance attention also includes the answers to two basic questions, the two most literal ones you can ask: *What's this poem about?* and *What's it say?* It seems to be about life in this world and the best way to live. The speaker doesn't see the world as a happy place.

- **Glancing-under-the-hood attention:** Step beyond asking the literal questions to asking *how the poem works* and *how it makes you feel.* This is where the real fun starts. Here is where you troll for metaphors, similes, symbols, allusions, all those poetic turns that lead to wide, deep meaning. Having found them, you try to figure out what they imply, the world of meaning that radiates from them.

  You may notice the simile in the first line of the Abû-l-`Alâ' al-Ma'arrî poem: "[T]his world is like an unburied corpse." This simile is followed by a metaphor: "And we're the dogs barking round it." The world (human experience) is like a corpse that "we" (all people) feed on like scavengers with nothing better to eat. These sentiments don't exactly speak well for the world. But what, exactly, is it implying about people? Asking such a question will lead you to the next level of attention.

» **Longest, most-loving-glance attention:** As its name implies, this is when you hold that loving glance longest, dig deepest.

Here, follow the sense of the metaphor, and you find that Abû-l-`Alâ' al-Ma'arrî actually has a little philosophical advice: *Don't get too involved with "this world."* ("If you stay out," he says, "you gain.") (Oooo: it sounds, doesn't it?, like a game of dice or cards, where there is risk in getting in and relative safety in staying out. Another metaphor.) That way, when you suffer (and everybody either gets "mugged" by night or "rolled" by daylight, which brings "disasters"), you can at least control your own behavior.

Longest, most-loving-glance attention is a wonderful place. We can't tell you how much we enjoy going there. Such intense attention means you care.

Paying attention brings many rewards. We proposed a main message in Abû-l-`Alâ' al-Ma'arrî's poem: Don't get too involved in the world, and your sufferings will be less. But then we read, "If you stay out, and hunger, you gain." This line is a *paradox* (that is, two things appear to conflict or contradict, and yet they coexist as if both were true). You gain if you stay out — but staying out also leaves you hungry. We *love* that. It's one of those moments poetry can give you. A weary speaker advises you to stay apart from the world — but then admits, to some degree, that it will be hard. Feel all the experience behind those words?

TIP

Pay close attention. Watch both what a poem is doing and how it does it — and later, pay close attention to your conclusions and how you draw them. You bring intense attention to things all the time. Bring it to poetry sometimes — after bringing it to your job, your favorite TV show, your loved ones, the purchase of underwear, skateboarding — and you may gain and *not* be hungry.

Poems that make you feel (instead of making an outright statement)

Consider this poem by William Wordsworth. Notice how it gives you an experience but doesn't offer bold statements or insights:

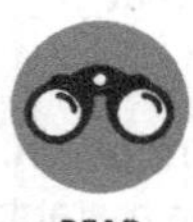
READ ALOUD

The Solitary Reaper

Behold her, single in the field,
Yon solitary Highland Lass!
Reaping and singing by herself;
Stop here, or gently pass!
Alone she cuts and binds the grain,
And sings a melancholy strain;
O listen! for the Vale profound,
Is overflowing with the sound.

No Nightingale did ever chaunt,
More welcome notes to weary bands,
Of travellers in some shady haunt,
Among Arabian sands:
A voice so thrilling ne'er was heard,
In spring-time from the Cuckoo-bird,
Breaking the silence of the seas,
Among the furthest Hebrides.

Will no one tell me what she sings? —
Perhaps the plaintive numbers flow,
For old, unhappy, far-off things,
And battles long ago:
Or is it some more humble lay,
Familiar matter of to-day?
Some natural sorrow, loss, or pain,
That has been, and may be again?

Whate'er the theme, the Maiden sang,
As if her song could have no ending;
I saw her singing at her work,
And o'er the sickle bending; —
I listened, motionless and still;
And, as I mounted up the hill,
The music in my heart I bore,
Long after it was heard no more.

TECHNICAL STUFF

With first-glance attention, you discover William Wordsworth (1770–1850) is an English poet renowned for writing about nature, landscape, and emotional responses to them. Many of his most famous poems are set in the Lake District of England or other beautiful places. And you may have discovered these unusual words and their meanings:

- **Highland:** An area of Scotland with high, striking hills and moors.
- **the Vale profound:** Another way of saying "the profound (deep) valley."
- **chaunt:** A different spelling of *chant.*
- **ne'er:** A poetic way of saying *never.*
- **Hebrides:** A group of islands in the west of Scotland.

- **plaintive numbers:** Melancholy rhythms.
- **lay:** Song.
- **Whate'er:** A poetic way of saying *whatever.*
- **o'er:** Another way of saying *over.*
- **mounted:** Climbed.

Wordsworth's poem plunges you into the midst of an experience. The speaker of the poem sees a girl working in the fields and hears the melancholy song she sings. A vivid picture: the highlands, the deep valley, the girl's work as she reaps the grain. And you get a general feeling about her song: The speaker says it is beautiful and melancholy, and that it echoes throughout the valley.

The speaker compares her song to that of two birds: the nightingale and the cuckoo. (Both the nightingale and the cuckoo are mentioned in poems throughout history. Do your research, and you'll find that the nightingale is famous for its melodious warble, and the song of the cuckoo usually announces the coming of spring, with all its joy and rebirth.) Yet the girl's song outdoes them both. Clearly, the speaker (evidently just a traveler passing through) is charmed and maybe a little intoxicated by the tune. The girl sings as if "her song could have no ending." The speaker stops for a moment, then climbs up the next hill and leaves the scene, with the memorable song in his heart.

The speaker tells you everything *but* the meaning of it all. Notice he doesn't even know what the song is about. He asks whether anyone will tell him, but there's no answer (certainly not from the girl, who keeps working). He *speculates*: Is it a song of war? Or something humbler? An old song? Or something new? He gets no answers to these questions, either, and neither do you, the reader. Even so, when the traveler leaves, the song stays with him "long after it was heard no more."

Many poems, like "The Solitary Reaper," simply present an experience and leave you to interpret it. Perhaps no interpretation is necessary. Maybe Wordsworth simply wants you to bask in the picture: girl in the midst of nature, singing a song.

TIP

What should you do with such poems? *Let yourself have the experience.* Envision the landscape of the Highlands; sense the rhythm of the girl's scything; hear the echo of her song throughout the deep valley. There's a mystery to the scene. You can't get to the bottom of it — but then, you can't get to the bottom of music either. Some songs stay with you long after you hear them. Some songs impart emotion from melody alone, even without the words. There is a sweetness to this momentary encounter. Neither girl nor traveler have anything to do with each other directly, but something memorable has happened — to the traveler and to you.

REMEMBER

"The Solitary Reaper" does not make an outright, explicit statement — although it leads you into a singular, compelling experience. Many experiences are like that: they simply *are* and resist further explanation. What matters is how you respond. The poem is like the song: You can't really tell what it means, but it stays with you long after you've read (or heard) it.

Music: Sounds and rhythms that lead to meaning

We've been using the word *music* to mean the total of the sounds and rhythms in a poem (see Chapter 3): the rhymes, the chimes, the line endings, the pauses, the patterns of stress and unstress. You don't have to know the labels to enjoy the sounds, any more than you have to know the number of a symphony to appreciate the music.

Related to *aural* (heard) music, as we've said, is the *visual rhythm* of the poem — its shape, the line lengths, and the impact of all that word-sculpture on you (see Chapter 4). The way a poem *looks* — its physical arrangement — is part of its message. Shape conveys feelings, just as sounds do. A poem written in bursts of brief lines strikes you differently from one that sprawls across the page in long lines.

REMEMBER

In poetry, form and *content* (what the poem contains — images, message, viewpoint) are mixed up in each other. Form is content and content is form.

Here's a passage from W.S. Merwin's poem "Leviathan" with a lot of exhilarating music in it. This fact for free: It concerns a whale. Read it aloud, paying attention to the sounds you hear and the rhythms you feel.

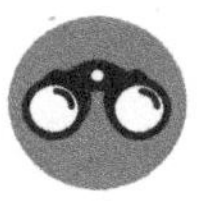

READ ALOUD

This is the black sea-brute bulling through wave-wrack,
Ancient as ocean's shifting hills, who in sea-toils,
Travelling, who furrowing the salt acres,
Heavily, his wake hoary behind him,
Shoulders spouting, the fist of his forehead,
Over wastes gray-green crashing, among horses unbroken,
From bellowing fields, past bone-wreck of vessels,
Tide-ruin, wash of lost bodies bobbing,
No longer sought for, and islands of ice gleaming,
Who ravening the rank flood, wave-marshalling,
Overmastering the dark sea-marches, finds home,
And harvest.

Feel the hugeness of the whale. Part of what's bringing that hugeness across is the poem's music, its sounds, its rolling rhythms. You can't really read these lines quickly. How quickly can you even say, "This is the black sea-brute bulling through wave-wrack"? The words force you to go slowly: The repeated *b*s and *r*s give your mouth a lot to do.

Read that first line again, aloud:

> This is the black sea-brute bulling through wave-wrack

Your mouth is working like a whale's jaw in a squid school! W.S. Merwin, among the most honored of U.S. poets, wants it that way. He has put slow, solid, heavy music in there to weigh down the lines so you move like a . . . well, like a whale. The lines are *describing* a whale, but they're doing more: They're *embodying* a whale.

REMEMBER

Music is seldom there only for its own sake. It can reinforce, represent, or even *be* the meaning of the poem. It's never just pretty, just window-dressing. Why not? Because poetry is *dense* (intense and compressed) and hasn't a syllable to spare.

Rhyme is an instrument that leads us to meanings as well. Here is a poem by Robert Frost (shown in Figure 5-1), a poet whose work has beckoned millions of readers with its descriptions of the New England way of life, its sensitive depictions of nature and the ways of the human beings Frost writes about.

READ ALOUD

> Nothing Gold Can Stay
>
> Nature's first green is gold,
> Her hardest hue to hold.
> Her early leaf's a flower;
> But only so an hour.
> Then leaf subsides to leaf.
> So Eden sank to grief,
> So dawn goes down to day.
> Nothing gold can stay.

So small yet so profound. The lines are short, and they rhyme in *couplets* (pairs of lines). Each rhyme is part of the meaning; each line packs a punch at the end. *Gold* is what nature can't seem to *hold* for very long. The *flower* of the early leaf lasts only for an *hour*, reinforcing the message. Next, the magic: Frost shifts from the *leaf*, which is what became of the flower, to Eden, the fall of humanity, and how things can't seem to stay at their best for very long. This little poem's tightness, its regular rhymes and rhythms, drive home the point.

FIGURE 5-1: Robert Frost.

Library of Congress/Public domain

Poetry is as much sculpture as it is music. Poets build their poems in specific shapes for specific reasons, and those shapes — the *visual rhythm* — become part of the poem's message and impact. A good example is Poem 15 from a series titled "A Coney Island of the Mind," by Lawrence Ferlinghetti, which concerns poets themselves:

READ ALOUD

Constantly risking absurdity
                                    and death
          whenever he performs
                                  above the heads
                                                    of his audience
the poet like an acrobat
                    climbs on rime
                              to a high wire of his own making
and balancing on eyebeams
                            above a sea of faces
          paces his way
                            to the other side of day performing entrechats
                              and sleight-of-foot tricks

and other high theatrics
and all without mistaking
any thing
for what it may not be

TIP

When reading this poem, slow down between lines, take your time, communicate Ferlinghetti's delicate, humorous tone. Notice the rhymes (not at the ends of lines, but in the middles!). And look up *entrechats* (we'll save you a step: it means an athletic ballet move in which the dancer leaps in the air and crosses his or her legs, or beats them together, several times).

Try our three kinds of attention on the music of poetry as well:

- **First-glance attention:** Who was Lawrence Ferlinghetti? When and where did he live? What's the poem about? What's it say?
- **Glancing-under-the-hood attention:** What are the big effects? The metaphors, symbols, images? What meanings do you get, what feelings, from these elements?
- **Long-loving-glance attention:** Ask, "What does the music add to the poem? What kind of music is there? Vowels? Consonants? Rhyme? Rhythms? Any interesting sculpture? How does the poem's form contribute to its content?

There's music galore. Read these lines aloud again:

READ ALOUD

and balancing on eyebeams
above a sea of faces
paces his way
to the other side of day

Next, train our three aspects of attention on these few brief lines:

- **First-glance attention:** Lawrence Ferlinghetti (1919–2021) was the longest-lived and among the best-known of the Beat poets (look *them* up). Writer, political activist, and businessman, he created and ran City Lights Bookstore in San Francisco. It's still going! Go buy a book of poems! He also wrote a little blurb for the first edition of *Poetry For Dummies!* And wow, that is some crazy form, wild and swinging. Some very interesting shape-building is going on — the wide-flung lines, all that open space, the lack of punctuation.
- **Glancing-under-the-hood attention:** Nice music: a lot of long *a* and *i* sounds. *Why* the long *a* and long *i* sounds? Perhaps to establish tension: that high-wire walker may fall any second. Or maybe to recall the sounds a thrilled crowd

makes as the high-wire walker performs. As for the visual rhythms, the freewheeling lines, hanging mobile-like in the air, reinforce the risk and daring of the poet's high-wire act.

TECHNICAL STUFF

In fact, Ferlinghetti once said that he was influenced by the artist Alexander Calder (look *him* up), famous for his many modernist mobiles. Ferlinghetti actually was trying to write word-mobiles!

» **Long-loving-glance attention:** Now you get to balance on the high wire of your own imagination. How is this poem's form entangled in its content? The spacious, jagged arrangement of the lines recalls the height and depth and risk surrounding the poet, which reinforces the excitement (and a little of the fear) in the poet's heart, and the anticipation in the reader's heart, when a poem begins. And how is the poem's content reflected in its form? The poem's content is playful and profound at the same time. It's an example of the risk poets take each time they write.

Speculating as You Read

Speculation. Is. The. Gold.

To interpret poetry is to go from literal/explicit to figurative/implicit. Most poems have a *literal* or *explicit* level, on which things are stated straight out, they happen, and no one can argue about it. In Robert Browning's poem "The Pied Piper of Hamelin," the guy with the pipe leads the kids out of town, and they're never seen or heard from again. That's the literal, explicit event in that poem, and if someone says, "No, he was playing a saxophone," or, "No, they all return as investment bankers," we can say, "Er, um, it's a pipe, and it says here they left and didn't come back."

But poetry has another world of meaning — one that isn't certain. You feel it and know it's there, you surely do, but it takes some work to say *how* you know or exactly *what* you're feeling. So you *speculate* — you speak, not in certainties, but in a provisional way about what you *think* you see. You start from concrete evidence (that's crucial), but you soon branch out from that evidence to build *theories* to account for your feelings.

REMEMBER

When you speculate about poetry, you never know for sure if your interpretation is right, but you're building on clues and intuitions to make an educated guess.

People speculate constantly in their daily lives: They speculate about people, about love and courtship, about music. They interpret street signs: "PED XING" or "ROAD WORK LANE ENDS 17 FT MERGE LEFT NOW." They interpret telephone schedules at hotels: "Local calls touch 8 plus area code plus local number. Hotel surcharge of $0.75 per call, for calls up to 20 minutes. $0.10 charge for each additional minute after the first 20 minutes (per call)." And poetry cries out for interpretation, too.

TIP

"Oh, come on," you may be saying. "Are you really saying *no* interpretations are ever wrong?" No: right and wrong answers do exist. Remember the Pied Piper above? That was no sax he was blowing. If you said, "Homer's *Iliad* is not set in 1956 Brooklyn," congratulations, here's your prize, you'd be right. But what's *that* worth? Much of the time in the poetry world, right answers either don't exist or (as with our two examples) aren't that interesting. So set aside all this business about "right answers" for a moment. Instead, think about interpretations that pay attention and really say something useful. When working up your interpretations of poetry, try for something that is:

- **Comprehensive:** It takes in as much of the poem as possible — its form; the speaker, theme, plot, problem, or character(s); the implications of the metaphors and figures of speech; the music (sound, rhythms, and so on) and visual aspects — the wild, swooping acrobatics of Ferlinghetti (see Ferlinghetti's poem, "A Coney Island of the Mind," in the preceding section), say, or the compressed profundity of Frost.
- **Accurate:** It tries to say nothing that is contradicted by something else in the poem, including its meaning, its form, or the historical and biographical facts surrounding the poem and its writer.

Mastering Speculation

Some people think that when you're interpreting, you're trying to figure out what the poet intended in the poem. Others say you can't ever be sure what the poet intended. But *we* recommend coming up with intelligent ways to account for the feelings the poem *gives you when you read it*. Try to explain what you think the poem is doing and how the poem does it.

TIP

When you interpret poetry, you do the same thing you do when you interpret anything:

- Understand the explicit, literal meaning.
- Consider what's implied, unsaid, or suggested — often by asking attentive questions about the poem.
- Build an interpretation based on your speculations about what's implied.

You may not take these steps in order. You may do some steps more often and others less, but all are involved in the interpretation of poetry.

Understanding the literal

If the poem in front of you tells a story or seems to have a fairly explicit topic (one that's *given* to you), take note. You need it. It's essential. That literal meaning, however, may be pretty complicated. But that's what's beautiful and worthwhile about poetry.

Here is a poem by Edward Arlington Robinson, among the finest poets in U.S. history. Watch what the poem explicitly lays out for you.

READ ALOUD

Richard Cory

Whenever Richard Cory went down town,
We people on the pavement looked at him:
He was a gentleman from sole to crown,
Clean favored, and imperially slim.

And he was always quietly arrayed,
And he was always human when he talked;
But still he fluttered pulses when he said,
"Good-morning," and he glittered when he walked.

And he was rich — yes, richer than a king —
And admirably schooled in every grace:
In fine, we thought that he was everything
To make us wish that we were in his place.

So on we worked, and waited for the light,
And went without the meat, and cursed the bread;
And Richard Cory, one calm summer night,
Went home and put a bullet through his head.

On the explicit or literal level, this poem tells the story of a high-class, rich, much-admired man who, contrary to all expectations, commits suicide. But that isn't all: The *speaker* in this poem, the voice telling it to us, is "We people on the pavement," and the people have a story, too, which Robinson explicitly lays out: They admire Richard Cory, they "wish that [they] were in his place," and they have lives filled with work and disappointment, fairly explicit in that line "went without the meat, and cursed the bread," an echo of a biblical image of misery.

Getting at what's implied

The literal part of a poem is important, but it's not all there is. In "Richard Cory" above, the explicit story invites a further feeling in the poem, emanating from the words and Robinson's orchestration of them. The feeling isn't explicit, but it's pretty strong nevertheless.

When you have strong feelings as you read a poem, start *interrogating* the poem. Step back and ask global questions about things like setting, speaker, character, and situation:

- **Where does the poem take place?** An American town.
- **What kind of town?** Some of the people are ordinary ("people on the pavement") and others aren't (Cory is "imperially" slim, which has overtones of royalty, picked up in the phrase "richer than a king").
- **What's the problem or conflict here?** The ordinary people wish they were like the richer, extraordinary ones. They find their lives hard and disappointing (implied in the phrase *went without the meat*, as if meat were something they expected to have and didn't get, to be replaced by "bread," a second-best food that is "cursed"). Yet one of the extraordinary people, one of the most admired, kills himself. That delivers an unexpected, uneasy feeling, surprise, or anxiety over the workings of fate. Maybe you can identify a source for that feeling later.

"Richard Cory" suggests a whole world of class divisions based on wealth. Cory isn't a king, but he is *like* one. People look at him, assume he's simply somehow "different," and they want to be in his place. Nowhere does the poem contain the phrase *class divisions* or *envy*, but nevertheless you can feel these forces at work.

Speculating about what's implied

Okay, so you've discovered issues relating to class and social life in general. Keep asking questions. What questions you ask depends on the poem. Often, you'll be asking about what isn't there, what doesn't happen, what is surprising or confusing.

For example, you may ask, "How well do the 'people of the pavement' know Richard Cory?" Not well, it seems. Almost all the adjectives describe his *outward* behavior and appearance. He glitters when he walks. He is "imperially slim." There is a hint of surprise, as if the "people of the pavement" expect Cory to be a showoff in his dress and condescending when he speaks to them. Instead, he dresses "quietly" and speaks in a "human" way.

What *aren't* you getting here? Possibly this: None of these words really penetrate to Cory's personality or intimate concerns. He keeps to himself. He is civil to people but not self-revealing. He is known to be rich and have everything everyone wants — but notice what we *aren't* told about him. He doesn't appear to work for a living. No mention of parents, mate, children, or any emotion or love in his life. Cory's life is too distant; the "people on the pavement" can't guess what's going on inside him. They are concerned with their own hard lives, which arouse resentments in them.

The last line of the poem comes as a shock. Notice the speaker doesn't say, "He shot himself." "Put a bullet through his head" is more explicit, which increases the shock. It's a violent moment in a quiet poem, *so* violent that you may want to retrace your steps and see how the poem led to that point. When you do, you may realize that the poem gets *darker* as it goes on, until you reach the final stanza, with its working, cursing, and gunfire.

Many people have taken away this implication from "Richard Cory": All his riches couldn't buy happiness. This is a perfectly good moral to the story, if you're looking for one. But see how much more our *speculations* have revealed: the frustrations of class, the deceptive nature of social life, the way people can hide great suffering from others, the brute facts that we envy other people and sometimes hate our own lives. Speculation delivers a lot, and a lot more that's worthwhile, than a simple moral.

REMEMBER

When interpreting poems, start with what's explicit. Then begin to consider what's suggested or implied and speculate on those suggestions. Try to build up an account of why you feel the way you do.

Searching for the Subject

With "Richard Cory" (see the earlier section, "Understanding the literal"), you can identify several subjects: social life, class, alienation (the feeling of being apart from people). When you've said, "I think the subject of this poem is X," you now have a direction to take in your speculations — that is, what does the poem *do* with that subject?

Some poems don't have subjects. Some are just wild howls of happiness or playful games with words. But it's hard to use words (even if they're flung all over the page) and not involve some aspect of the world and human life.

Tuning In to Tone

Tone (see Chapter 3) is the poem's emotional atmosphere. To figure out the tone of a poem, watch your own responses. Many readers are obedient. If a poet says they should be happy, they'll be happy. If a poet is angry, readers will feel that anger.

The tone of "Richard Cory" (discussed earlier in this chapter) is *ironic.* How do we know that? In three ways:

- **Many readers get a fatal, surprised feeling at the end of the poem.** This kind of feeling is a common response to irony.
- **The poem presents things that are contrary to expectation (one of the definitions of irony).** Readers see what the townspeople expect of Richard Cory and contrast it against his very different reality. The people assume Cory is happier than they are — partly because they themselves are miserable. His suicide suggests that he is even *un*happier than they are — and that's ironic.
- **Readers can spot the trouble with Cory before the townspeople do.** All the while the townspeople are assuming Cory is happy, the poem is giving us little reason to agree. If you're paying attention, you may feel trouble far in advance of anyone else in the poem. That's called *dramatic irony,* in which the reader guesses a truth of which the characters in a poem or story are unaware.

Notice, in the midst of the last, very eventful stanza, the "one calm summer night." This is even more irony. You may expect that a night of suicide somehow would be a violent night — but it isn't. The night of Cory's suicide recalls the "quiet" way he dressed and the "human" way he talked. Cory kept himself in reserve. There was no sign of trouble about him. And the night he kills himself is quiet, too.

How does all this irony help you interpret the poem? It makes you realize how little you know about people, how deceiving their exterior self-presentation may be. All may be quiet and calm on the surface but desperate and raging beneath. You realize the extent of human unhappiness — even in the midst of wealth. In the end, you get a profound sense of how human life works. The message is sad, but it is much larger than the scope of this short poem.

Being Alive to Language

Stay alert for symbols, metaphors, images, and surprising turns of speech as you read poems (see Chapter 4). These are all opportunities for interpretation. Take advantage!

In a graveyard, Hamlet lifts up the skull of Yorick, a jester who used to carry young Hamlet around on his back. That's a symbol, an invitation to *interpret.* Skulls often symbolize death or the passage of time, two things Hamlet is worried about.

When in "Coal," American poet Audre Lorde writes

> Some words live in my throat
> breeding like adders

you see a metaphor (the words living in the throat) followed by a simile ("breeding *like* adders"). Let's interpret: If a word "lives" in a throat, it grows, but maybe it never gets out, always stays in the throat, is never expressed. And the image of snakes breeding — especially poisonous snakes like adders — suggests ugliness, wildness, and danger. Connect that with never being expressed, and you may begin to think of the speaker as frustrated, angry, with dangerous things to say.

Following the Music

Very often, a poem's music is a direct guide to interpretation. Music helps establish a poem's emotional weather.

Listen to some smooth, ravishing music, from Alfred, Lord Tennyson's poem "Now Sleeps the Crimson Petal":

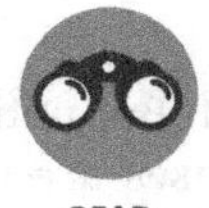
READ ALOUD

> Now sleeps the crimson petal, now the white;
> Nor waves the cypress in the palace walk;
> Nor winks the gold fin in the porphyry font.
> The firefly wakens; waken thou with me.

Tennyson's lines are liquid and whispery, with plenty of *s*, *l*, and *f* sounds. Those sounds are physical things and are partly responsible for the poem's impact. As melody and harmony in a song spur emotions, so do the sounds in a poem. The setting is the fall of evening, and the speaker calls to someone else to awaken. If you feel as though Tennyson's lines are slow, quiet, perhaps sensuous, the whispering music can help you account for that feeling.

Rhythm, too, can prompt interpretation. John Donne's Holy Sonnet 14 begins with four lines that assault you with their insistent rhythms:

Batter my heart, three-personed God; for You
As yet but knock, breathe, shine, and seek to mend;
That I may rise and stand, o'erthrow me, and bend
Your force to break, blow, burn, and make me new.

The lines punch and punch as the speaker calls on God to intervene decisively in his life. You can connect this hammering rhythm to the speaker's emotional state. Ask: Why would a speaker address God this way? Well, look at the little God seems to have done so far ("knock, breathe, shine, and seek to mend") and compare it to what the speaker wants: a violent overwhelm "to make me new." Perhaps the speaker feels his sin is so great that unless God takes such measures, he will not be saved. Those rhythms lead us to his agony and desperation.

Rhythm also informs these lines by Lucille Clifton. Listen as the words tumble forth from a speaker trying to explain her poetic gift:

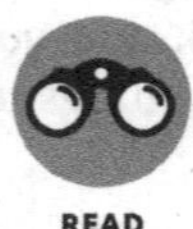

i don't know how to do
what i do in the way
that i do it. it happens
despite me and i pretend

to deserve it.

but i don't know how to do it
only sometimes when
something is singing
i listen and so far

i hear.

The rolling lines convey the speaker's joyful gratitude for her gift. But notice the three strong *pauses* after the fourth, fifth, and ninth lines. (Pauses are part of rhythm, too!) That pause between "pretend" and "to deserve it" emphasizes the speaker's awareness that she *can't* deserve such a gift. That pause suggests *humility*. She knows it may not be a permanent gift, as the pause between "so far" and "i hear" suggests. I hear *so far*, but it could change at any moment.

In traditional forms and open-form verse alike, you can use a poem's rhythms to figure out a poem's message, or at least your reactions to the poem.

Considering Narrative Elements

Many poems tell a story, bringing into play all the aspects of narration — speaker, setting, situation, plot, and character among them. Here we track the narrative elements in this poem by Eileen Myles.

The Honey Bear

Billie Holiday was on the radio
I was standing in the kitchen
smoking my cigarette of this
pack I plan to finish tonight
last night of smoking youth.
I made a cup of this funny
kind of tea I've had hanging
around. A little too sweet
an odd mix. My only impulse
was to make it sweeter.
Ivy Anderson was singing
pretty late tonight
in my very bright kitchen.
I'm standing by the tub
feeling a little older
nearly thirty in my very
bright kitchen tonight.
I'm not a bad looking woman
I suppose O it's very quiet
in my kitchen tonight I'm squeezing
the plastic honey bear a noodle
of honey dripping into the odd sweet
tea. It's pretty late
Honey bear's cover was loose
and somehow honey dripping down
the bear's face catching
in the crevices beneath
the bear's eyes O very sad and sweet
I'm standing in my kitchen O honey
I'm staring at the honey bear's face.

"The Honey Bear" certainly has a *speaker*, an "I" who makes the tea and tries to pour in the honey. Whenever you see speakers, ask questions. What kind of person is this, and how do you know? You may discern loneliness (the repetition of the phrase *my very bright kitchen*), insecurity ("I'm not a bad-looking woman/I suppose"), and self-dissatisfaction.

The poem has a clear *setting* also — a bright kitchen in a woman's residence. Is her place a house or an apartment? The tub is in the kitchen, so you can imagine it's a small place, maybe a studio apartment in a city like New York.

The poem has at least two *allusions* — to Billie Holiday and Ivy Anderson. Research those names and you'll find that both were great jazz singers of the mid-20th century. OK . . . go *listen* to them sing. (That's research, too!) You'll find they often sang sad or bluesy songs, which may fit this scene.

The speaker is straightforward and conversational, with some clever turns. A few statements could have more than one meaning. "It's pretty late" —does she mean the time of night *or* the time in her life? The speaker tells of her impulse "to make it sweeter." Does *it* refer to the tea or to her life? And "O honey" could be an exclamation at the mess, an address to the reader, or a call to an absent lover. Does anyone else get the sense we're at a solo birthday party? How and where?

Ask: Exactly how it is that the cover gets loose and honey "somehow" drips over the bear's face? Note the line breaks:

> and somehow honey dripping down
> the bear's face catching
> in the crevices beneath
> the bear's eyes

They seem to follow, step by very, very slow step, the drip of the thick honey. Is the speaker being careful as she pours? What may be distracting her? Consider her state of mind. Honey dripping all over the bear's face (and what else drips down a face?) may be a metaphor for the speaker's emotions.

TIP

With this poem, as with any other, interpret by paying attention to what the poem says and does and your responses to it. And then the fun begins — building a bridge of speculation between the poet's words and suggestions and your reaction. Interpretation is one of the best parts of reading poetry!

You may feel insecure at first, but you'll get to like the feeling. A good poem can be as sweet as a honey bear with the cover loose.

Interpreting "The Knot" by Susan Stewart

Born in 1952, Susan Stewart is an emerita professor of English at Princeton University. She has written a life's worth of witty, always insightful poems.

The Knot

The problem was how to begin with the end
and then it turned out there were two ends:
the end within the continuing
that, continuing, enveloped
the end. You passed yourself
coming and going, went through
one loop, then another,
what was behind drawn
through at a
slide until
it rose
before you, sprung.
Tangle like a bramble,
like a rose. Start,
start again against
the tight-
ening. A knife
could give up
on patience, but you
were born among
the dull and
kind, who wait
for Spring, and
lightening
and lightning.

1. Symbols, anyone? Want to start with the title? Okay, start with the title. What "Knot" are we talking about? Or what knots? If we take knots as a symbol, what are the "loops"?

2. Do those first four and a half lines make you a little dizzy? Try imagining yourself holding a piece of rope that either has a knot in it already (which needs untying) or needs a knot tied in it. Clearly, when you do either thing, ends and

beginnings switch places, and, yes, you're holding a piece of rope with two ends. And in tying a knot, the ends must continue, must go places, so, check, the "continuing" does envelop the ends . . . it works out!

3. Let's say that "you" is the person dealing with the "knot." What do we learn about this "you" person described in the last six lines?

4. Now let's look at that knife. Most of this poem is concerned with untying knots. Using a knife would be quicker (as it was for Alexander the Great in the story about the Gordian Knot). But this option is rather a brute method. It abandons what the rest of the poem presents as an interesting, if puzzling situation: working a way out of knots, entanglements. Sure, we could take the short cut of cutting the knot. But what does the poem seem to imply about that option? What gives you that feeling?

5. Back to "you," who is compared to the knife that "could give up/ on patience." Strange way to talk. Knives usually don't decide things. Oh, wait, maybe "a knife" is a symbol. For what, though? And "you" definitely do not "give up" the way "a knife" could. What's happening with this comparison, an impatient knife and "you"? Consider the word "dull." How is "you" dull? Is dullness necessarily a bad thing here? After all, "you" is willing to wait.

6. This poem is an absolute garden of *tasty line-endings*. Sentences snake around the end of a line and come into new worlds in the next line. Read "The Knot" aloud; take your time. Note all the different feelings you get from the line-endings and enjambments. To start, read aloud lines 5-12, from "You passed" to "sprung," a delectable snarl. As we read, we follow "You" and "yourself," literally passing each other in the physical line, "coming and going." Isn't that delightful? As readers, we, too, go "though/ one loop, then another." And *do*, please, spend a little time with the last four lines, which fetch up hard at "sprung." What is "springing," anyway? Is it a metaphor, too? Is it the same as "Spring," or is "Spring" a kind of "springing"?

7. Whatever "The Knot" may be, seems as if it's hard both to tie and to untie. There are difficulties. Where do you see difficulties?

8. Is there a volta in this poem? A change? Where does it happen?

9. We go from "tightening" to "lightening" to "lightning." Your comments? Does that progression have any benefits for "you," the person dealing with the knot? How do we know? What might these be?

2

An Intelligent Hustle through Poetic History

IN THIS PART . . .

Become a reader with the open mind, tools, and skills to appreciate poetry from all times and places.

Start tracking written verse through its amazing five-and-a-half-millennia-long journey, from the oldest poems to Golden Ages worldwide.

Journey through poetic history with knights in shining armor, damsels in distress, haiku and ghazals, and the balanced, lucid verse of the European Enlightenment.

Track poetry as it encounters the Industrial Revolution and a rapidly changing world.

Stride into the 20th century, a hundred years of poetry from the United States to China.

Arrive in the 2020s, as poetry, poets, and the poetry world meet a communications age and a pandemic — emerging changed yet better than ever.

IN THIS CHAPTER

» Assembling the tools you need to understand older poetry

» Learning about the poet's life and historical background

» Mastering unfamiliar language

Chapter 6

Connecting with Poems from the Past

Who would ever close their minds to all the great poetry written before their own times? And yet some readers do. Yes, it's sometimes more difficult. Often you can't just sit down and start reading. Preparation is involved. Reference works. Dictionaries.

But be of good cheer! Of course you'll be drawn to poetry of our time, speaking of the concerns and stories of our age. Of course. That's natural. There are, however, many reasons you'll also want to read poetry from the past. We'll just suggest three very good ones:

» You can't fully understand poetry of your own time without having some knowledge of what came before: the traditions, the big names, and the big events.

» Do you really want to walk away from so many fine writers? Miss out on all that wonderful poetry — almost all of it now available in modern translations or editions that help you with the background, the vocabulary, the poetic forms? Bye-bye, Shakespeare! Get away, Emily Dickinson! No way, Enheduanna, Homer, Horace, Ovid, Virgil, Dante, Bashō, Chaucer, Milton, Pushkin, Hugo, Baudelaire! See you never, H.D., Elizabeth Bishop, Gwendolyn Brooks, Anna Akhmatova — you made the mistake of not living in my century!

(Look some of these poets up; they're great.) Anyone who turned their backs on all that good stuff would miss out on so very much.

» Most important: If you turned your back on all those voices, all those centuries of lovely, world-defining poetry, you'd have only a *partial* idea of what poetry itself *is*.

So why not stay open to the poetry of all ages and peoples? What you'll find, with just a little work, is that what's human is *always* interesting. Much of what's in ancient Sumerian, Hebrew, Greek, Egyptian, Chinese, and Indian poetry will speak to you. You'll have much to laugh and cry with in the poems of the Italian Renaissance and the English Romantic Period. Let the Roman poet and dramatist Terence (c.184 BC – c.159 BC) be your guide: *Humani nihil a me alienum puto*, "I consider nothing human alien to me."

In this chapter, we offer guidelines on working with older poetry. After all, the 21st century represents only one of the 50 centuries from which we possess poetry. Each one has wonders to offer. Keep an open mind, and you'll find greatness before you.

Gathering the Tools You Need

REMEMBER

As of this writing, we are living in a great era of translation. It has never been easier to get into the great voices of the past, from around the world. Want to read some Sappho? All of her is online. Homer? Ditto. Who is this Rūmī, anyway? This Li Bai? Enter those names into your friendly local search engine and explore.

When reading poetry, try to have the following resources by your side, either online or in print:

» **Anthologies of literature (see Chapter 1).** These are collections of poetry from various cultures, periods, areas, and genres. Many have good historical surveys and other background information.

» **An encyclopedia.** Again, good information is a keyboard stroke away. Thank you, AI!

» **A good dictionary.** Many readers have both a modern dictionary and an *etymological* dictionary — one that traces the history of words. Both can come in handy when reading older poetry. Yep, it's all online.

TIP

You may also want to have several other helpmates nearby, especially if you want to dig a little deeper into your reading:

- **A dictionary of classical *allusions* (see Chapter 4),** references based on the literature and mythology of the ancient world.
- **A companion to literary study,** such as the *Oxford Companion to English Literature* or the *Cambridge History of Literature*. Online versions require subscriptions, but it's more than worth it.
- **A dictionary of poetic biography,** which offer short biographies of poets throughout the ages. One good example is the *Oxford Companion*.
- ***Poetry For Dummies*** or some other excellent all-purpose guide.

Understanding Older Poetry

Older poetry poses special challenges in three areas, each of which we can state as a question for you, the reader:

- **Biographical background:** Who was this poet?
- **Historical context:** What was the world the poet lived in and referred to in his or her poems?
- **Language:** What are all these unfamiliar words, allusions, and turns of phrase? What do they mean? Where do they come from?

These are interesting questions for poetry of *any* period. So be methodical as you read. Before reading older poetry, till the field a little. Get to know poets and their worlds. Do this every single time. It always helps.

Meeting the poet

Do all you can to lessen the distance and difference between you and the poet. Since the poet you're reading can't make the introductions, reach out yourself and offer a hearty, "Howdy, neighbor!"

For example, if you're interested in reading a song of Sappho or a play by William Shakespeare, you'll need to know their birth and death dates: Sappho, something like 630 BC–570 BC, and Shakespeare, 1564–1616. Read introductions to these poets and their lives and times. Thank you, AI! Thank you, local library! Thank you, friend or teacher who knows this stuff!

Sappho? She was a Greek-speaking singer, musician, and poet who lived on Lesbos, an island at the far eastern edge of the Mediterranean. She is one of the earliest European writers for whom we have a name — she lived a good 200 years before, say Plato (c. 427 BC–347 BC). Sappho became one of the most famous singers and musicians in the archaic Greek world. She was a leader among a group of women who practiced prayer, song, dance, comportment, and the ways of desire. We have maybe five complete or almost-complete poems of hers, and a bunch of very sweet fragments. Figure 6-1 shows an image on an ancient vase, showing Sappho playing a *barbitos* (a kind of harp or lyre), ca. 470 BC.

FIGURE 6-1: Figure on a vase found in Akragas, Sicily; Staatliche Antikensammlungen, Munich, Germany.

Image Public Domain; source: picryl.com.

Shakespeare, shown in Figure 6-2, was an Englishman of the Elizabethan and Jacobean era (that is, he lived during the queenship of Elizabeth I and the kingship of her successor, James I). He moved from his provincial town of Stratford to London, and he became a playwright and a shareholder in a theater company called the Lord Chamberlain's Men (later, the King's Men), who performed at the famous Globe Theatre. All this has bearings on his plays and poems.

FIGURE 6-2: William Shakespeare.

Library of Congress/Public domain

You'll learn that Sappho worshipped the gods of the Greek world, especially Aphrodite, goddess of desire. You'll learn, too, that Shakespeare was a Christian. Each was raised in the belief systems specific to their respective times. Sappho's got a chummy relationship with Aphrodite, whom she's always asking for help or support. Shakespeare's Christianity may help you understand why Hamlet, whose life is pretty painful, hesitates to commit suicide.

Discovering the poet's life and times

The more you learn about history and how it is reflected in poetry, the more you'll become interested in it — and the more you'll probably want to discover. Kenneth Fields, a fine poet and teacher, was fond of telling his students that "poets and readers of poetry have to know *more about more* than ever before."

Poetry concerns life, and life includes lots of things: language, botany (know the names of those flowers!), fashion (dost thou know what a *wimple* is? or a *buskin?* or *chopines, jodhpurs,* or *cravats?*), architecture *(keystones, Doric columns, naves, buttresses?)*, mythology (Eros, meet Cupid; Zeus, meet Jove), science (see Roald Hoffman's "Deceptively Like a Solid," in Chapter 4), and just about everything else.

When reading poetry of the past, find out immediately:

- **When the poem was written and when it was published (if it was).** The two dates could be quite different.
- **What was happening in the world when the poem was written.** This includes the historical currents, the politics, anything that could shed light on the poem. If you're reading some of Walt Whitman's Civil War poetry, reviewing what you know of the American Civil War makes sense. If you're reading Dante's *Divine Comedy,* knowing the background of politics in Florence, Dante's native city-state, *and* why he was kicked out, would make sense. The poetry of Anna Akhmatova and Maria Tsvetaeva sings all the more when you learn about the harsh world of early-20th-century Russia.

This information helps you appreciate the poem better; few poems are entirely uninfluenced by their times.

Practicing what we preach

Here's a piece of older poetry, "To Lucasta, Going to the Wars," written by Richard Lovelace (1617–1657). Here's a tip: It's not Lucasta going to the wars — it's the speaker.

To Lucasta, Going to the Wars

Tell me not, Sweet, I am unkind,
That from the nunnery
Of thy chaste breast and quiet mind
To war and arms I fly.

True, a new mistress now I chase,
The first foe in the field;
And with a stronger faith embrace
A sword, a horse, a shield.

Yet this inconstancy is such,
As you too shall adore;
I could not love thee, Dear, so much,
Loved I not honor more.

Lovelace's English is not too different from ours. The differences are gentle and slight. *Tell me not* means *Don't tell me.* And *that* in line 2 means *because.*

Now you have to rearrange words a little. In modern English, this would be, "Don't tell me, Sweet, that I am unkind because I . . . ." Because I what? Look for the verb — there it is, at the end of the stanza. Now rearrange it: "Don't tell me, Sweet, that I am unkind because I fly." And you may already know that *fly* can mean *leave*. What is the speaker leaving? "The nunnery / Of your chaste breast and quiet mind." But what's a nunnery? *Nunnery* was a word with various meanings, including "an abode for nuns," or more generally, "a place of retreat." So he calls his beloved's "chaste breast and quiet mind" a place of retreat. *That's* what he's leaving to go to war. He's asking her not to call him unkind.

Nunnery and *fly* may have rhymed in 1649, or Lovelace may just be using a *sight rhyme* on the *y* in the two words.

In the next line, slide *I chase* next to *True,* and you'll get the thoroughly modern "True, I chase a new mistress now." It's a clever, sad metaphor, right? War is his new beloved, so the "first foe in the field" is his new mistress. He must conquer his love for Lucasta and then go to war. That's why you get "And with a stronger faith embrace" in line 7. "Stronger than what other faith?" you may ask. What other faith does the poem deal with? The faith between the speaker and his "Sweet." In leaving her and going to the wars, he (the poet pretends) is changing one faith (one pledge of love) for another. Now he loves his horse and shield more than his Sweet.

This, by the way, is called a *conceit* — a comparison that runs throughout the whole poem. Lovelace's conceit compares this man's faithfulness to Lucasta with his faithfulness to the demands of honor.

Look up *inconstancy* in line 9, and you'll find out it means *faithlessness.* The speaker is inconstant because he is leaving his human mistress for his new mistress of war. Yet he claims that his human mistress, too, will "adore" this inconstancy. Not many people like "inconstancy" in their lovers, so why would Lucasta? Lovelace, clever poet, has brought us right up against a paradox. The answer lies in the last two lines. "I could not love thee, Dear, so much" is easy. But the next line — "Loved I not honor more" — may seem confusing. *Loved I not* is the same as *If I didn't love* or *Unless I loved.* Now try it:

> I could not love you, Dear, so much,
> Unless I loved honor more.

It's clever, and full of paradoxes. You can feel the difference between Lovelace's world and ours. His speaker loves honor more than he loves his Sweet, and further, he expects her to *adore* that fact. And, most likely, she would. If he showed cowardice by not going to the wars, he wouldn't be worth loving. His love of honor is what gives value to his love of her. He expects her to know this, and to realize that he goes, partly, to *prove* his love for her is worthwhile.

Taking it up a notch

After spending some time with this poem, you can see that it's a well-turned piece with unexpected elements. Don't stop there. Reach out. Hit that encyclopedia and find out what was happening in England in 1649. You'll find out that "To Lucasta" was published at the end of the English Civil War, also known as the Great Rebellion (1642–1651), which overthrew King Charles I (he was beheaded) and led to rule by the Puritans (1649–1660). So war was *definitely* in the air.

Knowing something about the poet definitely pays off as well. Seek, and ye shall find that Lovelace was the son of a wealthy family in the county of Kent. He supported the King against the rebels, and he was indeed a brave soldier, being wounded, captured, imprisoned, and exiled. The sad thing is that his side lost. By the time he was released, he was a ruined man. This poem was published eight years before his death.

Hit your keyboard, or your friendly anthology or history of English literature, and you'll discover that Lovelace is said to belong to a group called the Cavalier Poets. They strove to write short, compressed poems of a glittering clarity — a good description of "To Lucasta."

There's even a story behind the name *Lucasta.* Lovelace was engaged to a woman named Lucy Sacheverell. His pet name for her was *Lux Casta,* which in Latin means "chaste light." (Aha! Remember "thy chaste breast"?) Alas, when a false rumor got out that Lovelace had been killed, Lucy married someone else. While in prison, Lovelace wrote a series of poems to Lucy, using her nickname; this poem is one of them.

Now the poem has a great deal more meaning than it did when we first read it. Lovelace suffered the hardships of war and did uphold the honor of which this poem speaks. "Lucasta," seemingly slight at first, has revealed a moving story and depths of tenderness and courage.

Is this poem autobiographical? Apparently — but it also could stand for many people's departures for war. Its brevity, elegance, wit, and the burst of clarity at the end are an affecting package. The extra work, we hope you agree, is more than worth it.

REMEMBER

Know the poet, and you'll get to know the poem better.

Mastering unfamiliar language

Poets of the past write in the traditions of their times, which may differ from the traditions of our own. They may also write in older language. Those *poets* aren't going to change, so *we* must reach out to them and master their language as well as we can. This task usually isn't that difficult, and lots of nice people (known as editors) have done the work for you. Your book of Homer, Dante, John Keats, or Emily Dickinson probably contains:

» **Introductions** by the editors of these books, offering biographical information, historical background, and overviews of the poets' work.

» **Glosses** (translations of unfamiliar words) in the margins.

» **Notes** either at the bottom of the page or in the back of the book. The notes explain historical or biographical issues arising in the text.

TIP

Use these guides well; they'll help you as you journey through the poetry. If a note in the back of the book is interesting — for example, if you want to learn more about the English Civil War — follow your interests and read up. You may also consider listening to a podcast, watching an online course, or taking one in person class.

Older language poses three kinds of challenges: allusions, inversions, and vocabulary. In the following sections, we take a look at each.

Allusions: Have you heard the one about. . . .

As described in Chapter 4, poets *allude* (refer) to the world outside their poems all the time — history, other writers and literature, popular culture, anything that will help them create metaphors or enliven their work. But they were then, and you are now, which means you have to work a little to learn the sources and relevance of their allusions.

LOOKING IT UP: WHEN POETS WANT YOU TO DO A LITTLE LEGWORK

In his epic poem *Paradise Lost*, John Milton wanted his readers to feel the gentle sweetness of Adam's words to Eve. So he wrote that Adam spoke:

with voice
Mild, as when Zephyrus on Flora breathes

A little research will tell you that *Zephyrus* is the Western wind, which blows in spring and brings long-dormant nature to life. *Flora* is the goddess of the world of flowers and plants. Adam breathes sweetly on Eve, and she comes to life — a gorgeous moment, and ambiguous, too, because of their later marital discord!

TYING ONE WORK TO ANOTHER

Allusions also act as shorthand for larger stories and contexts the poets' readers may know; they help set the material of the poem on a larger stage. Here's a passage from Shakespeare's *The Merchant of Venice.* Lorenzo, a young Christian man from Venice, is wooing Jessica, a Jew and by law not allowed to marry him unless she converts to Christianity. It's a forbidden, thrilling love. Lorenzo says:

The moon shines bright. In such a night as this,
When the sweet wind did gently kiss the trees,
And they did make no noise, in such a night,
Troilus methinks mounted the Troyan walls,
And sigh'd his soul toward the Grecian tents,
Where Cressid lay that night.

Shakespeare obviously thought his allusion to Troilus and Cressid would help his audience enjoy this moment between the two lovers. But *you* won't enjoy it until you find out who Troilus and Cressid are! Here:

- *Cressid* is short for *Cressida,* name of a fictional widow living in the city of Troy during the Trojan (here, "Troyan") War.
- The Greeks were attacking Troy because Paris, prince of Troy, had stolen Helen, the wife of a Greek king.
- Cressida falls in love with Troilus, a brave knight of Troy. While war grinds on, they have a secret, passionate affair. For the Renaissance, these two were the defining type of the doomed lovers. We think of Romeo and Juliet; the Renaissance thought of Troilus and Cressida.
- Troy trades Cressida to the Greeks in return for some prisoners. Poor Troilus can't say anything. All he can do is pine away after his beloved, whom he'll never see again. Why won't he? Ever heard of the Trojan Horse? Troilus will die as his city falls, and the Greeks will take Cressida away. Their story is awfully sad and beautiful. Geoffrey Chaucer wrote a wonderful poem (and Shakespeare an equally wonderful play) about it.

Now you can see why Lorenzo and Jessica, a Christian and a Jew, may see Troilus (a Trojan) and Cressida (now with the Greeks) as a fitting comparison. Knowing the hopeless frustration of Troilus, you can resonate more to Lorenzo as he pictures Troilus climbing the walls of Troy and sighing at the Greek tents where his beloved is being kept. Knowing this allusion binds you more closely to the characters because you better understand their feelings — as allusions are supposed to do!

Inversions: Confused you are?

Older poetry was pretty forgiving regarding word order. The *conventions* of the time (the generally accepted rules) allowed poets much more leeway. Consider this anonymous line from the English Renaissance:

> My mind to me a kingdom is

Now, you may ask yourself, "Why didn't the poet just write, 'My mind is a kingdom to me'?" Excellent question. Here are a couple of answers:

- **The poet has chosen to write in *iambic tetrameter,* in which each line rolls out in four iambs (see Chapter 4).** An *iamb* is a rhythmic unit that goes duh-DUH, so four of them are duh-DUH, duh-DUH, duh-DUH, duh-DUH. The second line has no such regular rhythm: "My mind is a kingdom to me" rolls out duh-DUH duh-duh-DUH-duh-duh-DUH. It's nice — and clear enough — but it won't fit the form.
- **The inversion allows the word *kingdom* to get a special stress, which the "straightened out" version doesn't have.**
- **You're dealing with differences in poetic taste and convention.** Renaissance readers apparently liked a little inversion. They found it a mark of the poet's ingenuity as a craftsman. A plain English line like "My mind is a kingdom to me" appeals to readers today, but it may not have struck many Renaissance readers as poetic.

Straightening out a phrase like "My mind to me a kingdom is" certainly isn't very difficult. Your mind to you not too twisted by it is — is it? That's about how hard it is to straighten out most inversions.

Vocabulary: Methinks thou doth protest too much

When languages change, vocabulary changes. New words are created (like *podcast*, *rizz*, *influencer*, or *wannabe*), old ones fall into disuse (like *rumble-seat*), and some words change meaning (the word *perspective* was used to mean *telescope* in Shakespeare's time). So older poetry may challenge you to uncover unfamiliar words — or older meanings of familiar ones — and create your own understanding of the poetry as you move along. Discovering new words makes reading a poem a little slower — but *much* more rewarding.

Reading Older Poetry: Three Basics

TIP

Keep in mind these three basic aspects of reading older poetry. It's not necessarily a 1-2-3 affair — you can and will take these steps in any order, and you'll repeat all of them as you get to know a poem. But they are phases in the process of understanding a poem from the past:

1. **Do a cold reading.**

   Sit down and read what's in front of you. Read it aloud (because poetry is meant to be read aloud) (see Chapter 2). Reading aloud tends to slow you down (which is always good), revealing answers to quandaries and other difficulties.

2. **Translate the poem's meaning.**

   As you read the poem the first time, take into account any glosses or notes. What you're doing here is creating your own version of the poem, one you can understand. Translation involves three activities:

   - **Mapping the poem:** Here, you determine the parts you *do* understand and identify the parts you don't. We refer to the parts you don't understand as the *blanks*.
   - **Filling in the blanks:** When you've identified the words, phrases, or facts you need to uncover, go find the definitions, the information, the understanding, and apply what you find out to each blank in the poem until every blank is filled.
   - **Creating your own version of the poem:** You've made unfamiliar language familiar, and you've discovered enough about the poet's life and times to illuminate the poem. Now you un-invert the inversions and put unfamiliar material into your own words. ***Note:*** This is just an interim, provisional version. When you've created *this* version, you're better able to return to the original and experience it for itself.

3. **Reread the original aloud in its original form.**

   You now let the original words snap back into place, so to speak. Returning to the poem and rereading it in its original glory is crucial, because that, and only that, is the poem itself.

Here are seven lines of Middle English poetry written by Geoffrey Chaucer around 1400. Don't let the title stop you: *Compleignte* is *complaint*, and *Hys* is, you guessed it, *His*. So, this poem's title is "Complaint to His Purse." Try reading it at one go:

READ ALOUD

Compleignte to Hys Purse

To you, my purs, and to noon other wight,
Complaine I, for ye be my lady dere.
I am so sory, now that ye be light,
For certes, but if ye make me hevy cheere,
Me were as lief be laid upon my beere;
For which unto youre mercy thus I crye:
Beeth hevy again, or elles moot I die.

When you map these lines more closely, you see that they contain exactly eight words most modern speakers probably couldn't figure out; the rest are simply spelled a little differently. If you "blank out" the passage (and replace unfamiliar spellings with modern-day ones), you might get:

To you, my BLANK, and to BLANK other BLANK,
Complain I, for you are my lady dear.
I am so sorry, now that you are light,
For BLANK, but if you make me heavy cheer,
I were as BLANK be laid upon my BLANK;
For which unto your mercy thus I cry:
Be heavy again, or BLANK BLANK I die.

Not bad. Out of 60 words, you're probably unfamiliar with only 8. (*Note:* We changed "ye be" to "you are.") Some of the blanks fill in fairly easily.

TECHNICAL STUFF

Chaucer's English was pronounced *very* differently from modern English. Mastering the pronunciation of older forms of language may require a teacher. What we're trying to do here is to help you piece together an understanding of the passage as well as we can. By all means, listen to a professional reader read this delightful poem with original pronunciation: `https://youtube.com/watch?v=D_iP8Stx6bU`.

You can navigate most of the first line with a little imagination. *Purs* is simply *purse* without an *e*. *Noon other* is just *no other* in a slight disguise. But what is *wight?* That's the first blank for which you may need a dictionary or some other help. And that's what we're here for: It means *man* or *person*.

You're halfway through, and here's what you have so far:

To you, my purse, and to no other person
I complain, for you are my lady dear
I am so sorry, now that you are light

Wouldn't *you* be sorry if your purse was empty? Notice that the word *light* is being used playfully. The speaker is pretending his purse is his lady. In Chaucer's day, women were called "light" if they were unfaithful or promiscuous. And his purse, having nothing in it, is definitely causing him pain. "Complain I," he writes, an inversion for "I complain." Easy.

Look up *Certes*, and you'll find it means *Certainly* or *surely*. And *but if* means *unless:*

> For surely, unless you make me heavy cheer

Chaucer continues his fun with the light/heavy idea. The purse is light, causing him pain. So now he wants his purse to make him *heavy cheer* — cheer him up, so to speak, by getting heavier.

The next line — "Me were as lief be laid upon my beere" — is tough: You'll find that *Me were as lief be laid* means "I'd just as soon be laid," and *beere* is an unfamiliar spelling of the word *bier*, meaning the platform on which a coffin is laid for a funeral. In other words, unless his purse gets heavy, he'd just as soon die.

The next line is almost modern — "For which unto your mercy thus I crye." And the word *Beeth* means *Be*. It's a command, hurled pleadingly at his purse — "Be heavy again!" A little imagination may reveal that *elles* is our modern *else*. But *moot* is a tough one: It means *must*.

You've now made your own version of Chaucer's stanza:

> To you, my purse, and to no other person,
> I complain, for you are my lady dear.
> I am so sorry, now that you are light,
> For surely, unless you make me heavy cheer,
> I'd just as soon be laid upon my bier,
> For which, unto your mercy now I cry:
> Be heavy again, or else I must die.

Now, knowing this poem much better, return to the original and reread it. Your understanding will (we hope) be much greater than it was after your initial reading.

Oh, and hit AI, or the books, or the library, and learn about Geoffrey Chaucer, one of the best. You'll realize why we once read, written on a barroom wall, this surprising graffito: "Chaucer rules, OK?" He does! OK!

REMEMBER

If you reach out, you can connect with poets across many centuries. Cultivate your skills with older poetry, and the emotions, insights, and stories in their work will strike you as fresh as this morning's news.

IN THIS CHAPTER

» Identifying the different periods of poetry

» Knowing the important poets from each period

» Figuring out where to find poetry from every era

Chapter 7 From Enheduanna to the Golden Ages

In this chapter and the next, we tell the story of 5000 years of poetry in about 7000 words. Here, we take on the first 4700 years — a tough job, so we have to move fast. We at least want to give you a notion of where poetry has been and where it's going. We've divided the past 5000 years into 10 periods of poetry — arbitrary, yes, but at least it helps us keep on track as we ride along. We define each period and recommend some of the standout poets and poems of each era.

Your assignment, should you choose to accept it: Pick one poet or poem mentioned in each era — and read! These writers were speaking to their own times, but they all still have a lot to say today.

REMEMBER

Poetry from distant times wasn't written in English. Much was written in languages deep in time, some no longer used except by scholars. To read poetry from the far past, most of us have to rely on translations. Because poetry activates all the resources of language (as we've been seeing), some of a poem's best aspects — sound as well as meaning — may be "lost in translation." So, when we read a translation of a poem, we are reading a paraphrase of the original. And there is no one "right translation": different translators will likely produce different versions of the same poem.

The Pre-Homeric Period (3000 BC–1000 BC)

Some scholars say the oldest poetry was sung. Some think it grew out of religious rituals. Still others think it grew out of the work life. Whatever its source, poetry bore — and still bears — an intimate connection with music.

Mesopotamian poetry

The earliest poetry we know of comes from around 5000 years ago, from the Mesopotamian culture, which gave us cities, the wheel, the circular clock, and writing. They developed the *cuneiform script*, a writing system based on triangular indentations made in clay tablets. Only in the last two centuries did we discover and learn to translate the poetry of these people. These poems were probably already ancient when they were set down in writing, so when you read them, you are seeing even further into the past than 3000 BC.

Mesopotamian poetry apparently was meant to be sung to a harp or a lyre. The earliest poet for whom we have any kind of name is Enheduanna, "High Priestess of Nanna." Enheduanna composed powerful hymns to Nanna, the moon goddess of Mesopotamian religion. Reading her words is exciting because they are the earliest we can trace (so far!) to a person with a (nick-)name.

Here is a passage in which Enheduanna praises the daughter of Ishtar:

READ ALOUD

You are lofty like Heaven. Let the world know!
You are wide like the earth. Let the world know!
You devastate the rebellious land. Let the world know!
You roar over the land. Let the world know!

Listen for the songlike qualities — the repetitions ("You are . . . You are . . . You . . . You . . ."), the *parallelisms* (thoughts expressed in the same grammatical form, as "You are lofty . . .," "You are wide . . .," "You devastate . . .," and "You roar . . ."), the refrain ("Let the world know!"). These things suggest that this poetry may have been sung by bards or choirs.

Standouts: *Gilgamesh* is a series of epic tales about a real-life king who founds the city of Uruk. The two most famous episodes of this "first of all epics" concern Gilgamesh's descent into the underworld, in search of his dead friend Enkidu, and an episode in which the world is covered by a flood.

Egyptian poetry

The poets of ancient Egypt kept going for a long time. Their work spans about three millennia (3100–30 BC), and it comes in many forms. It concerns myths and gods and adds something new: personal poetry on attraction and courtship.

Only one, matchless sister,
Prettier than anyone —
Look: like the Star-Girl rising
To begin a blessed year.
Walks in the glow of her skin.
Lovely eyes she looks through;
Lovely lips she speaks with
And not a word too much.
Long neck, glowing
Nipple, sapphire hair,
Arms honey-gold;
Her fingers, lotus blossoms;
Firm midriff, dulcet bottom,
Her legs a book of her beauty;
Walks earth with pretty step
And her hug snares my heart.
Men turn their necks away,
Dazzled with her countenance.
Man who clasps her, happy
As the richest, readiest boy.
Watch her: she's going somewhere
Like a goddess, the Only One.

Standouts: The astonishing *Hymn to the Sun* by King Amenhotep IV.

The beginnings of poetry in India

Around 1500 BC, Sanskrit-writing scribes in what is now called India began to set down the Vedas, epic religious hymns concerning the deities and religious ideas of the Aryans, a tribe that recently had invaded the Indian subcontinent. These epics were called *Vedas*, from the word *veda*, meaning "knowledge." Over almost 1000 years, a series of Vedas grew that became the great foundation of both Hinduism and the Buddhist tradition.

MOUTH-TO-MOUTH POETIFICATION

How did poetry get passed along before there was writing? By memory and voice. Folklorists and anthropologists call this process *oral transmission*. Poetic history is full of incredible feats of memory. The *Mahabharata,* the sacred epic of India, is one of the longest poems ever, yet it was not published until the 19th century, more than 2500 years after its composition! Millions of people simply *remembered* all or parts of it. To qualify for the position of scribe to some of the potentates of India, you had to be able to recite thousands of lines from the ancient Vedas by memory. Many scholars believe that several of the world's great epic poems — including *The Iliad* and *The Odyssey* by Homer, *The Song of Roland* (the French national epic), and *The Poem of the Cid* (the Spanish national epic) — were originally orally composed and passed along.

In the 19th century, two scholars heroically rescued orally-transmitted epics from oblivion. The Serbian epic known as *The Battle of Kosovo* memorializes a terrible battle on the Field of Blackbirds in 1389, when the Turks overwhelmed the Serbs. Thanks to Vuk Stefanović Karadžić, who collected scraps and shards of the epic by interviewing monks, shepherds, and traditional singers known as *guslari,* the epic cycle was collected and published. The Finnish doctor and poet Elias Lönnrot roamed throughout Finland for 20 years, collecting remembered scraps of Finnish epic and lyric poetry, which he finally published as the *Kalevala* (1849).

In the early 20th century, scholars studied Balkan shepherds who were able to recite thousands of lines of poetry from memory while they tended their sheep — a clue to the way *The Odyssey* and much other great poetry survived the ages. There's still a lot of orally transmitted poetry in Asia, Africa, and elsewhere. And here, too! Even though much of it is printed, rap and hip-hop are essentially forms of oral poetry. And let's not forget Cowboy Poetry, much of the earliest of which was sung on the range.

Here are a few lines from the Vedic account of creation:

There were no things;
There was no nothing;
There was no atmosphere
Nor the heavens beyond the air.
What was concealed?
Where was it hidden?
Who guarded it?
Was it hidden beneath the waters?
Was it the unfathomable deep?

The last and latest parts of the Vedas are called the *Aranyaka* and the *Upanishads.* Together, they are known as the *Vedanta* ("the end of the Veda"). The Vedas are the beginning and the bedrock of all Indian poetry.

Alongside the Vedas and likely just as old is the *Mahabharata.* This vast epic concerns a war between the Kurus (forces of good) and the Pandus (forces of evil). (Yes, they're relatives.) All people from India know stories from the *Mahabharata.* It contains tales of the most familiar figures in ancient Indian mythology, including the god Vishnu, the creator/destroyer Shiva, the monkey-god Hanuman, and the hero Rama. Within this mega-epic are two mega-masterpieces:

- *Bhagavad-Gita (Song of the Blessed One):* Its main figures are the hero-warrior Arjuna and his chariot-driver, who is really the god Krishna. (Make sure you tip the driver!)
- *Ramayana:* This epic tells the story of Rama, his wife Sita, and their battles against the forces of evil.

The *Bhagavad-Gita* is probably the poem out of India that the Western world knows best. Thousands of copies have been distributed by people wanting to spread its vision and message. Here is the very end. Arjuna, greatest of warriors, has witnessed God as God really is. He can't stand it. He cries out for God to assume a more human form. God does, and this dialogue ensues:

Arjuna said:

"O Worshiped, O Agitator, O World-Mover,
This, Your Gentle Human Form,
I see now. Thoughts composed,
I am to my nature restored.

The Blessed One said:
"This Form of Mine, very hard to see,
you have seen. Even gods forever,
This Form long to behold.

Impossible to see as you have seen Me.
Study won't do it, not whips or
slashes or fasts, not gifts
or burnt bulls.

O Scorcher of Enemies, Arjuna,
only by devotion, one-mindedness,
am I possible to be known,
seen, entered into.

Whoever work for Me alone, Me
the Goal, devoted, are set free from
attachment to all things, no enmity.
It is me they enter."

A world of disorder, evil, and suffering. A glorious deity who creates and destroys. And the mother of all battles. And that is but a tiny part of the sprawling, ancient Mahabharata.

The Biblical and Homeric Periods (1000 BC–400 BC)

Poetry from the Biblical and Homeric periods is well-known around the world — but you may not have ever thought of it as poetry before. Read on.

Biblical poetry

Poetry from this period, comprising maybe the best-known of all ancient poetry, makes up a good part of the Old Testament. This rich poetic culture drew on a tradition spanning 600 years (1000–400 BC).

Most English-speaking people know the Psalms from the King James Bible. Here is a passage from the book called Ecclesiastes (3:1–5) or Koheleth ("The Preacher").

READ ALOUD

For everything there is a season,
 and a time for every matter under heaven:
A time to be born, and a time to die;
A time to plant, and a time to pluck up what is planted;
A time to kill, and a time to heal;
A time to break down, and a time to build up;
A time to weep, and a time to laugh;
A time to mourn, and a time to dance;
A time to cast away stones,
And a time to gather stones together.

So *that's* where that song came from. . . .

There is grandeur, balance, and clarity in this passage. There is grandeur in the sweeping vision of so much of human life; balance as the poet works with pairs of opposites (birth/death, planting/harvesting, killing/healing, and so on), and clarity in the simple, straightforward language. That's why so many readers have felt this passage resonates with truth.

Standouts: The Old Testament is revered for great philosophic poetry (in Ecclesiastes), religious tales (the Book of Job), prophetic books (Isaiah, Amos, Micah, and others), and beautiful erotic poetry (known as the Song of Songs or the Song of Solomon). The authorized King James Bible is the great traditional source for the poetry of the Old Testament in English.

Homeric poetry

The word *Homeric* refers to Homer, traditionally supposed to be the author of *The Iliad* and *The Odyssey.* These two epic poems were first written down around 680 BC. Both have been translated extremely well several times, and they're works you should definitely add to your must-read list.

The Iliad is the story of the Trojan War. We join the Trojans and Greeks in the last few days of a terrible nine-year war, and (hardly a spoiler), the Trojans are not going to win. It's a stirring tale with maybe the greatest cast of characters in history. Heard of Helen of Troy? Achilles? Hector? Agamemnon? Odysseus? All here. *The Odyssey* (which has been called the best story of all time) tells of the postwar wanderings of the Greek hero and trickster Odysseus. He has a series of adventures with an unforgettable gallery of gods and magical beings. Meanwhile, his faithful wife, Penelope, waits for him at home on the island of Ithaca. You may prefer reading these works in school with the help of an instructor, or in a reading group, or you may just want to look for a good translation and start reading by yourself. Both are really, *really* good to read.

The Iliad is not just a war story. Each battle scene, each death is singular, with a pathos all its own — as in this one, in which an unlucky young soldier encounters Agamemnon:

READ ALOUD

Then wide-ruling Agamemnon ripped the spear
From his hands, wrenched it away, wild as a lion,
Hacked the boy's neck with his sword,
Undid his limbs. So he fell there, slept a bronze sleep,
Unlucky boy, far from his wedded wife
Who helped the townspeople so, far from her

Of whom he'd had no joy yet. For her
Sake he had given up much.

In a few lines, you get a young man's life in the moment of his death.

HOW YOU CAN *HEAR* THE *ILIAD*

People ask us all the time: "How can I learn about Shakespeare?" That one's easy: Go see a play. Go see several. Hang with Shakespeare fans and talk to them.

People also ask, quite a bit: "How can I learn about the *Iliad*?" Here is your instruction manual.

The Iliad is one of the oldest written-down poems in European history. Though written down, it is really oral, an image of a world without writing. For centuries, these tales were told aloud, transmitted from mouth to ear. The *Iliad* may have begun the story of writing, but it embodies the history of reading aloud.

In 2023, Emily Wilson became one of the first women to publish a translation of the entire *Iliad* into English. *Isn't that great?* It is written in verse that just *rolls*, at a brisk, noble pace, just like the original. Wilson said reading aloud was a huge part of her *Iliad*. She read aloud to herself as she went. She read to groups. And now you can *hear* her translation, read by Audra McDonald, a person blessed with a memorable, mellifluous speaking voice. It is a thrill, let us tell you. McDonald's reading even won the 2024 Audie Award for Literary Fiction & Classics. Of *course* it did.

Your instructions:

Step 1: Assemble a friend or six or do this with you. Why do it alone? The *Iliad* would make a challenging and rewarding centerpiece for a poetry reading group. *Get a guide:* If you know people comfortable in the world of the archaic Greeks, invite them to come talk to the group.

Step 2: Purchase or check out or borrow the book: *The Iliad*, translated by Emily Wilson. It's everywhere. Go get it.

Step 3: Acquire by purchase or checkout, but not theft, the audio version: *The Iliad,* read by Audra McDonald. It's published by Audible Publishing.

Step 4: Play it and read along. Wilson has notes and a glossary in the back of the book, so if you want to know more about someone or something, pause and look it up. Take it little bit by little bit. It could be the best 20 hours and 20 minutes you ever spent.

The beginnings of Chinese poetry

Chinese ancient history was dominated by a series of dynasties, in which a single family provided a line of rulers. The Zhou Dynasty (1046–256 BC) saw the first emergence of literature and culture. The first important anthologies of Chinese verse, including the *Shijing* or *Book of Songs*, were in circulation between 1100 and 700 BC. The work of the man thought of as China's first great poet, Qu Yuan, emerged at this time. Tradition has it that he wrote the collection *Nine Classic Songs* and the beautiful lament *Li Sao* ("Encountering Sorrow"). During what's known as the Eastern Zhou (770–256 BC), two great religious leaders/*philosophers*/poets emerged. The first was Laozi (his name means "Old Master"), reputed founder of Taoism. The book known as the *Tao Te Ching* or *The Way of the Tao* is associated with him, although it may well be an anthology. Many of its compressed, poetic sayings are true mind-worms:

> Rule a large nation
> As you'd cook a small fish

You have to guess what he means. One good guess: Rulers should rule gently, with care, and not overdo it.

Confucius (Chinese name: Kong QiuKong) lived from 551 to 479 BC and became an important teacher, administrator, and jurist. He was also crucial for the history of Chinese poetry, because he collected and edited much of the ancient Chinese writings.

The Archaic and Classical Periods (750 BC–AD 476)

These two periods embrace the high points of Greek and Latin poetry. The story of these two great languages and cultures makes up a golden six centuries of recorded history.

Greek poetry

Greek poetry of the Archaic and Classical periods is just a heap of treasures. Many readers feel that the Greek poets, among the first poets in Western European history, set a standard for creativity and excellence that has yet to be equaled.

Lyric poets

The Greek lyric poets flourished for eight centuries. One of the earliest and best is Sappho, who lived around 600 BC. Almost all that remains to us are five or so complete poems (see Chapter 6) and fragments — bits of her poems quoted by later writers. In what remains of her work, we hear a fresh, direct, and almost contemporary voice.

Here, Sappho pleads with Aphrodite, goddess of erotic desire, to come down and help her with a woman who will not love her. Few gods in any poem ever spoke with such loving mock-irritation:

Rainbow-throned, deathless Aphrodite
Wile-weaving Zeus-daughter, I pray:
don't overwhelm with anguish and grief,
Mistress, my heart

but come here, if ever, if anytime
you from far away heard my voice
and left your father's golden house
in your yoked chariot.

Lovely swift sparrows spinning with
whirring wings carried you above
this dark earth down from the sky
mid-air and soon got here. You,

Blessed, smile on your deathless face,
asked, "What is the matter with you this time?
Why are you calling this time? What
in your craziest of hearts

do you want this time? Who am I
supposed to sweet-talk into
taking you back this time?
Who wrongs you, Sappho?

She runs from you? Soon she'll
chase you. She spurns your gifts?
Well, instead she'll give them.
She doesn't love?

Oh, yes, she will, soon, be she
never so unwilling."
                    Come
to me and now, free me from

these griefs of longing. All
my heart longs after, make
it happen ... and you, yourself,
be my battle-mate.

Magic, isn't it, to hear such a strong voice from 2600 years ago?

Standouts: In addition to Sappho, other luminous lyric poets of this period include Anacreon, Pindar, Theocritus, and Callimachus.

Dramatists

The classical-era Greek dramatists wrote in verse so powerful that the plays of Sophocles *(Oedipus Rex; Antigone; The Trojan Women)*, Aeschylus *(The Oresteia Trilogy)*, Euripides *(The Bacchae; Medea)*, and Aristophanes *(Lysistrata; The Frogs)* are still being produced today. If you ever have the opportunity to see any of them performed, go!

Latin poetry

One of the towering presences in classical Latin poetry is Virgil, who wrote *The Aeneid* (very much a Roman version of *The Odyssey*), as well as philosophical poems that involve farming (the Georgics) and herding sheep (the Eclogues). Many fine translations of *The Aeneid* exist.

Another great epic poet is Lucretius, who wrote *On the Nature of Things*, a wild and wildly beautiful philosophical poem that seeks to explain everything from the gods to vision to human history.

TECHNICAL STUFF

Latin, unlike Greek, was not a language naturally given to beauty or delicacy. It was given to sentences like "the farmer and his wife have bought the horses" or "the walls of the city soon were destroyed by Caesar's brave men." Yet, in the hands of the poets, Latin became a flexible, musical poetic language. Among the Latin greats are these three:

- **Catullus:** He wrote playful, troubled poetry to his beloved Lesbia.
- **Horace:** Perhaps the greatest of all Latin lyricists, he wrote a wide range of philosophical, erotic, and descriptive poetry.

» **Ovid:** His *Metamorphoses* tries to explain the universe as a place of end-less transformations. Ovid's erotic poetry (the *Amores,* the *Book of Love,* and others) is some of the best out there, in our humble opinion.

Late Antiquity and Golden Ages (AD 476–1000)

In late antiquity, the Roman Empire began to crumble, and the Goths, Visigoths, Ostrogoths, Lombards, and everybody but the Philadelphia Eagles overran the Romans. We don't call these the Dark Ages anymore. A lot of beautiful poetry was being written; in Europe, most of that poetry was in Latin. And this era was anything but dark for poetry in the Middle East and Asia, which witnessed golden ages in Arabic, Japanese, and Chinese verse.

The *Manyoshu* and Japanese poetry

Japan saw two great ages of poetry and two great anthologies: the *Manyoshu* (compiled around 750), which includes the work of Kakinomoto Hitomaro and Yamanoe Okura, and the *Kokinshu* (around 905), which includes the wonderful verse of Ono no Komachi. She wrote in a form known as *waka*, something like a tanka (see Chapter 8). Here's a lovely example:

They say autumn nights
are long, but what do "they" know?
We'd barely met, your
eyes, my eyes hardly began
to gaze when, just like that ... dawn.

This Ono no Komachi is good, right? Online there's plenty of her. Find. Love.

The *Manyoshu* contains some of the finest love poetry ever. It's also a vivid document of a thriving poetic culture. Schools of verse arose. Poetic competitions, something like modern poetry slams (see Chapter 10), were established, complete with prizes and revered poets as judges. Groups of poets wrote cycles of poetry together, including the playful *tanka chain*, an intricate braid of poems in which poets responded to one another's work. In this era, the long Japanese tradition of poetry by women reached the first of many high points.

This anonymous poem from the *Manyoshu*, written in the voice of a mother whose son is going on a journey, gives some idea of the delicate depth of Japanese poetry of this period:

If snow falls on the far field
where travelers
spend the night,
I ask you, cranes,
to warm my child in your wings.

The *Manyoshu* is still widely considered the apex of classical Japanese verse.

The poetry of India

The Gupta Empire (AD 322–550) is sometimes called the "Golden Age of India." It spread across northern India and involved a revival of Hinduism and the establishment of standards for literature and art. Among the most famous poets of this era is Kalidasa, who wrote plays and poems still performed today. Sanskrit became the basis of Indian literature, philosophy, law, and culture. Poetry in Sanskrit was written for 2500 years. Much poetry in Sanskrit is philosophical and scholarly, but there is some remarkable love poetry, plus a strong tradition of poetry by women, including Vidya, who lived between the 600s and 800s and is revered for her poetry about the emotions and the natural world.

Arabic poetry

Arabic poetry was vital even before the advent of Islam. Around AD 550, Imr El-Qais, "The Wandering King," wrote his influential odes in the anthology *Mu'allaqah (Necklace-Beads)*. Here are a few lines of his, from "The Great Ode," one of the earliest and most famous of all Arabic poems. The speaker, torn with love for a woman, watches her pack up to leave and realizes it's hopeless:

Here was the place I watched her
Load her camels for going. Here, by thorn trees
Was I stung, tears as bitter as desert gourd.

Two friends waited, already swaying on camelback.
Man — they called to me — don't let this grief kill you.
Better to bear with patience what pain may come.

With the establishment of Islam, Arabic became a transnational language of poetry, law, religion, and culture from the Middle East to Asia. Muhammad (AD 570–632) was the prophet and founder of Islam. The holy book of Islam, the Koran, is filled with sacred poetry. It is the basis for much Islamic law and life.

The golden age for classical Arabic poetry spanned 600 years (AD 600 to 1200). At its height, it was being written from Spain to India. The great poets' verses have become sayings and idioms far and wide. The written poem is often considered an artwork in and of itself. Many are the verses of intense desire, the desert landscapes, the laments for great kings and fallen warriors.

Two great poets of the early Islamic era are Umar Ibn Abi Rabiah and Al-Khansa, the major female poet in classical Arabic. During the dynasty of the Ummayad caliphs in Damascus, Syria (AD 661–750), Arabic poetry reached new heights; during this period, the *ghazal* (pronounced *guzzle*) was introduced. This playful, sensuous verse form, excellent for love poetry and mystical poetry, spread throughout the Middle East and Asia, and today it is practiced all over the world.

During the dynasty of the Abbasids, centered in Baghdad (AD 750–1055), Arab poets encountered the influences of Greek, Roman, and Persian poetry. Great poets included Al-Mutanabbi and the Syrian poet Abû-l-`Alâ' al-Ma'arrî.

China: The T'ang Dynasty

The T'ang Dynasty was the setting for what's known as the Golden Age of Chinese poetry. Du Fu is one the best-known poets in the world, as are Li Bai, Wang Wei, Bai Juyi, and Li He. The emperor Xuanzong was a great patron of poets.

Other fine poetry was written in the Han, Sung, and Ming dynasties.

LI BAI AND THE MOON

The famous Chinese T'ang poet Li Bai (AD 701–762) lived a life of wandering and spontaneity. He was said to embody the Taoist and Zen ideal of *wu-wei* (literally, "doing nothing"). He also claimed to be a kinsman of imperial princes. He was even appointed at one time as a court poet to the emperor, but he lost his position because of his wild, drunken behavior. Yet he wrote surprisingly insightful, highly imaginative poems during his drunken bouts. He wrote often of longing and nature: The moon appears in more than a third of his poems. As irony and (some might say) poetic justice would have it, Li Bai drowned one evening when he fell out of a boat. He was trying to embrace the moon.

Old English

Our earliest traces of *Old English* (once known as *Anglo-Saxon*) appear in anonymous stone inscriptions from around the 600s.

Beowulf, an epic, is one of the finest poems ever. It tells the tale of a warrior, Beowulf, and his showdowns with a series of monsters. Most famous of these is Grendel, who has the bad luck to get into Beowulf's clutches. Old English verse was *alliterative*, based on repetition of initial consonant sounds. Here, the first two half-lines repeat the initial *s* sound, the second line has two *m* sounds in it, and so forth.

READ ALOUD

Soon he saw — that shepherd of sorrows —
that he'd never met in all middle-earth,
all ways of the world, a warrior who wielded
a grip this grievous, so strong he groaned
in frenzy, fear, no breaking free.
He hurt to be home flee to his hideout,
lair of devils — but no such doings
as he'd done before in olden days!

The period also produced shorter poems, such as "Caedmon's Hymn," "The Battle of Maldon," "The Wife's Lament," "The Wanderer," and "The Dream of the Rood." (Look them up! Read!) The *riddle* was another common form in Old English poetry.

IN THIS CHAPTER

» Finding poetry of the Middle Ages

» Discovering poetry from the English Renaissance

» Seeing how reason and science affected poetry in the 18th century

Chapter 8
The Middle Ages through the 18th Century

The term *Middle Ages* was made up by historians in the Renaissance to describe the period between their own time and the fall of Rome (AD 476). They thought of Rome as a period of greatness, and their own as a rebirth of that greatness (and it surely was great).

The Middle Ages was a time of great discoveries, including the invention of written music and the beginnings of what we call science. It was also a time of great learning and great poetry. This period was not only a European thing. In Japan, one of the earliest novels we know of (one that contains more than 700 poems!) was written by a court lady. Persia, in the meantime, was home to some of the greatest poets in history.

We use the word *renaissance* to mean a rebirth, rediscovery, resurrection. When we speak of a "renaissance" woman or man, we mean a person who is very good at many things. That's what the capital-R Renaissance was all about: a sense that a brand new artistic golden age was at hand, a delirious thirst to learn and read and write and paint and sculpt as much as you could. Great epics were written, some of them historical, and some, like Edmund Spenser's *Faerie Queene,* all imaginary. Love poetry rose to yet another peak. And the art of the drama, generally considered a kind of poetry, rose to a peak with Shakespeare and many other great dramatists and poets across Europe.

It's not so much that the Renaissance *stopped*. It just kind of morphed into the Enlightenment, a refreshing celebration of clear-eyed reason. The poetry of that age rests on balance, perception, and emotion that sees itself clearly. Some people think the Renaissance discovered the modern notion of the self — but the Enlightenment perfected it. Its poetry shows it.

Poetry of the Middle Ages (1000–1450)

The poetry of this period helped create the world you live in. Our notion of *love itself* may have arisen at this time. The Middle Ages was dominated, in Europe, by the Catholic Church and its official language, Latin. It was indeed an era of belief, an era of mighty myths and battles, and also an era of great humor and compassion.

Standouts: *The Tale of Genji*; *The Song of Roland*; *The Poem of the Cid*; the Nibelung cycle; *Tristan und Isolde*; *Parzifal*; Bertran de Born, Arnaut Daniel, Walther von der Vogelweide, and Giovanni Boccaccio; Francesco Petrarca, Dante, Geoffrey Chaucer, Omar Khayyam, Rūmī, Hafez, and Ghalib. Poetry in Europe.

During this period, however, European poets began to write extensively in their native languages. The major modern European languages all had their beginnings (as literary languages, anyway) during this time. The *Poem of My Cid* appeared in Spanish around 1100. French got up and running with the epic battle poem *The Song of Roland.* German produced both courtly love poetry and *chivalric romances* such as *Parzifal* and *Tristan und Isolde.*

TECHNICAL STUFF

Courtly love poetry concerned personal love and was written by and for people belonging to the courts of kings and nobles. Some scholars believe that the love poetry of the 12th century — especially that of the Provençal poets, such as Bertran de Born and Arnaut Daniel — may have helped create our very concept of love as it is now known and practiced.

The *chivalric romances* were tales of knights and their kings and damsels. They spread throughout all the languages of Europe, and they gave us the tales of King Arthur and the Round Table.

Italian had a true golden age, including the lyric poetry of Petrarch. And perhaps the finest poet of the age, Dante, wrote *The Divine Comedy.* In this epic religious poem, the speaker finds his way into a guided tour through Hell, Purgatory, and Paradise:

READ ALOUD

In the midst of the road of our lives,
I found myself on a darkened path
With the right way lost.
Oh! It is so hard to say how savage
And bitter and rough that road was
That, as I think of it, the fear returns.

In English, Geoffrey Chaucer wrote *The Canterbury Tales* and *Troilus and Criseyde*.

Arabic and Persian verse — and the Rūmī supernova

In the Middle East, this era was the high point of Arabic and Persian poetry, including the work of Omar Khayyam, Rūmī, and Hafez in Persian, and Ghalib in Arabic verse. One of the great poets of the Golden Age of Arabic verse, Muhammad ibn Ghalib al-Rusafi (who died in 1177), remains one of the most popular of all poets in the Arab world. Ghalib was a master of the *ghazal* (see the section, "Arabic poetry").

A special word on *The Rubaiyat* of Omar Khayyam (1048–1131). Here is a case in which poetry written in one era and place (12th-century Persia) has to wait a while — in this case, 600 years-plus — to achieve popularity someplace else (mid-Victorian England).

A *ruba'i* is just a quatrain, a four-line form rhyming AABA. The 1859 English translation of Khayyam's *Rubaiyat* by Edward FitzGerald (see Chapter 3, "If Poems Could Spit") contains four of the most famous in English:

READ ALOUD

A Book of Verses underneath the Bough,
A Jug of Wine, a Loaf of Bread — and Thou
Beside me singing in the Wilderness —

O, Wilderness were Paradise enow! FitzGerald's translation started a wave of new interest in Persian verse — a wave still cresting today.

That brings us to a second star rising out of Persia: Jalāl al-Dīn Muḥammad Rūmī (1207–1273), better known simply as Rūmī. He was a jurist, theologian, and Sufi mystic whose verse apprehends the universe and its God with ecstatic love and joy. Good English translations of Rūmī started appearing in the mid-20th century, bringing readers a poet whose appeal transcends time and borders. His figure of "the Beloved," one of the greatest metaphors in history, fuses together the people one loves here on earth, Love itself, and God, the beloved of all beloveds:

You found me once again,
you thief of hearts. In drunken ecstasy,
you searched the bazaar and found me.

Even through sleepy-lidded, Love-drunk eyes,
you spotted me. I ran to the tavern.
You found me.

Why do I run when no one can escape you?
Why hide when you've found me a hundred times?

I thought I could lose you in a crowd of people,
but you find me even in crowds of secrets,
even behind my own masks.

What a blessing to be sought and found by your eyes.
What luck to be caught in your twists and turns —

loving seer, persistent seer,
towering cypress of countless gardens,

I was pulling a thorn from my foot
when you found me.

You showered me with flowers
from your fertile beds.
Dear nightingale,
your melodies opened my ears.

Like a ladle wanting its fill of light,
I plunged into the moon's halo.
At the bottom of that bottomless pot, you found me.

Like a deer fleeing a lion, I ran through the desert.
Deep in the mountains, you found me.

Wounded, I shed my blood on every path.
You followed the drops and found me.

I was a hooked fish writhing in the waves.
At the end of the line, you found me.

You roam the skies and catch galloping deer.
With all that skill and patience,
you found me.

The moment you found me,
you gave me a cup brimming with Love's wine,
heavy enough to match the weight on my soul.

Every sip lightened it.
Every sip, a balm.
I drank till empty.
My soul took flight.

I have no mind, no ear, no tongue today.
The source of thought and word found me.

In the lucid tumble of original images, the concentrated pace, many 21st-century readers hear in Rūmī a poet who sounds modern. But this 800-year-old poem is in fact a ghazal (see the section "Arabic poetry," and Chapter 11), and that repeated *you found me* is the *radif*! Rūmī's star has never been higher.

THE TALE OF GENJI AND GENJIPOEMS.ORG

In Japan, one of the masterpieces of world literature, *The Tale of Genji*, was written by Lady Murasaki Shikibu (around 970 to around 1014 or 1025), a lady in waiting at the imperial court. Often considered to be one of the first novels in history, *Genji* also included hundreds of poems, known as *waka*, sent by the characters to one another. The full impact of Shikibu's poetry did not hit the West until spring 2025, when `https://genjipoems.org` went online. Over nine years, led by J. Keith Vincent of Boston University, a team of students, volunteers, experts, and technicians collected all 795 *waka* in *Genji* and organized them according to the character who writes them and other data points. Each waka is accompanied by five different translations. And visitors to the site can add their own versions!

(continued)

(continued)

Here is Book 3, Poem 1. Prince Genji sneaks into a mansion, hoping to meet Utsusemi (her name means "cast-off cicada shell"), a woman he desires. But she escapes him. The dejected prince leaves this poem:

> Dew on the wings of
> A molted cicada shell
> In the secrecy
> Of a shady tree. Secret,
> My sleeves grow damp with my tears.

The *waka* begins with the empty cicada shell — a graceful pun on Utsushemi's name. Cicada and woman are both gone. In a lovely echo, Genji's grief is "secret," echoing the "secrecy" of the absent beloved.

In Book 8, Genji writes to a woman with whom he has fallen in love.

> You love the beauty
> of moon-set amid late-night
> mists — clearly I see
> that our togetherness is
> no mist, but strong, enduring.

Her character has conquered him, persuading him that, in spite of everything against it, their togetherness will last. Against the "late-night/mists" is the clarity of Genji's belief, "no mist."

Maybe now Shikibu's poetry will become as celebrated as the novel itself.

Chinese and Japanese poetry

In China, the Sung Dynasty (960–1280) ushered in a great era of innovation in forms and styles. One of the finest of Sung poets is Xin Qiji.

Another great anthology of Japanese verse, the *Shin Kokinshu*, appeared in 1265. In the 1300s, the great dramatic tradition of the Noh play began.

The European Renaissance (1450–1674)

The *Renaissance* (French for "rebirth") saw a resurgence of interest in the Greek and Latin writers, and an explosion of knowledge in the arts and sciences. The Renaissance started at various points in Europe, including Italy, France, and the north, working all around the continent. In Italy, great epic poems emerged, as well as many fine lyric poets, including the artist Michelangelo himself. In Spain, an incredible period of dramatic poetry, or plays in verse, started up in the 16th century. Lope de Vega is probably the best known poet from that period. The great French dramatic poems were written in the 17th century by Racine, Corneille, and Molière.

The English Renaissance

The English Renaissance brought the world such writers as Shakespeare and Sir Walter Raleigh, but dozens of other first-rank poets were working in England as well, some of whom were good playwrights, too. Dramatic, lyric, epic, and historical poetry all flourished. Many of the poetic forms we find most familiar today became firmly established among English poets. *Blank verse* (unrhymed iambic pentameter) was the form in which Shakespeare and many of his fellow dramatists wrote their plays. Ballad forms appeared both in folk poetry and in the popular songs and madrigals of the time. And the sonnet was an international craze; poets across Europe wrote thousands of them.

Standouts: We can't possibly list them all here. If you want to get a true feel for the Renaissance, read Shakespeare, as well as the poetry of Sir Philip Sidney, Edmund Spenser, John Donne, Ben Jonson, and George Herbert (see Chapter 4). The high point and end of the English Renaissance was John Milton's *Paradise Lost*, a vast religious epic. You could fill a good-sized bookstore with the great dramatic poetry of the period: Christopher Marlowe's *Faust;* Shakespeare's *Romeo and Juliet, Hamlet,* or *The Tempest;* Jonson's *Volpone;* Pedro Calderón de la Barca's *Life Is a Dream;* Pierre Corneille's *Le Cid;* Jean Racine's *Phèdre;* and Molière's *The Misanthrope.* Even with all that, you've only just gotten started.

Poetry on three continents

Across the Atlantic, people were writing poetry in the English colonies of North America, including Mistress Anne Bradstreet (1612–1672), who published her first book of forthright, charming poems in 1650. She thus became the first published "American poet." In "A Letter to her Husband, Absent upon Publick

Employment," she compares their union to that of turtledoves or the fish called mullets, who at that time were believed to be monogamous species:

Together at one Tree, oh let us brouze,
And like two Turtles roost within one house,
And like the Mullets in one River glide,
Let's still remain but one, till death divide.

Bradstreet's fresh directness — turning the ordinary experience of household, family, and self into poetry — foretold the future of American verse. She began a line of American poets that would include, among many others, Emily Dickinson, Sylvia Plath, Kay Ryan, Natalie Diaz, and Tracy K. Smith.

As for South America, before the Spanish and Portuguese conquerors over-ran the continent, ancient poetic cultures already were in full flower. In what is now Guatemala, the Quiche Mayans compiled the *Popul Vuh*, an account of the history of the Mayans from the creation of the world to the year 1550. Defeat and genocide inspired some beautiful poems, including those of the 16th-century Mayan text known as *Chilam Balam:*

Before the conquerors came
there was no sin,
no sickness, no aches,
no fevers, no pox.
The foreigners stood
the world on its head,
made day become night.
There were no longer
any lucky days
after they came into our lands.

A great deal of South American poetry meditates on the pre-Columbian, the mysteries and wisdoms of indigenous peoples. From Mexico to Brazil, the facts of a violent colonial past, along with the rainforest and the jungle, are still realities in poetry today.

This period was a crucial one for poetry in India. The Mughal Empire (1526–1857) not only spread Islam throughout the subcontinent but also introduced Arabic and Persian poetry, which had a huge impact on verse in several languages.

Japanese poetry saw the birth of one of its greatest practitioners during this period. Matsuo Bashō (1644–1694) became a recognized master of the form known as the *haiku* (see the section "Japan: The haiku tradition continues," later in this chapter, and Chapter 13), as well as a celebrated teacher and judge of poetry. His poetic journals, interspersing prose commentary with wonderful haiku, remain favorite readings throughout the world.

The 18th Century

The 18th century in Europe was dominated by an intellectual movement known as the *Enlightenment* — so named because people were placing greater and greater confidence in the power of human reason to improve life and discover the truths of nature.

Standouts: Jonathan Swift (the same man who wrote *Gulliver's Travels*), Samuel Johnson, John Dryden, and Voltaire; Issa, Bashō, and Buson.

Reason, science, and a changing world: The English Enlightenment

As of 1700, the age of science and technology had just begun. The Industrial Revolution was ahead, as was the American Revolution, the world wars, the Digital Age, and much else. Poetry benefited from all these developments, and poets developed new ways to express life in their changing circumstances.

Some readers think that, coming between the vastness of the Renaissance and the brilliance of the Romantic era (see Chapter 9), Enlightenment poetry is a disappointment. Not so! We like the stateliness and balance of the poetry of the Enlightenment.

Listen to these lovely couplets from Alexander Pope's *Essay on Criticism*, a long poem on how to form judgments about poetry. He's recommending that the first thing any poet (or critic of poets) should do is be awake to Nature:

READ ALOUD

First follow Nature, and your judgment frame
By her just standard, which is still the same;
Unerring Nature, still divinely bright,
One clear, unchanged, and universal light,
Life, force, and beauty must to all impart,
At once the source, and end, and test of art.

You can feel in these lines the Enlightenment's quest for clarity and perfection. The form here is *rhymed couplets*, very stately, very regular. Poets of this era shared the Enlightenment faith that clear-sightedness and reason could lead to a new era of understanding. That's the "universal light" provided by Nature — it's the truth itself. In the Enlightenment, poets and scientists alike strove toward that light.

Japan: The haiku tradition continues

In Japan, the *haiku* tradition was upheld by two of the very greatest of poets, Yosa Buson and Kobayashi Issa (see Chapter 1).

IN THIS CHAPTER

» Discovering Romanticism, Symbolism, and the beginning of modern American poetry

» Knowing standout poets from each period

» Figuring out where to find poetry from every era

Chapter 9 Poetry During the Industrial Revolution

The 19th century saw the Industrial Revolution reach full throttle. Great strides in technology created great wealth and great poverty, as well as many social and political changes across the world. Poetry, too, was changing rapidly. This chapter covers the three developments that marked this eventful poetic century: Romanticism, Symbolism, and the beginning of modern American poetry.

The Romantic Period

Some readers get confused by the term *Romantic.* People in the Romantic period were not any more inclined to love than those who lived in other periods. The word *Romantic* came to mean a new, often revolutionary outlook, emphasizing the importance of personal emotions, the inspiration of the artist, innovation in ideas and the arts, and unity with nature (which in some writers came near to a religion). Some of these developments emerged as a reaction to the Industrial Revolution.

The Romantic era is one of the three or four greatest periods in the history of poetry. In Europe especially, poetry was the most-read literary form. Several novels in verse, including *Don Juan* (by English poet George Gordon, Lord Byron) and *Eugene Onegin* (by the Russian poet Alexander Pushkin, shown in Figure 9-1) were international bestsellers. But the leading poetry of the era was lyric poetry, personal, intense, and titanic. When many people think of the image of The Poet, often they're thinking of Romantic poets and poetry.

FIGURE 9-1: Alexander Pushkin. Portrait by Orest Kiprensky, 1827.

Public domain. Source: Picryl.com

One of the great geniuses of this age, or any age, was Johann Wolfgang von Goethe. As a poet, playwright, novelist, philosopher, and politician, he helped create and sustain the notion of Romanticism and of the Romantic poet. His ideas about nature, the emotions, the soul, and the importance of poetry found their way into poetry all across Europe. Goethe was very prolific, and his lyric poetry fills volumes. Perhaps his best-known work is his monumental verse drama *Faust* (1808).

Pushkin's *Eugene Onegin* is one of the most successful of all tales told in poetry; it was and is an international success. The tale is unforgettable yet puzzling: Eugene, the main character, is by turns admirable and frustrating. Both he and Tatyana, the woman who loves him, pursue a doomed relationship. Pushkin wrote several verse tales, as well as important verse drama, including the historic *Boris Godunov*, a sort of ethnic creation myth for the Russian people.

HEARING PUSHKIN'S *EUGENE ONEGIN* READ ALOUD

This whole book, we've been saying poetry is meant to be read aloud, and we've been encouraging you to read it — and hear it read. Well, then, here's your biggest, best chance! *Eugene Onegin* by Pushkin is one of the finest poems ever, one of the finest novels, too. If you read Russian, go get it and read it aloud; Russian-speakers say it is transporting.

On the off-chance that you don't read Russian, you can find the best English translation of *Onegin* and hear a marvelous reading while following along in your book.

Your instructions:

Step 1: Procure *Eugene Onegin, A Verse Novel,* translated by James E. Falen. Part of the Oxford World's Classics series, this translation is one of the best. Order it online, or at your bookstore . . . or check it out at your friendly, sweet-smelling library.

Step 2: Locate *Stephen Frye Reads Eugene Onegin* (`https://soundcloud.com/search?q=EUgene%20onegin%20fry`). It's located on the platform Soundcloud. Once you have registered (it's not too hard), search for "Eugene Onegin Stephen Fry," and it should pop right up, part by part. Writer, comedian, actor, and public star Frye has a rich, sonorous, kind voice, and *he knows how to read!* Put on thy headphones or earbuds, open thy book, click on thy Play arrow, and begin. Each chapter takes around 40 minutes. Spread the pleasure out as much as you wish. Organize a *Eugene Onegin* reading group. You may well get hooked on this tragicomic tale.

As with Shakespeare in English, so with Alexander Pushkin in Russian. Almost every Russian can recite some Pushkin. He was a true innovator, a fiery figure just as good at love poems as he was at vast epic tapestries. And he had a miraculous ear for the music of the Russian language.

In the British Isles, Romanticism brought in a rush of fresh, visionary poetry. Many of the best-known poets of this era are among the best-known ever: Scotland's Robert Burns and England's William Blake, Samuel Taylor Coleridge, William Wordsworth, John Keats, George Gordon, Lord Byron, and Percy Bysshe Shelley. Each had his own voice, but there was an energy in common, a refreshed vision of the universe and humanity's place in it, a revolutionary fervor, a feeling of new beginnings.

Here's "Love's Philosophy" by Shelley. Watch how he begins with a joyful vision of all creation as one — and focuses down to his own interests:

READ ALOUD

The fountains mingle with the river
  And the rivers with the Ocean,
The winds of Heaven mix for ever
  With a sweet emotion;
Nothing in the world is single;
  All things by a law divine
In one spirit meet and mingle.
  Why not I with thine? —

The gusty pleasure of this verse, the way the poet connects the joy in nature with his own desires — that's a Romantic moment.

The Romantic period brought about a revolution in the kind of language poets used. England's Wordsworth and Germany's Friedrich Schiller, among many others, sought simpler, more direct language. The *ode* — passionate, serious, elaborate, meditating on nature as a way to explore the human soul — was perhaps the era's most characteristic verse form. Because of its emphasis on *sincerity* and emotion, *lyric poetry* — shorter, often songlike poems usually of a personal nature (what most people today think of when they think of poetry) — became the dominant genre and has remained that way. Sonnets were widely written for the first time since the Elizabethan period (the time of Shakespeare); epics, when written at all, tended toward personal subjects rather than public events.

Standouts: Johann Wolfgang von Goethe and other German Romantics, including Friedrich Hölderlin, Friedrich Schiller, and Heinrich Heine; the plays, verse novels, and lyric poetry of Russia's Alexander Pushkin; Victor Hugo, the huge presence in French Romantic poetry; Giacomo Leopardi of Italy; Robert Burns of Scotland; the English Romantic poets, including William Blake (*Songs of Innocence and Experience*), William Wordsworth, Samuel Taylor Coleridge ("Kubla Khan," "Rime of the Ancient Mariner"), John Keats ("Eve of St. Agnes," "Ode on a Grecian Urn"), Percy Bysshe Shelley, and Byron. *Read some!*

The Victorian Period

The Victorian period was a time of big changes in society. Victoria was the queen of England at this time, but the changes during her queenship were worldwide. The Industrial Revolution — and the intense ambivalence it caused — was in full swing. The United States was growing up. Science and technology were transforming human life at an astonishing rate, and many poets wrote about those changes. A heightened interest in human psychology led to the popularity of the *dramatic monologue*, in which a speaker delivers what appears to be a speech about his or her personal situation. England's Robert Browning; Alfred, Lord Tennyson; and Matthew Arnold all wrote masterful dramatic monologues.

Standouts: English Victorian poets, including Alfred, Lord Tennyson (*In Memoriam* and much very accomplished poetry); Robert Browning and Elizabeth Barrett Browning; Christina Rossetti; Matthew Arnold; Gerard Manley Hopkins; the French Symbolists, including Charles Baudelaire *(Fleurs du Mal),* Jules Laforgue, Tristan Corbière, Arthur Rimbaud, Paul Valéry, Paul Verlaine, and Stéphane Mallarmé; Americans Walt Whitman and Emily Dickinson (well-represented in many fine anthologies); and Japanese poet Masaoka Shiki.

The Symbolist movement

In France, a poetic movement called *Symbolism* got under way. Symbolist poets sought to evoke states of feeling through their poetry, rather than spelling out exactly what their poems meant. They were interested in the intense, almost magical spell language could cast on the beholder, and they explored new uses of metaphors and images in an effort to get language to mean new things.

Symbolist poets build entire poetic worlds out of intensely private symbols. Poets had done something like Symbolism before. Some people consider the Romantic English poets Blake or Shelley, or maybe Hölderlin of Germany, as early Symbolists. But the capital-*S* movement began in 1857 with the publication of *Fleurs du Mal (Flowers of Evil)* by Charles Baudelaire. It culminated with the Big Four of French Symbolism: Arthur Rimbaud, Stéphane Mallarmé, Paul Verlaine, and Paul Valéry. These poets come close to creating a *completely* symbolic world, evoking states of feeling or awareness, often without specific, locatable meanings. Their poetry *suggests* things, in other words, but it directly states very little. That's difficult to do.

Read this stanza from "Memory" by Arthur Rimbaud:

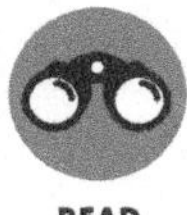

READ ALOUD

Longing for thick, young arms of pure grass!
Gold of April moons in the heart of the holy bed! Joy
Of abandoned woodyards by the river, prey
To August nights that made the rotten things sprout!

Each of the images in this passage is full of emotions — crowded, conflicting emotions. You can't really tell what the images *mean*, exactly, but still you can feel longing and joy. This stanza is mainly a group of symbols, but you're not told exactly what the symbols are meant to stand for. Because the poem is titled "Memory," you can assume these are pictures from the speaker's memory, with which the speaker associates various states of feeling. The idea is to feel your own way along these surprising bursts of images — to feel the implications, the suggestions that arise.

The layering of these symbols, one on top of the other, was key to the 20th-century movement known as *Modernism*, in which the *meaning* of a poem sometimes bounced among images rather than being stated straightforwardly. This required a more agile reader capable of following a series of complex associations. It also helped create the public image of modern poetry as being something *difficult*.

As a movement in France, Symbolism reached a peak in the 1870s and 1880s, but it never really went away. It was a bridge into 20th-century poetry. Two of the finest Symbolist poets, Valéry and Paul Claudel, wrote poetry well into that century. Among the 20th-century poets in whom Symbolism is a strong influence are India's Rabindranath Tagore (see Chapter 10), France's Marguerite Burnat-Provins; Austria's Rainer Maria Rilke (we love his poetry helplessly); Nicaragua's Rubén Darío; Russia's Marina Tsvetaeva; Ireland's William Butler Yeats; U.S. poets Wallace Stevens, T.S. Eliot, Hart Crane, and Adrienne Rich; Mexico's Octavio Paz; and Chile's Pablo Neruda.

American poetry: Whitman and Dickinson

Leaves of Grass, written by U.S. poet Walt Whitman (shown in Figure 9-2), was a book mostly of long-lined, *open-form* poems (see Chapter 14). Whitman kept editing and re-editing it his entire life. Although lengthy, *Leaves of Grass* is inviting and comfortable to read. Its hearty, often rollicking verses cast a vibrant, personable shadow over world poetry for the next 175 years.

Dip anywhere into Whitman's poetry, and a celebratory gust of wide-openness hits you in the soul, as in these lines from "Spontaneous Me" in *Leaves of Grass:*

READ ALOUD

Spontaneous me, Nature,
The loving day, the mounting sun, the friend I am happy with,
The arm of my friend hanging idly over my shoulder,
The hillside whiten'd with blossoms of the mountain ash,
The same late in autumn, the hues of red, yellow, drab, purple, and
light and dark green,
The rich coverlet of the grass, animals and birds, the private, untrimm'd
bank, the primitive apples, the pebble-stones,
Beautiful dripping fragments, the negligent list of one after another as I
happen to call them to me or think of them

FIGURE 9-2: Walt Whitman.

Mathew Benjamin Brady/National Archives/Public domain

You don't see traditional end-rhyme or regular meter in Whitman's open-form verse. (It has a great deal of rhythm but no strict meter repeated from line to line.) Just as traditional meters and stanza forms had characterized poetry of the previous 1300 years, Whitman's expansiveness, his inviting, free manner, his boundary-busting, led the way into modern poetry.

Meanwhile, living in her parents' house in Amherst, Massachusetts, Emily Dickinson was writing short, intense poems that experimented with rhyme and form, fearlessly exploring death, immortality, pain, and paradox, as in Poem 1732:

READ ALOUD

My life closed twice before its close;
  It yet remains to see
If immortality unveil
  A third event to me,

So huge, so hopeless to conceive
  As these that twice befell.
Parting is all we know of heaven,
  And all we need of hell.

In her personal life, Dickinson was as inward as Whitman was outward, but her tight, short, concentrated poems are just as original as his. She seldom sought publication, and the first collection of her works appeared in 1890, four years after her death. She blended a very nearly modern compression with ballad forms and rhymed stanzas related to the hymns she heard in church. Whitman and Dickinson are, for many people, the beginning of American poetry.

Shiki and the New Style in Japan

Japan had always been an isolated country and culture. But in the latter half of the 19th century, that began to change. In 1868, the Emperor Meiji was restored to the throne after a long period of Shogun rule. Leaders began to reorganize and modernize Japanese society and customs. Japan opened up to Western influences, especially to French Symbolism. A movement known as the *New Style,* an attempt to forge a new, contemporary Japanese poetry, arose in the 1880s.

One of the most important figures in Japanese poetry of this period was Masaoka Shiki. He was a scholar of both Japanese poetry and Western poetry. Shiki undertook to purify the rules of *haiku*; his understanding is how most of us Westerners come to haiku. When Western poets write in this form, they are practicing the ways Shiki taught. Shiki was at the forefront of the movement to modernize Japanese literary art, and he wrote some of the century's best Japanese verse.

IN THIS CHAPTER

» Checking out ten Modernist poets

» Discovering new voices and the experimental forms of the Postmodern era

» Exploring the rise of hybrid forms during the Global era

Chapter 10
The Century of Poetry

The 20th century was the Century of Poetry. The world had never seen such an explosion of styles, such a diversity of audiences, such a widening of the poetic horizon.

What made the 20th century so poetic? The first half endured an economic depression bookended by world wars. Such upheavals called into question what people thought they knew. So did the global triumph of technology: the automobile and airplane, the atomic bomb, and the coming of the computer and the Digital Age. Several such innovations — radio, telephone, and television — helped spread information and learning. That started to change society, very rapidly, especially after the Second World War, with the rise and expansion of middle-class society in many countries. Poets could be in touch with one another's work more quickly and easily, which led to new influences and new combinations of subjects, styles, and traditions.

The Modern Era (1901–1945)

We know: It's weird to think that the modern period is *over*. But *modern*, used as the name of a period, means a specific combination of things:

- » Experimentation and innovation in poetry.
- » A radical break with the past; the notion that the old ways of writing couldn't address the novelty and chaos of modern life.
- » A profound interest in psychology and the forces of history.
- » The rising dominance of free (or open-form) verse as opposed to traditional forms.
- » A new interest in writing about the forbidden side of life. The poetry of Hart Crane, C.P. Cavafy, and Gertrude Stein, for example, explores homoerotic and homosexual themes.

Many people think of Modernism as starting a little bit before the First World War and ending with the bombing of Hiroshima and Nagasaki in the Second World War.

Standouts: Ezra Pound, T.S. Eliot, William Butler Yeats, Hilda Doolittle ("H.D."), Robert Frost, William Carlos Williams, Langston Hughes, Gertrude Stein, Wallace Stevens, Marianne Moore, André Breton, Jacques Prévert, Rainer Maria Rilke, Georg Trakl, Marina Tsvetayeva, Anna Akhmatova, Federico García Lorca, Leopold Sédar Sénghor, Rabindranath Tagore, Pablo Neruda, and Octavio Paz. And they are just the beginning.

REMEMBER

All the arts of the Modern Era wrestled with what *the modern* was. Poets worked to find fresh, unprecedented ways to embody and present the viewpoints, emotions, lives, and environments of people in the real world. Modernism was a continual search for the new, the unguessed, the masterstroke that unpacks new energies to bring alive reality and our response to it. It was a time of experiment, suffering, and triumph, especially in the world of the word.

The following sections provide brief introductions of ten important Modern poets. Find! Read!

Rabindranath Tagore

The poetic career of Bengali poet Rabindranath Tagore (shown in Figure 10-1) bridged the 19th and 20th centuries. A prolific writer of fiction as well as essays, travel diaries, and other nonfiction works, Tagore also wrote 100 books of poems. This mystical, philosophical poet was deeply influenced by the Bengali and

Sanskrit traditions — and also by French Symbolism (see Chapter 9)! For his visionary, sensuous poems, Tagore won the Nobel Prize in literature in 1913. He was knighted in 1915 but resigned that honor in 1919 in protest over the British massacre in Amritsar, in which British Indian Army troops killed hundreds of protestors. His well-known books include *Gitanjali*, *Songs of Kabir*, and *The Gardener*.

FIGURE 10-1: Rabindranath Tagore.

William Butler Yeats

The Irish poet William Butler Yeats transformed himself from a late Romantic poet to a Modern poet with a wild, vivid voice. One of the most-quoted of all Modernist poems is this one, in which the speaker seems to think the present is chaotic and the future is terrifying:

READ ALOUD

The Second Coming

Turning and turning in the widening gyre
The falcon cannot hear the falconer;
Things fall apart; the centre cannot hold;
Mere anarchy is loosed upon the world,
The blood-dimmed tide is loosed, and everywhere

The ceremony of innocence is drowned;
The best lack all conviction, while the worst
Are full of passionate intensity.

Surely some revelation is at hand;
Surely the Second Coming is at hand.
The Second Coming! Hardly are those words out
When a vast image out of Spiritus Mundi
Troubles my sight: somewhere in the sands of the desert
A shape with lion body and the head of a man,
A gaze blank and pitiless as the sun,
Is moving its slow thighs, while all about it
Reel shadows of the indignant desert birds.
The darkness drops again; but now I know
That twenty centuries of stony sleep
Were vexed to nightmare by a rocking cradle,
And what rough beast, its hour come round at last,
Slouches towards Bethlehem to be born?

Two notes: a *gyre* is a spiral, so the falcon is traveling in widening spirals, further and further away from the falconer. *Spiritus Mundi* is, for Yeats, the vast, prophetic world-mind, the source of inspiration and, here, nightmare. Try to imagine that "rough beast." Human head, lion body . . . what incredibly famous desert being is that? Is it a symbol for something? Published in 1923, this horror movie of the soul wades into the chaotic state of Yeats's Ireland and the world. The music, as in all Yeats, is unearthly and gorgeous.

Ezra Pound

This Pennsylvanian innovator helped the rest of the century's poets "make it new" (a favorite slogan of his). Influenced by Chinese and Japanese poetry, Pound focused on the *image* (a concentrated moment of revelation, epiphany, or complex emotion), enacting the *occasion* for emotion but not *commenting* on it. This may be his best example:

READ ALOUD

In a Station of the Metro

The apparition of these faces in the crowd;
Petals on a wet, black bough.

There it is: a single moment of vision and revelation. Faces come out of the crowd; instantly, you encounter an image from nature — unexpected, its connection with the faces unexplained. *You* must forge that connection yourself — think, perhaps, of how both the faces and the petals may be beautiful. That's a Modern moment.

Hilda Doolittle

The American poet Hilda Doolittle ("H.D.") was a protégée of Ezra Pound (see the previous poem!) and part of the movement Pound called *Imagism*. Sick of the "blurriness," "messiness," and decadence of late-19th-century verse, the Imagists tried to use images to make poetry tougher and more precise. Their main inspirations were Greek classical poetry, Japanese haiku, and French Symbolism.

One of the most memorable of the Imagist poems is H.D.'s "Oread":

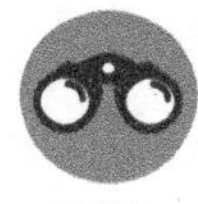
READ ALOUD

Whirl up, sea — whirl your pointed pines,
splash your great pines
on our rocks,
hurl your green over us,
cover us with your pools of fir.

TECHNICAL STUFF

An *oread* is a nymph of the mountains or woodland.

Imagist poems, at their best, were short, direct, and, like this one, breathtaking. A woodland nymph appears to be addressing the sea. Notice that exhilarating *metaphor*, waves as green and pointed "pines," — almost as if the nymph can understand an ocean wave only in terms of the forest. Feel the stinging reality. It's both a visual and tactile image *and* a metaphor for being overwhelmed by experience. And *that's* an image!

Marianne Moore

Famously eccentric, the American poet Marianne Moore (our third straight Pennsylvanian) carved out her own unmistakable niche in Modernism. Moore is perhaps the most consistently delightful of the era's poets. She keeps the reader off-balance, starting with her selection of topics.

She also is famous for her original stanza forms. The following stanza, from "The Monkeys," has six lines. Each line contains a set number of syllables: 15-16-10-10-10-11. And there is a rhyme scheme on top of that — the first two lines rhyme, the third line is unrhymed, the fourth and sixth lines rhyme, and the fifth line is unrhymed:

The Monkeys

winked too much and were afraid of snakes. The zebras, supreme in their
abnormality; the elephants with their fog-colored skin
and strictly practical appendages
were there, the small cats; and the parakeet —
trivial and humdrum on examination, destroying
bark and portions of the food it could not eat.

Notice how much fun Moore seems to be having: the title that also begins the poem, the "fog-colored" skin of the elephants, the behavior of the parakeet. Moore was a Modernist in her sheer originality.

T.S. Eliot

The American poet T.S. Eliot (shown in Figure 10-2) combined French Symbolism, a wide reading in the classics and English literature (especially the Metaphysical poets of the Elizabethan and Jacobean eras), and a frightening sensitivity to the modern world to create a new kind of poetry. "The Love Song of J. Alfred Prufrock," *The Waste Land*, and Eliot's religious poetry, including *The Four Quartets*, are among the monuments of the 20th century.

To many, Eliot's *The Waste Land* expresses the spiritual decay and moral paralysis of the 20th century. It's also a repository of the Modernist influences discussed in the previous sections of this chapter, including Symbolism and Imagism.

The Waste Land is a nightmare, like Yeats's "The Second Coming," yet with its own ineffable music:

READ ALOUD

Who are those hooded hordes swarming
Over endless plains, stumbling in cracked earth
Ringed by the flat horizon only
What is the city over the mountains
Cracks and reforms and bursts in the violet air
Falling towers
Jerusalem Athens Alexandria
Vienna London
Unreal

FIGURE 10-2: T.S. Eliot.

Wyndham Lewis/Library of Congress/Public domain

TIP

Take a tour of *The Waste Land* with a good teacher, who can help you breast the tide of its images and references (the poem comes complete with footnotes).

Marina Tsvetaeva

The Russian poet Marina Tsvetaeva's passionate, often tortured verse recorded love, suffering, and the sweep of history in jagged yet songlike poems.

In "The Poem of the End," she writes about a bridge, one of the most familiar of all symbols:

> Last bridge I won't
> give up or take out my hand
> this is the last bridge
> The last bridging between
> water and firm land

Bridges symbolize all sorts of passages — from youth to age, from ignorance to understanding, and (as here) from life to death. Can any single poem stand for the 20th century as a whole? This one might be in the running.

André Breton

The French poet André Breton helped create *Surrealism,* that explored the unconscious and its role in producing art.

For a brief taste of Surrealism, read this passage from Breton's "A Man and Woman Absolutely White":

READ ALOUD

> At the depths of the parasol I see the marvelous prostitutes
> On the side near the streetlamps their gowns are the color of polished wood
> They are walking a great piece of wallpaper
> At which one cannot look without that choking feeling about the heart of ancient floors in buildings being demolished
> Where a slab of marble lies fallen from the fireplace
> And a skein of chains is tangled in the mirrors

The images in a Surrealist poem may not work together in conventional, conscious ways, but thrown together they can produce startling mental associations. You look into a parasol and somehow see prostitutes. Depending on your associations regarding that world, you already may feel an element of the degraded and the forbidden. They are "walking" wallpaper, as if it were a dog — and suddenly you're standing in a demolished building. A strange sadness arises, that of endings, abandonment.

Notice how the poem challenges you to analyze *yourself* as you analyze *it.* Surrealism, thus, involves not just how poems behave and function, but also how human minds do — and that is part of its fascination.

Pablo Neruda

The Chilean poet Pablo Neruda led a whole generation of South American writers to renovate poetry in Spanish. Neruda (shown in Figure 10-3) created a poetry based on "the things of this world," as he put it. See and feel the concreteness of the images in his famous poem "Walking Around." The speaker is "tired of being a man," restless and sad, ready to burst out:

> The smell of barber shops makes me sob out loud.
> I want nothing but the repose either of stones or of wool

At the end, the speaker walks among the surprising, mundane things of the world:

> I stride along with calm, with eyes, with shoes, with fury,
> with forgetfulness,
> I pass, I cross offices and stores full of orthopedic appliances,
> and courtyards hung with clothes on wires,
> underpants, towels and shirts which weep
> slow dirty tears.

FIGURE 10-3: Pablo Neruda.

Jack Delano/Library of Congress/Public domain

Léopold Sédar Senghor

Senegal's Léopold Sédar Senghor combined French Symbolism with Surrealism and an awareness of African origins and traditions. With the poets Aimé Césaire (from Martinique in the Caribbean; an excerpt from Césaire's poem, "Since Akkad, Since Elam, Since Sumer," appears later in this chapter) and Léon Gontion Damas (from French Guiana in South America), Senghor helped found a movement called *Négritude*, focused on the many African heritages. Senghor eventually was elected prime minister of Senegal and served from 1960 to 1980, becoming the first black member of the Académie Française in 1984.

The Postmodern Era (1945–1989)

If the Modernist period was marked by anxiety and radical innovation, the Postmodern period was marked by irony. There was much to be ironic about. Big business dominated world politics, prompting poets to point out the many ways in which making money doesn't guarantee a good life. Many groups — including the Hiroshima poets of Japan, the Beat poets of 1950s America, including Allen Ginsberg (see Figure 10-4, and the sidebar, "Howling about "Howl""), and folk, pop, rap, and performance poets — insistently parodied and questioned the assumptions of the political establishment and the company man.

FIGURE 10-4: Allen Ginsberg.

Library of Congress/Public domain

The Cold War and the threat of global annihilation were seldom far from artists' minds. To many writers, this threat sapped life of all meaning, and despair was not far away. In poetry, a sense of the breaking up of the old and an uncertain future emerged in the poetry of many languages.

The Postmodern era was also an age of political contention. Protests against the United States' involvement in the Vietnam War spread worldwide. And local movements for human rights — which, in the United States, spawned the civil rights movement and feminism — produced a new generation of poets. In China, the failed revolution at Tiananmen Square in 1989 sent several poets into exile. Perhaps the best-known of these (and maybe the best-known Chinese poet of the late 20th century) is Bei Dao. He is one of a group known as the *misty poets*. They were more introspective than "official" poetry was supposed to be, more likely to examine their subjective lives.

A STEIN IS A STEIN IS A STEIN. . .

Gertrude Stein is one of the 20th century's best-known and most influential poets. She played a double role: as poet and as cultural hostess. In 1907, Stein moved to Paris, where, with her companion, Alice B. Toklas, she held a long-running salon, a meeting place for poets, artists, and thinkers, one of the central nodes of the Modern and Experimental eras. Picasso, Hemingway, and James Joyce were among her visitors. Many Americans became expatriate artists in the first half of the century, and the Stein/Toklas salon was a favorite resort. Stein encouraged and helped many standouts in 20th-century literature and art.

Stein also was and is a very influential Experimental poet. She constantly and boldly tested the distinctions between poetry and prose, writing stories, books of poems, opera librettos, and memoirs in a rhythmic ("a rose is a rose is a rose"), humorous ("I am because my little dog knows me"), and surprisingly philosophical and profound style. Her renown has never been higher than it is right now.

Photo by Carl Van Vechten, 1934.
Source: Library of Congress.

Bei Dao's poetry is full of protest. These four lines were dangerous ones for a poet to write in Mao's China:

Listen. *I don't believe!*
OK. You've trampled
a thousand enemies underfoot. Call me
a thousand and one.

If this poetry seems "Western," it's because Western poetry has absorbed so much from the Chinese tradition. That tradition is as large and various as the country from which it comes. As China changes, so does its poetry.

In Figure 10-5, Basil Bunting, one of the Post Modern greats, reads at the San Francisco Museum of Modern Art.

FIGURE 10-5: Basil Bunting reads at the San Francisco Museum of Modern Art, presented by the Poetry Center of San Francisco State University, April 29, 1976.

The Greats: Postmodern greats include Amiri Imamu Baraka, Robert Lowell, Elizabeth Bishop, Charles Olson, Allen Ginsberg, Frank O'Hara, John Ashbery, Basil Bunting, Gary Snyder, A.R. Ammons, Sylvia Plath, Anne Sexton, Robert Creeley, Adrienne Rich, Sharon Olds, Bob Dylan, John Lennon, Paul McCartney, Nicanor Parra, and Violetta Parra.

HOWLING ABOUT "HOWL"

In the summer of 1955, ringleader Beat poet Allen Ginsberg wanted to write a fearless poem that would sum up his life. He intended this highly personal work to be read by himself and a few others, and it wasn't originally intended for publication. But a few months later, he recited the first part of his now-famous poem *Howl* to a packed crowd at the Six Gallery in San Francisco. City Lights book publisher and poet Lawrence Ferlinghetti published *Howl and Other Poems* the following year, and controversy soon followed. Copies of the book were seized and banned by U.S. Customs and the San Francisco police. Ferlinghetti was arrested and accused of distributing indecent writings, and a long obscenity trial ensued.

With a host of prominent literary figures and the ACLU backing Ginsberg, Judge Clayton W. Horn ruled that the book was not obscene. The *Howl* trial was thus a landmark case for the freedom of speech and for the press. The national publicity surrounding the trial put Ginsberg and Ferlinghetti in the national spotlight, and *Howl and Other Poems* became a bestseller.

Poetry from the Spanish-speaking world

In the mid-1900s, poetry from Spain, Mexico, and South America started to grow in esteem and attention. Spanish poet and playwright Federico García Lorca, Mexican Nobel Prize winner Octavio Paz, Argentina's Jorge Luis Borges, Peru's César Vallejo, Brazil's Vinícius de Moraes, and Chile's two Nobelists (Gabriela Mistral and Pablo Neruda) were among this wealth of new voices. Each country, culture, point of view, and voice were and are very different — but all translate well into English and have their own ways of being of-the-moment.

Despite marked differences, the two Spanish poets below share in the Modern and Postmodern spirit of exploration and experimentation.

Traveler, Your Footsteps

Traveler, your footsteps
make the road, nothing else;
traveler, there is no road,
you make the road by walking.
By walking you make the road,
and, turning round, you see
behind you the path
you will never tread again.
Traveler, there is no road,
only wakes on the sea.

— Antonio Machado

Do you get a sense of folk wisdom, even Eastern thought? Machado studied all that, as this wise little poem shows. Next is a favorite at weddings, but that popularity is hardly limited to I-do's:

From *The Voice Due to You:*

Everything says yes:
the sky, its blue;
the blue of the sea,
seas, skies, blues,
with foam, with breezes,
one syllable, jubilant,

repeating without cease.
One yes answers yes
to another yes. Hear
vast dialogues repeat,
spanning the sea,
world to world: yes.
Read long yesses
through the air,
lightning of stork
feathers, so snowy
they fall flake by flake,
blanketing Earth with
an enormous,
white Yes. It is
the great day. Today
we can approach
that which does not
speak: pain, love,
the bone behind
the forehead: they
are the slaves of Yes.
It is the only word
the world grants them
today. Soul, quick
to ask, to grab for
the moment's maximum
crazy, asks for those
impossible things,
pleaded for, wordless,
so often, so long, so
today we will ask them
shouting, sure for
one day — today, only
today — that
the no's were false,

just façades, delays,
ignorant woofs,
and that behind them
slowly ripening
along with this longing
that begged for it
in vain, was the
grand delight: the Yes.

— Pedro Salinas

Women's voices

Along with the rise of the feminist movement, important women emerged in poetry everywhere. Americans H.D., Marianne Moore, and Gertrude Stein were three great pioneers. Among the many extraordinary North American women poets of mid-century, we may include the work of Muriel Rukeyser, Lorine Niedecker, and Elizabeth Bishop. Other fine women poets are Russia's Anna Akhmatova, England's Stevie Smith, Poland's Wisława Szymborska, Canada's Margaret Atwood and Nicole Brossard, France's Anne-Marie Albiach, China's Shu Ting, and Japan's Shiraishi Kazuko. South American poetry can boast of the work of Uruguay's Delmira Agustini and Mexico's Rosario Castellanos. And that's just a start.

As of about 1970, poets increasingly began to explore the lives of women and increase readers' awareness of how social or political realities affect women. Some of the most influential such poets include Sylvia Plath, Anne Sexton, Adrienne Rich, Carolyn Kizer, Marge Piercy, Alicia Suskin Ostriker, Sharon Olds, Louise Glück, and Judy Grahn. This strain of poetry, especially in Europe and the Americas, has remained especially strong and vibrant, especially as expressed in first-person autobiographical poetry.

A strain of feminist experimental verse evolved, in which poets explored the notion that there may be a characteristically feminist way of pushing the boundaries. Some of the most interesting women experimental poets include Kathleen Fraser, Beverly Dahlen, Maureen Owen, Joan Retallack, Lyn Hejinian, the sisters Fanny Howe and Susan Howe, Marie Howe (unrelated to Fanny and Susan), Norma Cole, Carla Harryman, Rae Armantrout, Mei-mei Berssenbrugge, Leslie Scalapino, Haryette Mullen, Erin Mouré, Cole Swensen, Myung Mi Kim, and Maxine Chernoff.

WOMEN'S VOICES AND PROTEST POETRY

Three of the most interesting writers of political protest poetry in this century were women, and all three suffered heroically under persecution, imprisonment, and exile. Noémia de Sousa (1926–2002) of Mozambique was very active in her country's struggle to free itself of colonial rule by Portugal. Her outspoken public statements, and her poetry critical of the ruling regime, brought official denunciation and persecution, and she was forced to live in exile in France and Portugal.

Cuba's María Elena Cruz Varela (1953–), self-taught and idiosyncratic, won her country's National Award for Poetry in 1989. Two years later, she published poems and essays critical of the Castro regime. She was thrown into prison, beaten, and starved. Since 1994, she has lived in Puerto Rico and also Spain, continuing to write poetry calling for freedom and justice in Cuba.

Naslima Tasrin (1961–) is a Bangladeshi poet. Her poems are feminist, often secular, and often critical of Islamic fundamentalism. (In fact, some of the mullahs, Islamic religious leaders of her country, offered to pay anyone who would kill her.) In 1994, she was driven into hiding. As of 2025, she was sometimes in the United States, sometimes (despite death threats) in India, continuing to write some of the best feminist protest verse in the Islamic world.

Experimental poetry

As the 20th century progressed, poets experimented more and more with new ways to make artworks out of language. Here's a Cubist poem, "Departure," written in France in 1919 by the French poet Pierre Reverdy, a forerunner to the Post-modern experimental poets. It's a good example of the poets experiment with the fragment.

The horizon slips down
Days are longer
Journey
A heart leaps in a cage
A bird sings
It will die
Another door will open
At the end of the hall
Where a star
Flares up

A dark woman

Lantern of the departing train

Reverdy condenses the feelings of taking a journey into a few shards of language like a Cubist collage. First, an awareness of horizon. The long days mean spring, summer, time to travel. The heart becomes a bird that leaps up and sings. Its death is predicted flatly; it's a shock. The poem turns there, as if from the knowledge of death. You are already looking out on the platform: There is a dark woman (more foreboding? or just waiting for a train?), and the train's lantern comes into view, "flares up." Or perhaps the lantern is the dark woman, who has become a star to lead the traveler.

TIP

If you want to read about the poetic theories behind such poetry, you may want to consult publications such as *Poetic Journal*, *L=A=N=G=U=A=G=E* (available through *The L=A=N=G=U=A=G=E Book*, edited by Charles Bernstein and Bruce Andrews), and *How(ever)*.

Prose poetry (another form of experimentation) enjoyed a major surge in popularity starting in the 1970s. Prose poetry is what it says: *prose* (defined as writing that runs from one edge of the page to the other) that exhibits the tension, pulse, vivid voice, and uses of language found in *poetry*. Here is a passage from *a.k.a.* by Bob Perelman. Watch how different kinds of language intrude on each other, how the passage starts to portray the way these languages relate to one another.

READ ALOUD

The speakers vibrate through the entire house. Brahms' lust scans the swept garden. Number streams down onto the trees. Born witness to his own fragmentation, a child breaks into speech. Hear against it a matter of course.

The reward you were tacitly promised when you began reading this sentence is now yours. You are that smoke. Black wisps of leaf tended by an orange flame, iced antennas against a starry sky. I dressed as a tiger and knocked at the varnished doors.

Here you have not one voice talking but a mosaic of voices. You're tossed among images, statements that seem to make sense and others that fall apart. The "you" in the second paragraph *seems* to be an address to the reader — but you can't really be sure. Perhaps it is some other "you," some person(s) known to or created by the poet alone. Again and again, your attention is brought back to how words and their relations bring out meanings as your mind considers them. Poetry in prose, or mixed with prose, has inspired some of the most ambitious work of the last 40 years. Perelman's *a.k.a.*; Lyn Hejinian's *My Life;* Ron Silliman's *Age of Huts;* Barrett Watten's *Bad History;* Beverly Dahlen's *A Reading;* Monique Wittig's *Lesbian Body;* Fanny Howe's *Lives of a Spirit;* Carla Harryman's *The Words;* Aaron Shurin's *The Paradise of Forms;* Bernadette Mayer's *Proper Name;* Leslie Scalapino's *The Return of Painting, The Pearl,* and *Orion*; and many, many more.

New York, Paris, Vancouver, and London have all had writing scenes where innovative poetry flourishes, but the San Francisco Bay Area was long the world's hotbed of experimental poetry, with many presses, reading series, and a faithful audience. Here's a poem, "The Mouth," by San Francisco Bay Area poet Laura Moriarty (shown in Figure 10-6) that moves between fragment and prose.

READ ALOUD

We have words
Over definition
Terror
Something to lose
Loose
In us
Harshness
Oracularity

A stone bath or wood room vivid and liquid ritual means the wished for repetition against the sense of what is said at the same time taking in the heart the belly the groin the mouth and legs the ass the chest and eyes.

FIGURE 10-6: Laura Moriarty.

© Emily Grossman

Notice the music, how the heavy syllables of the word *oracularity* almost separate in your mouth. Are you in the stone room of a Greek oracle or a hot tub? The parts of the body are opposed to the "sense of what is said." The "wished for repetition" may be a chant, a prayer "loose in us," or simply the refrain of a song. Could the words of that prayer or refrain be "over definition" in the sense of "beyond definition"? Would those words include this poem? The open form of this poem doesn't allow a single resolution; it is available to alternate interpretations.

Performance poetry

The 1980s saw a surge of interest in poets reciting their work in public. It was a world movement: For Ghana's Ama Ata Aidoo, Peru's Eduardo Calderón, and the Zuni storyteller Andrew Peynetsa, poetry is primarily to be spoken and heard. Up sprang an immediate, often impromptu poetry, often harsh or crass, designed to be delivered in a dramatic or histrionic way before an audience.

This kind of poetry made use of everything poets could get their hands on: music, television, movies, humor, slang, confession. Its main gods were poets such as Whitman, Neruda, Ginsberg, and Dylan — poets interested in a poetry close to the pace and impact of speech.

African American poetry has always had a strong element of performance, from the earliest days of slavery to the cultures of rap and hip-hop (see the sidebar, "From The Godfather of Rap to DJ Cool Herc"). One of the birthing moments of the performance poetry movement was the "choreopoem" *For Colored Girls Who Have Considered Suicide When the Rainbow Was Enuf* by Ntozake Shange, a major contributor to the Nuyorican Poets' Café (founded in 1974), a venue on the Lower East Side of New York for multicultural performance art. Shange combined popular culture, jazz, African and American history, feminist politics, urban legend, and dance.

Poetry slams became widely popular in the 1980s and 1990s. Very often, slams are competitive poetry readings in which audience reaction determines the "winning" poet. The slam was founded in Chicago in the 1970s by Marc Smith, at the Green Mill Lounge on Broadway Avenue. Prominent slams were held annually in Chicago, San Francisco, New York, and Boston. Several venues throughout the world put on annual slams to determine the champion poet of the year. Figure 10-7 shows a poetry slam aboard an aircraft carrier.

FIGURE 10-7: Logistics Specialist 3rd Class Desiree Alston reads a poem during a poetry slam held in the mess decks aboard the Nimitz-class aircraft carrier *USS Abraham Lincoln*.

Photo: U.S. Navy/Mass Communication Specialist 3rd Class Jeff Sherman. Public domain. Source: `Picryl.com`

NEW VOICES, NEW AUDIENCES

Langston Hughes. Photo by Jack Delano, 1941. Public domain. Courtesy of the Library of Congress.

Throughout the 20th century, poets from various cultural groups, often long repressed or discriminated against — ethnic and sexual minorities, women, the poor, the young — began to forge their own poetic identities. An aboriginal poetry scene emerged in Australia. In South America, indigenous peoples contributed some of the century's best verse, as in the agonized Surrealism of Peru's César Vallejo, a poet of mixed Inca and Spanish heritage. In India, a country of great poetic traditions, a dizzying number of poets began to publish in many languages. African poetry prospered on two tracks: an ancient oral tradition, and a newer written verse, including the work of Ghana's Kofi Awoonor, Nigeria's Christopher Okigbo, and Uganda's Okot p'Bitek.

Modernism deeply affected Chinese poets, but writers were prevented from participating fully in this world revolution by the political convulsions that shook China all century. Mao Zedong, leader of Communist China, was also an accomplished poet. Suspicious of the free-thinking, questioning experiments of Modernism, he imposed standards that stressed realism, folk poetry, and patriotism. That forced China's best poets to find a way to please the censors while writing exquisite verse. (Much the same thing happened in the European Communist countries.) An ironic, resigned, symbolic kind of verse emerged. Some of the poets of this period include Lu Xun, Hu Shih, Feng Zhi, and Yan Zhen.

In "Since Akkad, Since Elam, Since Sumer," by Aimé Césaire of Martinique, the speaker reflects on the way people of African descent have been made to carry the weight of their oppressors' history:

> I have borne the body of the commandant. I have borne the railroad of the
> commandant. I have borne the locomotive of
> the commandant, the cotton of the commandant. I have borne on my
> woolly head (which does so well without a pad) God, the machine, the route —
> the God of the commandant.
> Master of three roads I have borne under the sun, I have borne in the mist I
> have borne
> over smoldering shards managing ants
> I have borne the parasol I have borne the explosive I have borne the iron collar.

In the Arabic-speaking world, the Tammuzi poets looked for a way to break away from tradition and explore modern experience in Arabic poetry. Two of the most famous

(continued)

(continued)

Tammuzi poets are Lebanon's Yusuf al-Khal and the astonishing Syrian poet Ali Ahmad Sa'id, known as Adonis, author of the following passage:

> thus I no longer hesitate to say:
> "the I and the other
> are me,"
> and time is but a basket
> to collect poetry

In the United States of the 1920s, the Harlem district of Manhattan saw the rise of a distinctive African American culture expressed in all the arts. This decade of activity came to be called the *Harlem Renaissance.* Poets such as Claude McKay, Countee Cullen, and Langston Hughes (shown in the figure in this sidebar) first came to widespread notice. As the century closed, African American voices were among the most prominent of U.S. poets, including Robert Hayden, Gwendolyn Brooks, Maya Angelou, Amiri Imamu Baraka, Lucille Clifton, Al Young, Yusef Komunyakaa, Rita Dove, June Jordan, and Audre Lorde.

The Global Era (1989–2001)

As of the *Global era*, poetry began to take part in the Internet age, the connected era in which worldwide influences joined together in poetry to mix traditions, ethnicities, and genders. Mixtures — that's what global poetry explores. Television, radio, and movies taught people how to think in rapidly shifting images; confusing and exhilarating, they mixed almost anything with almost anything else. Global poets tried to tap into both the confusion and the exhilaration.

Forms joined with other forms, new with old, to make all sorts of hybrids. And performance poetry challenged written poetry as the premier poetic form of the age.

Anne Waldman, who began her career in the Postmodern era, is a bridge to the Global era. Her poetry, as in this passage from "Iovis XIX," often shifts back and forth in history, tone, and mood, and it's usually well worth the ride:

my friend dark night a result
friend a light of me combine
to find alas no woman at the table
of Israel, of Lebanon, Palestine
how do they sleep? of Syria
& shine or shrink the tale as of void
& radio it says hands-on broadcast
a hundred deejays wait, not one a woman
the scholar & savage equal points of light
rub dry sticks together
a sham, a delusion, kind of affectation
never felt lonesome in it

At first, you may find this poem hard to read. But read it aloud — or hear Waldman, a remarkable performance poet, read it — and it becomes clearer. The question isn't "What is this *about?*" but rather "What's *happening* here?" Notice how ideas and images interrupt one another and rub together. There is even rhyme: *combine / Palestine / shine.*

In Waldman's poem, you get images from politics (the absence of women), personal life, popular culture. You can even catch glimpses of *statements,* as when the speaker tells of a world in which "the scholar and savage" may be "equal points of light." (Both may have important things to tell us — both rub "dry sticks" together, the savage to make fire, the scholar to enlarge human knowledge.) And in a whirling, infinitely active, always interesting world such as ours, the speaker says he or she "never felt lonesome." It would be difficult to feel lonely, with all these different voices around.

The Greats: Global greats include Miguel Algarín, Victor Hernández Cruz, Charles Bernstein, Ron Silliman, Lyn Hejinian, Arkadii Dragomoshchenko, DJ Kool Herc, Dr. Dre, Patricia Smith, Ntozake Shange, Barrett Watten, Fanny Howe, Norma Cole, Francisco Alarcón, Kathleen Fraser, Erica Hunt, Michael Palmer, Tom Raworth, Emmanuel Hocquard, Rosmarie Waldrop, Ammiel Alcalay, and Anne Waldman.

FROM "THE GRANDFATHER OF RAP" TO DJ KOOL HERC

The Global Era saw poetry that rhymed and poetry that didn't. Here we celebrate rap and its close cousin, hip-hop; they frequently rhyme. Musician and poet Gil Scott-Heron is rightly called "the grandfather of rap." He intoned poetry to jazz as early as his 1970 album *Small Talk at 125th and Lenox.* There, he first performed "The Revolution Will Not Be Televised." On his 1971 album *Pieces of a Man*, he redid it backed by an all-star band including Ron Carter, Hubert Laws, and Herbie Hancock, creating one of the most influential performance works of the 20th century. "The Revolution Will Not Be Televised" is a superb example of *allusion*, a history lesson calling out everything from Bullwinkle Moose to Willie Mays to Francis Scott Key, along with ad slogans for Coca-Cola, Liquid-Plumr, and Hertz car rental.

Rap emerged in the South Bronx, New York City, around 1973, when a Jamaican-born New Yorker known as DJ Kool Herc figured out a way to control the spin of multiple records while rapping out verse. DJ Kool Herc's innovations electrified ancient African American forms of performance poetry. Did he know his invention would take over the world? Well, it did. Democratic, danceable, and, powered by that little invention, the Internet, rap quickly spread everywhere.

IN THIS CHAPTER

- » Understanding why The Digital Age is such a great time for poetry
- » Seeing which new and old forms of poetry particularly mark this age
- » Getting a taste of collaborative poetry, poetry inspired by other arts, and the translation explosion
- » Welcoming the rise and flourishing of the online poetic community

Chapter 11
Poetry in the Digital Age

The Digital Age (2001–) is a continuation of The Global Era — more of the same, but faster, hotter, empowered, and impassioned. But there *was* something different, again a technological innovation (or a world of them), that changed the poetry world itself. At least initially, the Digital Age was called the *communication age*: the era of smart phones and portable media in which everyone with these tools could publish their work globally, instantly, all the time.

Would something as old-school as poetry find its place in the Digital Age? It surely would — but then it had been living in the digital world since that world first appeared, as described in Chapter 10. All that mixing, all that cross-fertilization, all those new voices, faces, topics, and techniques: the Digital Age is the Age of Poetry. It also turned out that when the Pandemic of 2020-2023 hit, and poets couldn't get out so much, they went online, found new venues, new colleagues, new events, and they started getting busy!

New Voices and Viewpoints

Poetry has always been for everyone, and yet often it has seemed like a white man's toybox. In 1965, George Oppen (see Chapter 4) wrote that "indeed/ a poet's room/ Is a boy's room/ And I suppose that women know it." No longer. These days, when reaching out in all its forms is easier than ever, poets reach out all over the world to other poets, new audiences, and new places in which their work can appear. Of course, as always, there are plenty of fine male poets. But there are other poets, too. The poetry world, again thanks to the Digital Age, hosts a greater range of voices and viewpoints than ever before.

Once upon a time, it was pretty hard for women poets, or nonwhite poets, or poets of different genders, to break into recognition. One glance at the recent major awards for U.S. poets, however, and it's clear that there's more and more and more room at the top and throughout the poetry world. It's thrilling to see Tracy K. Smith, Joy Harjo, Ada Limón, Lena Khalaf Tuffaha, Terrance Hayes, Martín Espada, Robin Coste Lewis, Craig Santos Perez, Don Mee Choi, and Arthur Sze among U.S. award winners. It's great to see Richard Blanco, Elizabeth Alexander, and Amanda Gorman (see Figure 11-1) get up there and read poems at presidential inaugurations. It's great to see Kendrick Lamar win a Pulitzer for his album *DAMN*. (True, it was in music, not poetry, but many people think of him as a poet.) It's looking a lot like the world.

FIGURE 11-1: Amanda Gorman reads at the Library of Congress, 2017. She would read her poem "The Hill We Climb" at the 2021 Presidential Inauguration.

Library of Congress. Public domain.

Collaborative Poetry

Poetry does not have to be a strictly solitary pursuit. The popularity of two or more people writing poetry together has been growing steadily since the 1990s. As of the 2000s, it's easier than ever to locate other poets and collaborate. The Surrealists (see Chapter 10) did it all the time, and some of our writing exercises are collaborative (see Chapter 15), but it's far more. Two heads are not just better than one — they are totally different, surprising, energizing. Many websites, including Wattpad, AllPoetry, and Jam Verse (focusing on haiku), have arisen as platforms for collaborative poetry-writing.

In a 2022 piece for The Poetry Foundation (`https://poetryfoundation.org/articles/157020/ekphrastic-poetry-analogy-noise`), Crista Siglin presents a collaborative prompt that involves not only poetry but also other arts:

- Draw/paint/sculpt alongside your partner.
- Write a stream of consciousness in response to your partner's piece.
- Trade texts with your partner.
- Reformat the texts into a different poetic format.
- Discuss outcomes.

During the pandemic of 2020–2023, the Woodberry Poetry Room at Harvard University announced a collaborative poetry project titled "Boston Renaissance," and 75 poets signed up "agreeing to be randomly paired with a poetry pen pal." Through the Enemies Project (`https://theenemiesproject.com`), poet S.J. Fowler has involved more than 600 poets in dozens of countries in a variety of collaborative endeavors. Check it out!

In an initiative started by Christopher Merrill, director of the International Writing Program at the University of Iowa, Merrill and six other poets — Marvin Bell, István László Geher, Ksenia Golubovich, Simone Inguanez, Tomaž Šalamun, and Dean Young — got together for a great collaborative venture. Each wrote a 15-line poem and read it aloud to the group. Poets made various uses of the material, and the result was a collection of 80 poems, published as *7 Poets, 4 Days, 1 Book.*

Some collaborators have gotten well-known doing their together thing. Denise Duhamel and Maureen Seaton, for a good example, started writing poetry together in the 1990s, publishing their joint poems in *Exquisite Politics* (1997), *Oyl* (2000), and *Little Novels* (2002). In 2007, Duhamel, Seaton, and David Trinidad (see Chapter 13) edited the very first anthology of collaborative verse, *Saints of Hysteria: A Half-Century of Collaborative American Poetry.*

Poetry and the Other Arts

Poetry has always hung out with music, and music with poetry. But what about other arts? Painting? Sculpture? Dance? Can we get together? In the 21st century, the answer is increasingly yes.

Many poets have collaborated with other artworkers to produce new kinds of art or refresh old kinds. Apart from music, the most popular kind of collaboration might be *ekphrastic poetry*, in which a poet writes in response to a painting, sculpture, drawing, or photo (see Crista Siglin's prompt in the preceding section, "Collaborative poetry"). This is an ancient practice. Even Homer does it in the *Iliad*: about 130 lines to describe the shield of Achilles! Goodness, it's breathtaking, one of the greatest ekphrastic poems ever. Book 18, lines 478–608: Look it up! Read!

Ekphrastic poetry is among the most popular forms of the early 2000s; once again, thank the Digital Age, which makes it easier than ever to discover artists and art to write about. Anne Carson writes "Hopper: Confessions," in which the painting of Edward Hopper (you know his *Nighthawks)* (look it up!) says howdy to *Confessions*, a biography written by St. Augustine. Several poets have been moved to write by famous photographs, including Dorothea Lange's *Migrant Mother*, *Napalm Girl* by Huynh Cong Ut, or *Afghan Girl* by Steve McCurry. Look up these famous photos and then search online for poems based on them — they're out there!

And we haven't even gotten *started* with the hundreds of art installations worldwide in which poetry hangs out with dance, painting, music, and any other art to make something new! It's very 2000s.

Translation

Elsewhere in this book, we went crazy about how translation in the 2000s has basically gone blooey all over the world. It's not too much to claim that in the first 25 years of this century we effectively *re*-translated the past. A good thing, probably inevitable: every era finds its own voice, and it's good to read new hearings of old musics. Respect to the Digital Age: It's easier today to connect with translators, experts, and resources.

In fact . . . remember Emily Wilson (see Chapter 7)? Well, to translate Homer, she did a *very 2000s thing.* As she went along, she *crowdsourced* some of her work, posting it on social media platforms — especially a place called Twitter back then — and sometimes even asked for responses and ideas.

It's hard work. No one is sure what Homer means sometimes, or what the best equivalents for his words would be in contemporary English. Wilson, though, put herself and her choices out there — in a way literally never possible before. Some folks were dismissive, mad, or unhelpful. Other times, healthy discussions occurred, and people offered a few useful suggestions. People knew it was different, even cool: In a *New Yorker* piece, poet Dan Chiasson called Wilson's social media presence "quietly revolutionary, a new kind of experience for readers, poets, translators, and really anyone who likes to watch knowledge take shape in an open format."

Take advantage of the world of contemporary translation. We have recommended very new translations of Dante, Rūmī (yay, Haleh Liza Gafori!), classical Chinese poetry (hurray for David Hinton!), Marina Tsvetaeva (Andrew Davis, yes!), and . . . well, you name it. Better yet, go *read* it.

New and Old Forms

Every era seems to have its favorite forms — shapes and kinds of poems that seem to stand for that time in the world, its history, and people's concerns. So far, the 2000s have been a lot like that. Here are four poetic forms that seem to speak for this era.

Sonnets, anyone? Beginning in the 1990s and cresting with the 2020s, interest, maybe even mania, crested for those square, pressure-packed poetry boxes called *sonnets.* Some sonnets were 14-line prose poems. Some rhymed at the *beginning* of lines, not the end. Many didn't rhyme. Among the great renewers is Terrance Hayes, whose 2018 book *American Sonnets for My Past and Future Assassins* offers 70 sonnet-adjacent poems that produce new music, new meanings:

I live a life
That burns a hole through life, that leaves a scar for life,
That makes me weep for another life. Define life.

The *cento* (a Latin word meaning "patchwork quilt") is a poem built from the words and phrases of other authors. Think of a cento as a *collage*. Melanie Weldon-Soiset weaves a lullaby from the lines of other lullabies:

A Lullaby Patchwork Quilt

Up above the world so high
Thy mother is shaking the dream-land tree
Now the wind is whispering
Stars begin to peep

Now the darkness gathers
With lilies o'er spread
Golden slumbers kiss your eyes
Soft and warm is your bed

Here's where each line came from; you probably have heard almost *all* these lullabies:

Up above the world so high ["Twinkle, Twinkle, Little Star," Jane Taylor, 1806]
Thy mother is shaking the dream-land tree ["Cradle Song," Ethelbert Nevin, 1887]
Now the wind is whispering ["Now the Day Is Over," Sabine Baring-Gould, 1867]
Stars begin to peep ["Now the Day Is Over," Sabine Baring-Gould, 1867]

Now the darkness gathers ["Now the Day Is Over," Sabine Baring-Gould, 1867]
With lilies o'er spread ["Cradle Song," Johannes Brahms, 1868]
Golden slumbers kiss your eyes ["Cradle Song," Thomas Dekker, 1603]
Soft and warm is your bed ["Cradle Song," Johannes Brahms, 1868]

These lines come from all over, from Brahms to "Twinkle, Twinkle Little Star," even a hint of Beatles, since the "Golden slumbers" line made it into the closing medley on *Abbey Road*. Intriguing new combinations arise. "Thy mother" is not singing to thee in thy bed; she's "Up above the world so high." Later, "mermaids" chant "in a canyon, in a cavern," far from where mermaids usually appear. It's both *like* and *unlike* a lullaby.

The *duplex*, invented in 2018 by wondrous poet Jericho Brown, has elements of ghazals, sonnets, hip-hop, and blues. A duplex is a series of couplets; each couplet has 9-11 syllables. The second line of each couplet is echoed in the first line of the next couplet, and the first line of the poem in the last line. Seems simple, but it can have devastating effects.

Rediscovery, renewal, connection, community: the first quarter of the 2000s showed that poets are always interested in form, following and breaking rules, mixing them up, both practicing and reimagining the old ways. Poets, now in better touch than ever, are making communities, writing poems, and working with editors, readers, and other poets in ways unimaginable when *Poetry For Dummies* first appeared. Thank you, Digital Age.

Chill subs and Other Poetry Communities Online

Those first 25 years of the 2000s saw an upsurge of online "communities" offering writers the chance to connect, share their work, learn about events, and find resources. It's not too much to say it: these communities have reorganized the way many poets write, submit their poems, and meet other poets.

In Chapter 16, we talk in detail about online poetry communities and their offerings. For now, just to give a taste, we examine one particularly encouraging example.

Chill subs (`https://chillsubs.com`) has as its subtitle "Making your writing life not so freaking exhausting." And that, really, is its mission: to help poets be poets with minimum stress, from composition all the way to submissions (thus the name *chill subs*). Figure 11-2 shows Benjamin Davis, cofounder of chill subs.

FIGURE 11-2: Benjamin Davis (seen here with Cookie), cofounder of chill subs, a 21st-century online poetry community with a rich offering of resources for poets.

The outfit was started in 2022 by Belarussian Web designer Katrina Kupp, who joined forces with Benjamin Davis soon thereafter. "I'd been writing and submitting for about 12 years when I ended up cofounding Chill Subs," Davis says. "Katrina created it, and I saw it and thought it was the coolest thing I'd ever seen. I started bombing her with massive emails about how chill subs could bring the literary community into a more modern space — and also break down psychological barriers around writing and submitting."

The outfit was started in 2022 by Belarussian Web designer Katrina Kupp, who joined forces with Benjamin Davis soon thereafter. "I'd been writing and submitting for about 12 years when I ended up cofounding chill subs," Davis says. "Katrina created it, and I saw it and thought it was the coolest thing I'd ever seen. I started bombing her with massive emails about how chill subs could bring the literary community into a more modern space — and also break down psychological barriers around writing and submitting." Kupp and Davis quit their jobs and now run the site with a staff of about 10 core members and "a whole lot of contractors and contributors."

This was all mid-Pandemic, when a lot of people in the poetry world suddenly were coming online more and more. "The poetry space needed it," Davis says. Reception has been great, and chill subs has grown crazy-fast.

The chill subs home page is uncluttered, offering you a chance to:

- Get published
- Promote your work
- Connect with other creatives
- Grow as a writer

. . . "all without having a mental breakdown," it adds cheerily.

Each of these pathways — Publish, Promote, Connect, Grow — is a chock-full, beautifully organized, happy-making world of resources unto itself. chill subs takes good care of its poets.

A good example is "Sorry For the Inconvenience — a Submitter's Guide to Lit Mags." The term of art at chill subs is *lit mags*, not *literary magazines* — "it's just to lighten up the tone," Davis says. (We like it! We'll use it a lot in chapters to come!)

You get to "Sorry for the Inconvenience" by subscribing to a Substack newsletter titled "The Forever Workshop." "Sorry" itself is free. The "Sorry" front page gives us one of the most attractive bullet lists the poetry world has ever seen, one that engages 80 percent of that world's most urgent questions:

- Why you should (or shouldn't) submit to lit mags
- Five ways to find lit mags (with all the tips, tricks, and bullshit)
- Everything you wanted to know (and plenty you didn't) about lit mag submission guidelines
- How to write the perfect cover letter and lit bio even though nobody cares

- What happens after you submit to a lit mag?
- Best method for organizing your writing according to some guy (me)
- How to match your writing to the right lit mag (without your head exploding)
- How to strategize and track submissions to lit mags
- What makes a "high quality" lit mag anyway?
- How to beat 20% of the competition every time you submit to a lit mag

In its welcoming, nutty way, this is actually revolutionary. In the pre-Digital Age, submission, even online, was largely a mysterious process. The two sides — submitters and editors — seldom communicated. Neither side knew as much as desired about the other. In "Sorry," we learn of ways to filter and choose likely lit mags, along with strategies to make the most of our chances. There are truly impressive, sensible approaches to doing your market research (see Chapters 16 and 17) and staying organized in your search for publication.

Asked what poets crave most, Davis says, "Honestly? Validation. Resources and community-oriented experiences. I think 'writing as a solitary act of genius' isn't the cool thing anymore. Everyone wants a writing partner, a live reading, or a retreat."

The days of community are here if you desire them. Connection is here if you long for it. A chance to write and get feedback, a chance to belong to groups of like-minded writers and readers — those are here, too. Poetry: Thousands of years old and still youthful, still growing. An amazing story, far from over. New stanzas are being written, right now, all over the world.

3

Writing Poetry and Finding Community

IN THIS PART . . .

Recognize the habits and promptings of your creative urge, putting it to use as you work on your poetic style and mastery.

Add to your skill set by learning the history and rules of writing six traditional forms of verse.

Add even more to your skill set by learning the attitudes and rules that help you write verse without traditional rhyme, meter, or form.

Work out at the poetry gym, with dozens of writing exercises exploring the many ways you can create a poem.

Go from poetry to people, as you attend poetry events, meet other poets, read your own work in public, employ social media to let the world know about your work, and even become part of a poetry community.

Assemble a strategy to send out your poems to be published, knowing when you're ready, where to submit your first tries, how to assemble your submission packet, what's involved in self-publishing, and what interests editors.

IN THIS CHAPTER

» Developing good habits as an aspiring poet

» Organizing your writing time

» Recognizing the creative urge when you feel it

» Turning raw material into poetry

» Staying in touch with what's happening in the poetry world

» Meeting other poets

Chapter 12
Calling the Muse

So, who gets to be a poet? Anyone who wants to. Anyone willing to read, write, work, and live with poetry. There is no entrance fee, no initiation ritual, and, last we looked, you can't get kicked out of the club.

So how do you go about doing this poetry thing? Jot down thoughts as they come, on old receipts, napkins, and scraps of newspaper? (Some fine poets, such as Frank O'Hara of the New York School, did it that way.) Or will you lose all those scraps of paper? Should you be more methodical? Write every day? Keep a journal? Revise and revise? Stay current with the latest in the poetry world? Find a mentor who will read your poetry and give you good criticism? Become part of a community of poets?

Something more methodical will likely serve you best. So, in this chapter we suggest ways to corral the creative urge and ride it toward poetry.

REMEMBER

Ignore any advice in this chapter if it doesn't work for you. These aren't rules; they're guidelines. Pick and choose! Build a *modus operandi* (a "way of working") all your own.

How to Live If You Want to Be a Poet

No *one* way of life works for every poet. But poets tend to share a few traits:

- **They have passion.** Poets care about something very much, and this passion drives their work. They may have passion for making words, or passion for a way of seeing. Some poets maintain a commitment to a public theme of some kind. Others carry a passionate attachment to life itself. Find a reason to care about something — or many things!
- **They think like poets.** Poets like to play with words. They think in images, metaphors, and music. They even find ways "behind the scenes" of their conscious minds, seeking divergent ways of thinking and forms of writing that shake them loose from habits and ruts.
- **They read a lot and write a lot.** Poetry is, above all, a *practice.* Reading and writing are central. If you're a poet, you'll do them.
- **They are sensitive people and work to enhance their sensitivity.** They practice paying attention. Some poets have explored alternative consciousnesses, which leads them into meditation, religion, drugs, and so forth. Not to recommend any of these; only to point out where poets have gone in search of the creative urge.
- **They are open to experience.** Curiosity makes the poet. It means that whatever you encounter, you do so with your eyes open.
- **They work hard to improve.** This work involves two major disciplines: *revision* and *learning from criticism*.
- **They associate with other poets. Not required** — but it's what poets do. As we cover in Chapter 11, the Digital Age has made meeting and hanging with other poets easier than ever. Visit several online poetry communities (see Chapter 16) and join one you like.

Reading Like a Poet

A poet who doesn't read is like a composer who doesn't listen to music. As the marvelous poet and teacher Gerald Stern once said, "The great poet who doesn't read — *il n'existe pas!*" ("He doesn't exist!"). So read a lot and then read some more. Here are some things to read, along with reasons why:

- **Classics in poetry and fiction,** to learn the traditions of literature. Start with Part 2 of *Poetry For Dummies,* 2nd Edition!

- **Online and print journals of art and culture — including lit mags** — to learn what's happening in the arts.
- **The latest in fiction and nonfiction,** to find out what writers are creating right now.
- **Newspapers (online or print) and major current-events websites, journals, and magazines,** so you know what's happening in the world.
- **Poetry,** lots of poetry, different kinds of poetry, poetry from all over. Reading a variety of verse — in different styles, from different periods and countries, by different kinds of people, about a variety of subjects — will show you the huge range of possibilities and also help you train your ear and eye, understand how poetry works, and build your personal tastes.
- **Junk, grocery-store paperback novels, and relaxation reading,** because it doesn't hurt.

Some aspiring poets are afraid to read, afraid of being influenced by other minds and voices. Go ahead and risk it! Hear those other voices, get a taste for those other minds, learn what's up in the world of poetry, so you can speak to the *present*. "But they're probably better than me." Remember what the jazz guitarist John Scofield said regularly to his students: "If you want to improve, get out and play with people who are better than you are." Makes sense, doesn't it?

Writing Like a Poet

There's no way you're a poet unless you find the time to write poetry and work at it — not just *making* poems but also *revising* them. If you're serious about being a poet, you can't just write poetry in bits and pieces — you have to schedule time to write.

Finding the right time and place to write

TIP

Carry around a digital recorder or a notebook. Use these tools as storage space for the stuff that rains down on your brain during the day — all the ideas and phrases and words that occur to you, but that you would forget if you didn't jot them down. Then transfer that material from your notebook into a journal during your writing time.

How long do you need to set aside? At least an hour. And if you care about poetry, you won't cheat yourself out of the time you need to write it. Decide the following:

- **When you're at your best.** Are you a morning, noon, or night person? Many poets get up *very* early — early morning is a poetic time (birds are singing, garbage collectors banging, and so on). Others wait until the depths of night. Know what works best for you.
- **What setting is best.** A quiet library? A park bench? A crowded café? Most folks need the following:
  - **A quiet place,** somewhere free of distractions and interruptions.
  - **Good lighting,** which can help your vision and your mood. We know someone who insists on "light over my left shoulder." Find out your druthers (preferences) and set them up.
  - **Writing tools,** such as a computer, pens, pencils, paper, a dictionary, reference resources (see Chapter 1), and so on.
  - **Comfort foods and comfort sounds.** Some people need music; others can't work with it on. Some folks need a snack nearby. Pay attention to what *you* require, and make sure you have it.

THE WAY POETS WRITE

Each poet has his or her own way of composing poetry. Here are five interesting ways:

- The Roman poet **Virgil** was said to walk through his gardens all day long, and by sunset, if he'd had a good day at work, he had produced . . . a single line.
- Elizabethan and Jacobean poet **Ben Jonson** said he would write out a prose paragraph stating the poem's content and *then* sit down and write the poem. Now that's discipline!
- Modern American poet **Theodore Roethke** had an interesting use for his bed. Whenever he got stuck while writing a poem, he would hop into bed, and when he felt he had solved his poetic problem, he would get up and start to write again.
- **Frank O'Hara**, a poet of the New York School, wrote a whole book of poems titled *Lunch Poems.* Seldom known to turn down a party, O'Hara would have lunch with his New York pals, then return to his job at the Museum of Modern Art, put a piece of paper in his typewriter, type out a poem, and then get back to his "real" job.

- African American poet **Maya Angelou** had a singular way of setting up her "office." She rented a hotel room, then left her house at 6:00 a.m. and tried to get to "work" (in her hotel room) by 6:30. She lay across the bed to write; after a while, she developed a permanent callus on one elbow. "I go into the room," she wrote, "and I feel as if all my beliefs are suspended. Nothing holds me to anything. No milkmaids, no flowers, nothing. I just want to feel and when I start to work I'll remember."

Recognizing the creative urge

For 5000-plus years, poets have described an agitated, exalted state, a peak experience, white-hot, out of which they created poetry. No doubt about it, this happens. Shakespeare appears to have written the first draft of *Hamlet* in about six weeks. (Doesn't it make you *sick?*) Rainer Maria Rilke, after working on his incomparable *Duino Elegies* for more than 20 years, finished them in an attic study in two incandescent weeks. Sylvia Plath's last six months alive, during which she wrote the tortured, supremely inspired poems in the collection *Ariel,* were of that white-hot variety.

Some think the creative urge is the voice of the Divine whispering directly into our souls. Others believe it's the individual's mind (yours!) working subconsciously, stitching experience, memory, desire, and language into a crazy quilt the poet somehow turns into poetry. Many creative people talk about access to the subconscious, even access to childhood. However you frame it, as a poet, you probably will find that *you eventually learn to trust your subconscious to come up with what you're looking for, to solve problems.*

REMEMBER

One good reason to have regular working habits is to visit your subconscious regularly, give it a chance to read itself, so to speak. Regular work habits make *you* better at reading what your subconscious is up to. Yet the subconscious doesn't keep office hours: It can also be dreamlike and elusive, so carry a pen and notebook with you wherever you go.

Sometimes you *know* you're "on": You taste that elevated, breathless excitement. At other times, however, the creative urge sneaks up on you. Unless you're very sharp, you may not even realize it's happening. Many of us, after all, just *think,* not especially paying attention to ourselves, just watching our mental movies. Then, maybe, we snap out of it: "Hey! Wait a minute! What was that again?"

TIP

Be awake to your own processes. Get to know when your mind is most open to the muse. The creative urge is likely to strike almost *any* time. But poets have often written about the following situations, which seem to lead to moments of intense creativity:

- **Whenever you're alive.** From overpowering elation to quite modest insights (say, an idea about a wheelbarrow wet with rain, something about which William Carlos Williams created a famous poem), connections and realizations can happen anytime. Sometimes words come at the very moment of experience; some poets say they need to write them down before the ideas fade. Others find having the experience and recollecting it later works best.
- **Between waking and sleeping.** Some folks keep notebooks by the bedside, to capture their thoughts when they're in transition from conscious to subconscious states and vice versa. Many people jot down dream and daydream material, scrawling in notebooks.
- **At uncanny moments.** Life is full of surprises, discoveries, crazy coincidences, the unexpected, or the strangely fortuitous or serendipitous. An enormous blue squirrel falls out of a palm tree right into your lunch. You suddenly go hang-gliding while drunk (do *not* try this at home!). You discover your six-year-old brother has a secret career as an oil tanker pilot. Talk about a wealth of *material.*
- **During intense diversions.** When you're really concentrating hard on something (a math quiz, or a tangled bike chain, or sawing at a tree limb 40 feet above the ground, or watching an exciting hockey game), your subconscious mind may try to slip in an image, a phrase, or an idea while you're not looking.

TIP

The subconscious often tries more than once. You may miss its suggestions the first time. But it often tries again, like a distant phone ringing. If the same image, word, or notion keeps surfacing now and then, pay attention to it. If you *know* that's how the creative urge tends to tap you on the shoulder, you can get better and better at recognizing it, grasping it, and using it in your verse.

Empty page, full imagination: Getting started

Some people can just turn to a clean page and start writing. If you're like that, fine. Get going. God bless.

Other people are stymied by the empty page. If you're part of this group, waiting for the creative urge can keep you from writing. Sometimes, sitting down and writing anyway, even when you can't think of anything to write about, is important — think of it as exercising muscles you'll need later. Besides, some of your best writing can come to you when you feel like you're plodding along in a rut, without anything to say.

If you need a warm-up, try one or more of the following:

- **Free-write.** Free-writing is a technique pioneered by Peter Elbow, a well-known teacher of writing. It's simple: Just put pen to paper or fingers to keyboard and write. What you write doesn't matter. If you can't think of anything, write, "I don't have anything to say, I don't have anything to say." Ten to fifteen minutes of free-writing often loosens people up, and you may discover you've written something interesting — in spite of yourself.
- **Rewrite a famous poem.** Go to your favorite anthology, select a poem, and put it in different words. Poet, teacher, and anthologist J.D. McClatchy recommended writing out the poem you've chosen — triple-spacing the poem on the page — and writing a response in between the lines. Then erase the original and work on your response to it as a separate poem — one *you've* created.
- **Try "Tzara's Hat."** Try this Dada/Surrealist game: Cut words out of a newspaper, draw them out of a hat, and arrange them in any way you want. Then write a poem reversing the words. One Surrealist game, The Exquisite Corpse, is a similar, collaborative game in which players add to a drawing or piece of writing without seeing the entire thing, leading to possibly surprising results.

If you're itching to start, start. Write what you're on fire to write. That's what this time and place are for. If you want to be *extremely* methodical, you could establish a pattern and do it the same way every time, like this:

1. **Begin with some exercises *or* copy material from your daily notebook into your journal.**

   Feel free to expand or work on anything as you do so.
2. **Read the previous day's work aloud.**
3. **Revise your previous work.**
4. **Generate new writing.**

Keeping a journal (again!)

Your poetry journal could be the Notes or Voice Memo apps on your smartphone, or a folder named Poetry on your phone, tablet, or laptop, or even that aforementioned digital recorder. What can you put into a journal? Here are some examples:

- **Drafts and revisions of poems.** A journal can be where you work from first thoughts to more finished versions of poems. Keep track of your versions (some poets number them; some use different colored pens or pencils; some simply start a new page when they start a new version). Watching your poems grow and develop may, in itself, reveal to you how your poetry takes shape.
- **Pasted-in newspaper articles, magazine art, drawings, and "found" objects.** Maybe you've come upon a random family photograph in the street, and that photograph suggests a poem to you.
- **Poems you've read and loved.** Why not build your own personal anthology? That in itself could yield inspiration.
- **Exercises in traditional forms.** Write sonnets, ballads, centos, haiku, tanka, ghazals, and other tightly formal poems. Pay your dues! Master these forms even if you'll never use them. They teach you the foundations of your craft. (See Chapter 13 for more on working with traditional forms of poetry.)
- **Lists of subjects to write about.** Just list them. Someday you could return to this list, select an item, and write a poem around it.
- **Sentences and phrases, bits and pieces.** Phrases ("the weather-facing wall") or sentences ("The only reason I have this job is to have this job") you overhear during the day, or fragments, thoughts, and ideas that just occur to you — all make great candidates for journal entries.
- **Words you never heard of before.** Expand your understanding of your chosen material: words. Write down words you'd like to use someday in a poem (like *frangible*) or sentences made up of unfamiliar words, just for their sound ("The frangible zerk mewled at the eumoirous thyristor"). Journals can be where you become more familiar with the possibilities of language.
- **Metaphors.** When metaphors occur to you with no poem around them ("the sea is the eyelid of the shore"), put them in your journal. They may come in handy later.

Moving from journal entry to poem

Some journal entries are complete poems the moment you write them. They just drop down out of nowhere, right into your brain. But most journal entries *aren't* poems just yet — they're the *raw material* for poetry, the stuff poetry is made *of*.

So how do you know when your journal entry has become poetry? You *never* know for sure. Many poets keep working and reworking their poems forever. But it's important to distinguish between a journal entry (in which you just say something) and a poem (in which you use language and thought to *make something new happen*).

Here's a passage from a journal:

> I'm feeling mad today because I love this guy and he isn't being that responsive. He seems to be acting like he's interested, but then it's as if he doesn't know anything is happening.

Sure, you may be able to imagine *situations* in which this could be poetry. (A couple of examples: What if this were your *dog* talking? What if this prose passage came smack in the middle of a Shakespearean sonnet?) But most of the time, entries like this are only the *beginning* of something poetic.

Arranging them in lines can't hide that fact:

> I'm feeling
> mad today because I
> love
> this guy and he isn't
> being that
> responsive. He
> seems to be
> acting like he's
> interested, but then
> it's as if
> he doesn't know
> anything
> is happening.

Even arranged into more interesting lines, it's still prose — just chopped-up prose. In this new form, the words are more fun to read — two lines even rhyme — but it's still not poetry yet. You're looking at the ore, not the processed gold (ore is good, gold is better).

REMEMBER

In poetry, some *event* takes place. Something *happens to the reader.* What that something is (a revelation, an epiphany, a redirection, a surprise, a paradox, an outrage, a jest) and how it happens is up to the poet. Emily Dickinson famously said she knew she was reading poetry "if I feel physically as if the top of my head were taken off." Poetry is *that* startling, that surprising; it can change the way you see things.

In the journal entry, you know the writer is feeling "mad" because she says so. But do you really *feel* it? On a scale of 1 to 10, with 10 meaning you resonate strongly to the poet's frustration, her passage is maybe a 3. Fine, she really wants this guy to open up to her — but you're *guessing* at her emotions, not *knowing* them.

Using her journal, the writer later came up with these lines:

I am an improvised
explosive
device triggered to
your front door come
out come out

Boom! A *lot* closer to poetry. Why? Because she has found a metaphor for her emotional state. Her emotional state is an *IED.* Think that metaphor through:

- **IEDs are a form of attack often associated with terrorists and often aimed at one person.** How is her love improvised and explosive? "I'm feeling mad" is only *talking about* anger; this metaphor is trying to *embody* it.
- **The writer is triggered to his front door.** She is so attuned to his movements, so sensitive, that any move he makes is meaningful. Note also the psychological overtones of "triggered."
- **The last words, "come/out come out," resonate with the game of hide-and-seek, ironically connecting the terrorist IED to a children's game. They also suggest she may really want the guy to "come out" by showing his feelings to her.** But if he does come out — blam! — she explodes. So, there we encounter some tasty *ambivalence* (the coexistence of opposing or very different emotions): frustration alongside relief (in the release of the pent-up emotions). Plus . . . she's dangerous.

TIP

The poet went from a straightforward journal entry to an *event.* Her progress suggests a few things about getting from journal entry to poem:

- **Think in images and metaphors.** This poet's first good move was to find a metaphor for her emotional state: the IED. That one metaphor says a lot more, and a lot more powerfully, than three lines of prose did.
- **Concentrate on *showing* rather than *telling. Embody*, don't just *say*.** This poet's second good move was to see that simply declaring "I'm feeling mad today" didn't bring her emotional state alive. She had to find a way to *involve* the reader in her frustration. Poetry thus often works by *indirection.* (As Emily Dickinson puts it, "Tell all the Truth but tell it slant.") Her poem never mentions

the word *love,* yet we get more of her passion than if the word *love* had come bopping in.

» **Think with music, rhythm, and form.** Another interesting move was to drop all punctuation. Now you, the reader, must work a little to group the words into understandable units — maybe become a little more conscious of each word. And say — how about that last line break? She *could* have written,

Come out,
Come out!

but instead she wrote,

come
out come out

which slows you down a little and forces you to punctuate the phrase in your mind (and give it the tone carried by an absent exclamation point). It maybe even lead to a smile when you realize who's talking, to whom, and why. She has involved you more. And that's what most poets want to do.

Choosing subjects

As you forge a personality as a poet, you'll find that *what* you write about and the *form* you write in are almost as important as *how* you write.

If you're struggling for things to write about, check out the following lists of subjects from two separate journals.

List #1	List #2
Friendship	Friendships based on making sure nothing goes wrong
Clothes	Why men wear clothes until they're just about falling off their bodies
Kittens	The first time I pulled back the blankets to get in bed and discovered that my cat had chosen that place to have her 13 kittens
Words	How odd it is to say the word *plentiful*
Butterflies	Seeing a real butterfly land on a plastic flower
Death	Having a cancerous blip scraped off my face, knowing it won't spread but still realizing that cancer has come visiting

List #2 is more specific. *Friendship* is fine, but what *about* friendship? What *kind* of friendship? *Abstractions* are not productive subjects for poetry. You may have fresher, more penetrating things to say, about *friendships based on making sure nothing goes wrong*: that's the stronger topic.

TIP

Write about anything you want, but when considering subjects for your poems — and when stockpiling subjects in your journal — follow these suggestions:

- **Choose limited subjects over broad ones.** Not *clothes* (broad) but *how men wear clothes until they're almost falling off* (amusingly limited).
- **Choose concrete and specific subjects over abstract and general ones.** Not *death* (abstract) but a *cancerous blip* (chillingly concrete). Not *words* (general) but the word *plentiful* (specific).
- **Choose original subjects over those you've seen before.** There are, we're guessing, about 12,571,813 poems about cats. But how many are there about cats giving birth in *your bed*?

These choices can help you discover better subjects and write better poems.

Rewriting until it hurts a lot better

Some poets want their poetry to be the red-hot, first burst from their minds. In the words of Allen Ginsberg, "First thought, best thought." Such poets are wary of tampering too much with the material they've produced in the initial heat of creation. But we've rarely met poets, no matter how devoted to the creative urge and the authentic, who didn't revise like obsessed demons. The superb poet James McMichaels once read a six-line poem to his class, after which he said, "I've revised this thing 300 times, and it *still* isn't ready."

REMEMBER

The creative urge is usually just the *beginning* of a poem. Ezra Pound compared the making of poems to sculpture: You start out with something promising and keep refining, chiseling away, getting rid of anything you don't need. Dorothy Parker called it "killing your babies." (Sweet metaphor, huh?)

TIP

Be ready to cross out *anything* if it doesn't work — no matter how reluctant you may be to part with it. And follow these three guidelines for revision:

- **Treat everything you write as provisional.** Nothing is set in stone; everything is subject to change at any time.

» **Be tough with yourself.** Cut out anything that:
  - You've seen in print before (the "George Orwell rule").
  - Seems trite or obvious.
  - Doesn't need saying or has been said or *implied* elsewhere in the poem.
» **Never keep something in your poem just because it helps you make a rhyme or fills out a meter.** Find a different solution instead of keeping anything second-rate.

TIP

Your subconscious is very useful in revision. You may close your journal, yawn, and turn in. But your subconscious is still working on that poem all the time, even while you're sleeping. If your subconscious finds something in the poem isn't working, that will occur to you here and there, sometimes consciously (as when you read it and immediately think, "That isn't working") and sometimes subconsciously (as when the offending word or phrase just keeps surfacing in your attention). Pay attention when such things happen; the subconscious is very often right.

REMEMBER

Make revision a large part of your daily writing routine. Revision is hard work. Sometimes, when you've revised, hardly any poem is left. But you learn a lot as you revise — about the poem in front of you, about yourself, and about poetry. So be open to revision — it's how you and your poems get better.

From "City Bus" to "City Bus": A case study in revision

Hayden Saunier takes us through her process in writing "City Bus," from first draft to final form. Read her first draft aloud and then read what she has to say about drafting it.

READ ALOUD

City Bus

I'm seated on the molded bench
behind you. Your shoulders sag
beneath an unseen weight as do
the shoulders of the woman in the knitted
cap across the aisle who must already
feel the coming cold inside her.
Exhaustion's cape drapes over all our
bones. The bus stops and kneels

for each of us and though
we do not know the other's
sorrows like we know our own, see how
our bodies sway side to side and lurch
identically, carried as we are, by the same
machinery, all the long way downtown.

Saunier discusses first-drafting:

> This first draft was a quick capture of the idea, trying to get it down.
>
> There was a rhythm in the first lines of this draft I wanted to maintain and develop, like the rhythm of a bus moving, stopping, moving, stopping, but with momentum. That's what propelled me into the poem. The "molded bench" was the detail that grounded me enough to start; it was a "sense memory" that grounded me in the details I needed to bring the reader onto the bus with me. A poem, for me, usually gathers itself around either an image or something by ear, like a phrase that rings. Here, the weighed-down shoulders and swaying bodies were images that drew me in.
>
> I've learned in a first draft to keep going once I'm in and follow where the poem leads as well as I can — even when I know it is lacking — and in this draft, I actually took my own good advice. I did not stop to edit, as much as my internal critical editor wanted. I could sense where the poem was trying to go — even if the shape and movement and closure of the poem were not there quite yet.
>
> I got it down and then waited a day before going back.

Saunier was doing what good poets do when they draft. She *resisted the urge to edit as she wrote the first draft.* Some poets do edit as they write, but many others simply follow where the brand-new draft is leading — especially if they have a "sense," as Saunier did, of "where the poem was trying to go."

She *let herself cool off from the intensity of creating the first draft.* Saunier waited a day, and then she returned to "City Bus," cooler, clearer, with a more objective eye. For thousands of years, poets have been recommending this practice. The Roman poet Horace wrote, "Keep back what you write for nine years." He didn't; no one does. But wisdom is wisdom: *Draft, cool off, return, and revise!*

Imagine now that Saunier has worked on "City Bus," not just once but many times. (She mentions "a few dozen re-drafts"!) Read the final draft aloud a few times, and then follow the handwritten comments referring to various parts of the poem.

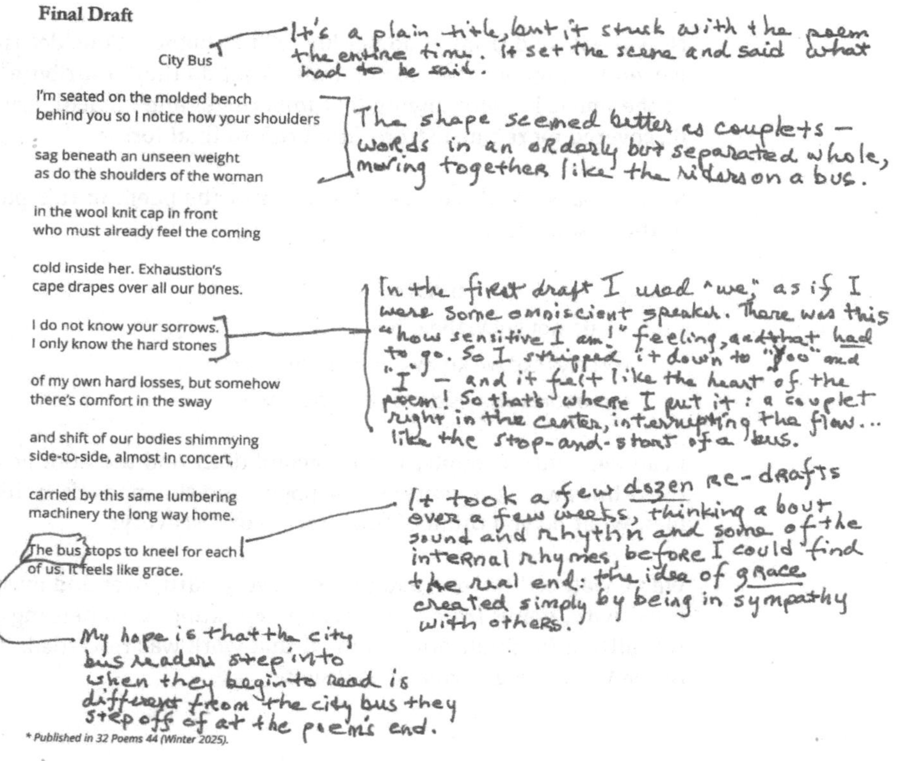

Final Draft

City Bus

I'm seated on the molded bench
behind you so I notice how your shoulders

sag beneath an unseen weight
as do the shoulders of the woman

in the wool knit cap in front
who must already feel the coming

cold inside her. Exhaustion's
cape drapes over all our bones.

I do not know your sorrows.
I only know the hard stones

of my own hard losses, but somehow
there's comfort in the sway

and shift of our bodies shimmying
side-to-side, almost in concert,

carried by this same lumbering
machinery the long way home.

The bus stops to kneel for each
of us. It feels like grace.

It's a plain title, but it stuck with the poem the entire time. It set the scene and said what had to be said.

The shape seemed better as couplets — words in an orderly but separated whole, moving together like the riders on a bus.

In the first draft I used "we," as if I were some omniscient speaker. There was this "how sensitive I am!" feeling, and that had to go. So I stripped it down to "you" and "I" — and it felt like the heart of the poem! So that's where I put it: a couplet right in the center, interrupting the flow... like the stop-and-start of a bus.

It took a few dozen re-drafts over a few weeks, thinking about sound and rhythm and some of the internal rhymes, before I could find the real end: the idea of grace created simply by being in sympathy with others.

My hope is that the city bus readers step into when they begin to read is different from the city bus they step off of at the poem's end.

** Published in 32 Poems 44 (Winter 2025).*

What do you think? How does the first draft compare with the final draft?

Saunier found a form — couplets — that *embodies and enacts* people rocking together on a bus. She felt that movement in the first draft and refined it as she revised. Where do you see, hear, and feel that movement?

Look at all those great line breaks! Think about what they mean and do. Look at "Exhaustion's/cape drapes over all our bones." What feelings does this enjambment give you? The first draft had "Exhaustion's cape drapes over all our/bones." How do the two choices *feel* different?

Saunier says she revised for music. Read the poem aloud. What kinds of rhymes and echoes do you see and hear?

Now read aloud from "I do not know" to "home." Consider the *o*- and *m*-sounds woven throughout the second draft. What do they contribute? What do you think of the music in "shimmying," "lumbering," and "machinery"? Do you think she discovered more music from first draft to final form?

Saunier says she discovered the center of the poem in this passage, near the end of the first draft:

though
we do not know the other's
sorrows like we know our own, see how
our bodies sway side to side and lurch

Read her central couplet in the second draft and the note next to it. She decided these lines were the center of the poem, and she made them into that central couplet. What do you think of this process of discovery?

We've watched Hayden Saunier work very hard, over and over, with patience and sensitivity, going from a promising beginning to something she felt good about submitting for publication. And all that work was rewarded: "City Bus" appeared in the Winter 2025 issue of *32 Poems!*

Getting Connected to the World of Poetry

Poets stay in touch with what's going on in the poetry world. It definitely is its own world, with news, events, stars, and controversies. Being part of this world — meeting people passionately committed to writing, reading, and listening to poetry — is a fine way to learn more, make friends in the art, and meet *mentors* (experienced poets and teachers who act as guides or counselors). Poetry need not be isolating; in fact, it can lead you to a fascinating community of like-minded artists.

TIP

How do poets stay connected to the world of poetry? Here are some ways:

- **They read.** Just as car mechanics read the latest *Auto Mechanic*, many poets read (online or even in that other mode, print) the latest *American Poetry Review, Conjunctions, New American Writing, Poets & Writers, The Poetry Project's Newsletter, Rattle, New Verse Review,* or other journals and sites related to the poetry scene. See what other people are writing and how they're writing it. Some poems you'll like, some you won't — but all will be instructive. Also, read the reviews in journals, such as those in *Poetry, The Hudson Review, or The New Criterion*. Lots of places now organize and collect reviews so you can see who is publishing and what readers think. These reviews can help you discover how poetry is getting talked about.

- **They attend poetry readings.** Readings happen at colleges and universities, museums, bookstores, bars, coffeehouses, and writing centers. Go. Better yet, go and read your own poetry.
- **They take courses.** Many colleges and universities offer creative writing courses. So do some community centers. Find out what's available in your community and take advantage of it.
- **They go to workshops.** A *workshop* is a small group session given by an experienced poet who discusses the work of the group and invites discussion. Usually, you have to send in a set of poems as an application and pay a fee to attend. Workshops are offered by colleges, universities, some bookstores and coffeehouses, and community arts centers. Some are even offered by writers in their homes. Workshops offer an intensive critique of your own poetry and that of other people. They are a good way to learn a lot at one time — and they bring you into contact with an experienced teacher and other writers.
- **They meet other poets.** Perhaps you know some guitarists. When they get together, *all* they want to do is talk about one another's guitars. Poets are into *their* art, too. When they congregate, they like to talk about who's publishing, what they're working on, what problems they're working out. Many writers like to be part of such a scene because they learn a lot from their peers.

REMEMBER

Don't fear your fellow writers. They're fascinating folks, with an interest in common. Knowing that a lot of other people share your interests and challenges is a good feeling, so make the effort to get to know other poets.

IN THIS CHAPTER

» Exploring traditional forms of poetry

» Respecting the tradition of formal poetry

» Making sense of the rules for the ballad, the psalm, the sonnet, the ghazal, the haiku, and the tanka

Chapter 13
Working with Traditional Forms of Verse

When many people think of poetry, they think of ballads, sonnets, rhyming couplets, iambic pentameter, ABAB, verses, stanzas, and refrains. What they're thinking of are *traditional* forms of verse — forms that have come down through the centuries, each form with its own rules and challenges. Open-form verse (covered in Chapter 14) is different every time you use it — in essence, you *create* a form each time you write. But with traditional verse forms, you accept measures, restrictions, and rules that have accrued through the years.

No matter what kind of poetry you end up writing, knowing how to write in traditional forms can be a great benefit. For one thing, it can help you appreciate the *fruitful music and tension* that come along with meter and rhyme schemes. Almost all these forms remain vibrant today — poets are still singing loud and strong through them, making them do modern tricks. Practicing traditional forms is an excellent way to:

» Work on the craft of poetry.

» Begin a writing session.

» Break writer's block.

» Write good poems.

TIP

RESPECTING THE TRADITION

As a poet, you'll write the way you want to write — and that's great. But when you're starting out, and when you're trying traditional forms, take the forms seriously and (at least at first) follow the rules strictly. Start by trying to find perfect rhymes (instead of something that comes close) and try not to vary many feet in your chosen meters.

Later, you can vary the rules — write a sonnet that doesn't rhyme or one that doesn't use meter, mess with the rhyme schemes, or use *slant rhyme*, daring to rhyme *shoe* with *snow*, for example (slant rhyme is an excellent way to tune your ear). But first get to know how trad forms help you organize your poems and reach for language in intense, creative ways. Let those old forms stretch you in new directions.

You're never done working with the traditional forms — you are always beginning afresh. Writing poetry is a lifelong apprenticeship, one to be savored.

Ballads

Traditional *ballads* are stories — often of a romantic or lurid sort —told in verse. Ballads still are being written that way, especially in the form of popular songs such as Bob Dylan's "Boots of Spanish Leather" and Richard Thompson's "1952 Vincent Black Lightning." To find these songs on YouTube, go to `www.youtube.com` and search by artist name and song title.

Ballads take many forms. A popular one is the four-line stanza in which the first and third lines are written in iambic tetrameter (four iambs) and the second and fourth in iambic trimeter (three iambs), with a rhyme scheme of ABXB (the third line, X, need not rhyme or may rhyme with A).

Here's what two such stanzas may sound like:

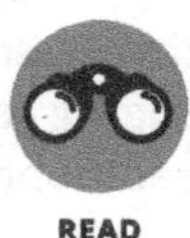

READ ALOUD

The winter moon had tipped and spilled
        Its shadows on the lawn
When Farmer Owen woke to find
        His only daughter gone;
She'd taken all the clothes she had
        Against the biting cold,
And in a note to him she wrote,
        "I've taken all your gold."

TIP

Using this stanza type, write a ghost story, mystery, suspense tale, news account, or heroic story (stories of the Knights of the Round Table and Robin Hood were written in this form). *Forget* "olden days" talk ("What ho, varlet! I shall smite thee in twain!") and make story and language as modern as you can. You'll see that this sturdy little form is excellent for carrying a tale.

Psalms

The singers who compiled the Psalms worked with a very interesting verse form. It consisted of *distichs,* verses of two lines. The lines could be of almost any length. The first line was a statement, and the second built on that statement, usually in one of three ways:

- **Amplification:** The poet *expands on* the first half by restating all or part of it in some way, as in Psalm 102:

  I am like a pelican in the wilderness;
      I have become like an owl among the ruins

- **Antithesis:** The poet states something in the second half that oppose the statement in the first half, as in Ecclesiastes 3:4:

  A time to weep
      and a time to laugh

- **Complement:** A complement balances two halves of a statement, as in Proverbs 19:21:

  A man may have many plans in his mind
      but the counsel of the Lord — that will stand

You, too, can write a psalm. The rules are few. Pick a very mundane event in your life and write it down straightforwardly in all the *first* (left-hand) lines of the distichs, leaving the *second* (right-hand) lines blank, like this:

Today I came down to breakfast
And I was hungry
So my mother brought me some cornflakes
She poured them in a bowl
And gave the bowl to me

Yawn! Now fill in the second lines. Use sameness, antithesis, and complement. Amplify, illustrate, question, comment, contradict the first halves in as many ways as you can think of:

Today I came down to breakfast
    Or breakfast came to me [antithesis]
And I was hungry
    Eating rose by rose the wallpaper [amplification]
So, my mother brought me some cornflakes
    Fighting off the cornflake-stealing hordes [amplification]
She poured them in a bowl
    Pouring them in the garden would be strange [antithesis]
And gave the bowl to me
    I accepted it, humble as cornflakes [complement]

The fun (and challenging) part is to create second lines that echo material in the first lines but also *transform* that material. You may find your second lines becoming humorous or surreal. The right-hand lines don't have to make sense or be logically related to the left-hand ones.

REMEMBER

Psalm-writing is a good way to get invention juices flowing, and it can yield interesting poems. Have fun with it. Break your own rules now and then. The idea is to think divergently.

Sonnets

They're back! Time to pay your dues. Try writing a sonnet.

TIP

Here are the rules. Your sonnet will:

- **consist of 14 lines.**
- **be written in iambic pentameter (duh-DUH-duh-DUH-duh-DUH-duh-DUH-duh-DUH).**
- **be written in one of various standard rhyme schemes.**

In the *Shakespearean* form of sonnet, the rhyme scheme is this:

A
B

A
B

C
D
C
D

E
F
E
F

G
G

Every A rhymes with every A, every B rhymes with every B, and so forth. You'll notice this type of sonnet consists of three *quatrains* (four-line stanzas) and one *couplet* (two consecutive rhyming lines of verse).

Ah, but there's more to a sonnet than just its physical build. A sonnet is also an *argument* — that, too, builds up a certain way. *How* it builds up is related to its metaphors and how the poem moves from one metaphor to the next. In a Shakespearean sonnet, the argument builds up like this:

- **First quatrain:** An *exposition* of the main theme and main metaphor.
- **Second quatrain:** Theme and metaphor are *extended* or *complicated*; often, some imaginative example is given.
- **Third quatrain:** A twist or conflict (technical name: *peripeteia*) occurs, often introduced by a *but* (very often leading off the ninth line).
- **Couplet:** Summarizes; leaves the reader with a new, concluding image.

One of Shakespeare's best-known sonnets, Sonnet 18, follows this pattern:

Shall I compare thee to a summer's day?
Thou art more lovely and more temperate.
Rough winds do shake the darling buds of May,
And summer's lease hath all too short a date.
Sometime too hot the eye of heaven shines,
And often is his gold complexion dimmed;
And every fair from fair sometime declines,
By chance, or nature's changing course, untrimmed;
But thy eternal summer shall not fade,
Nor lose possession of that fair thou owest,
Nor shall death brag thou wanderest in his shade,
When in eternal lines to time thou growest.
So long as men can breathe or eyes can see,
So long lives this, and this gives life to thee.

The *argument* of Sonnet 18 goes like this:

- **First quatrain:** The speaker considers the notion of comparing "thou" ("you") to a summer's day, and it's a bad idea. But he makes that metaphor anyway . . . and the beloved wins every time.
- **Second quatrain:** Shakespeare extends the theme, explaining why even the sun, supposed to be so great, gets obscured sometimes, and why everything that's beautiful decays from beauty sooner or later. He has shifted the metaphor, from summer in general to the sun specifically, and at last to "every fair," every beautiful thing.
- **Third quatrain:** Here, right at line 9, the argument takes a bold, brave turn with the familiar *But.* The main reason the speaker won't compare his beloved to summer is that summer dies — but the beloved *won't*. He refers to the first two quatrains — the beloved's "eternal summer" won't fade, and the beloved won't "lose possession" of his or her "fair" (beauty). So the poet keeps the metaphors going, but in a different direction. For good measure, he throws in a negative version of all the sunshine in this poem — the "shade" of death, which, evidently, his beloved won't have to worry about.
- **Couplet:** But hold on. Exactly how is his beloved going to escape death? In the *lines of Shakespeare's poetry*, which will keep the beloved alive as long as people breathe or see. This bold statement gives closure to the whole argument — it's a surprise.

And so far, Shakespeare's sonnet has done what he promised it would. See how tight, how complex, how well-organized, this little box of poetry is? Try writing a sonnet of your own.

REMEMBER

Poets are attracted by the grace, the concentration, and the challenge of writing sonnets. You may never write another sonnet in your life, but this exercise is more than just busywork. It does all the following:

- Shows you how much you can pack into a short form.
- Gives you practice with rhyme, meter, structure, metaphor, and argument.
- Connects you with one of the oldest traditions in English poetry — one still vital today (see Chapter 8).

WRITING EXPERIMENTAL SONNETS

Poets take the sonnet to some crazy places. David Trinidad's "Monster Mash" is a Shakespearean sonnet (it rhymes and maintains recognizable iambic pentameter) — made entirely of the names of old horror movies:

> Frankenstein, Godzilla, The Blob, Phantom
> of the Opera, The Wolf Man, The Hunchback
> of Notre Dame, Children of the Damned, Them,
> Queen of Outer Space, Creature from the Black
>
> Lagoon, Curse of the Cat People, The Mum-
> my, The Green Slime, The Brain that Wouldn't Die,
> Invaders from Mars, It! The Terror from
> Beyond Space, Dr. Cyclops, Freaks, The Fly,
>
> Bride of Frankenstein, The Invisible
> Man, The Mole People, Dr. Jekyll and
> Mr. Hyde, Mothra, The Incredible
> Shrinking Man, Dracula, The Crawling Hand,
>
> Attack of the Fifty-Foot Woman, King
> Kong, Tarantula, 13 Ghosts, The Thing.

Today, poets are using traditional forms in nontraditional ways. When you feel comfortable in a form, explore new avenues with it yourself.

Ghazals

The *ghazal* (pronounce it "guzzle" with a slight gargle on the *g*) is an Arabic verse form that has had a big impact worldwide. It came into European poetry through 19th-century German poets and got into English-language poetry in the late 1960s. Here are the rules:

- **Every line must have the same number of syllables; meter optional.** American and English writers usually settle on iambic pentameter or something close, but you can choose any number of syllables you like.
- **The poem is a series of couplets,** at least five, but there's no upper limit.
- **The first couplet rhymes.** For example:

  October: the horizon, grey and wide,
  Is staggering — you're dancing in the tide.

- **The closing words of the second half of the second line are repeated in the second line of each succeeding couplet.** It could be the last word, or a several-word phrase — it's up to you. This is called the *radif.* Here, our *radif* is "dancing in the tide." The *radif* is perhaps the most distinctive thing about the ghazal. It operates much like a short chorus, staying the same while the poem all around it is changing. An alert, responsive audience, once it knows the *radif,* will be good and ready to holler it out ("Dancing in the tide!") each time it comes round.
- **The remaining couplets don't have to rhyme, and they can shift around in subject and tone.** Make them as independent as you want, but always, come back to that *radif* ("dancing in the tide").
- **The *makhta,* or the poet's signature (first name, last name, or both) appears somewhere in the last couplet (optional).**

Here's a ghazal we wrote ourselves, following all these rules:

October: the horizon, grey and wide,
Is staggering — you're dancing in the tide.

My uncle died and left me twenty sheep
Stacked in my basement. Dancing in the tide

Of debts, divorce announcements, and debris,
I chuck it all, go dancing. In the Tide

There was a lottery coupon, and I won.
Now all my friends come dancing in the tide.

As ocarina orchestras obfusc,
Marina Watts goes dancing in the tide.

Ghazals are both free and patterned, traditional yet loose, closed yet wide open. For a ghazal that rocks, check out "You found me once again" by Rūmī (see Chapter 8)!

Haiku and Tanka

The Western version of the Japanese *haiku* form is, we hope, pretty familiar. In the form most often taught in the West, a haiku has three lines, of 5, 7, and 5 syllables respectively. Today's poets *do* observe the three-line rule but often don't observe the syllable counts.

Other things to observe:

- Avoid rhyme.
- Use enjambment: wind your sentences around the ends of the lines. In the example below, for example, we read "beneath a warrior's/helmet, a cricket," and so on.
- Try not to end all the lines with a single-syllable word.

Haiku present moments of vivid clarity emerging from an encounter with nature. Something is observed, triggering a complex of emotions. Those emotions, however, are signaled or suggested rather than presented directly. Here is one of the most famous examples, by that man again, Bashō:

beneath a warrior's
helmet, a cricket, stranger
to grace, is singing

We understand Bashō's haiku because we register *absences*. The warrior, the battle, the armies, all are in the past. The cricket, being "a stranger/ to grace," literally is ungracious, pitiless. All it can do is sing. The *tanka*, even older than the haiku, is another quiet, meditative form beginning with observation and ending with epiphany or complex emotion. Formally, a tanka begins like a haiku and adds two more lines of 7 syllables each. Those extra lines leave more room for experiment and exploration. Many poets find it natural, in writing tanka, to write a haiku, followed by the couplet, though you don't need to. The haiku may focus more on observation, the couplet on reflection:

Invisible hands
   caress my face; have I walked
through a spider's web

woven this morning to catch
   flies writhing or my surprise

IN THIS CHAPTER

» Defining *open-form* poetry

» Looking at examples of successful open-form poems

» Considering four approaches to writing open-form poetry

Chapter 14 Writing Open-Form Poetry

Some folks used to call it *free verse.* We're calling it *open-form poetry.*

Open-form poetry, particularly open-form verse in shorter lines, is the dominant verse form in the Western world. Most published poetry is in some kind of open-form verse. Much of the poetry people write in their journals is open-form.

In this chapter, we offer guidelines for writing open-form poetry. We discuss why your *attitude* and *approach* are crucial. We also point out some of the challenges awaiting the open-form poet. Even though such poetry allows for a great degree of independence and self-expression, poets who write in open forms have to earn every ounce of freedom by showing the greatest attention to detail in their poems.

Working Toward a Definition

Poetry with regular rhyme and shapes is "closed" in the sense that you choose a restrictive form and stick with it — which, as you see in Chapter 13, is often marvelous. But in the poetry we're examining in this chapter, we use the term *open* to acknowledge that poets look for natural, often changing, unpredictable rhythms and musics and physical shapes.

REMEMBER

The term *open-form poetry* makes two points the term *free verse* doesn't:

- As soon as you start writing a poem, you've *chosen a form*. You can't help it.
- As soon as you start writing open-form poetry, you discover all sorts of patterns and restrictions you're imposing on yourself.

See the sidebar, "'Free verse' versus open-form poetry," for a detailed explanation behind the terminology we've chosen for this book.

TECHNICAL STUFF

"FREE VERSE" VERSUS OPEN-FORM POETRY

You're probably familiar with the words *free verse*. They conjure up long lines flowing across the page, surging like emotions themselves. That certainly seems to be the case with English poet D.H. Lawrence's "Bavarian Gentians," an almost hallucinatory poem about a deep blue flower:

Bavarian gentians, big and dark, only dark
darkening the day-time, torch-like with the smoking blueness of Pluto's
    gloom,
ribbed and torch-like, with their blaze of darkness spread blue
down flattening into points, flattened under the sweep of white day

Pluto was the god of the underworld in Roman mythology; a *gentian* is a kind of flower, usually with deep blue leaves; and *Bavarian* means coming from Bavaria, a region in the south of Germany.

Most people believe that free verse — sorry, open-form verse — doesn't have to have rhyme or rhythm. You can just write. No more tightly constricting forms.

But take another look at Lawrence's poem: It has plenty of echoes ("the smoking blueness of Pluto's gloom"), plenty of rhythm ("Bavarian gentians, big and dark" or "darkening the day-time, torch-like with the smoking blueness"). Lawrence's poem doesn't have *meter* — regular, prescribed rhythmic patterns line after line — but there are lots of rhythms. And plenty of *patterns,* too: repetitions ("dark, only dark/ darkening the day-time"), consonant sounds, choirs of vowels ("down flattening into points, flattened under the sweep of white day"). What a feast — and how *worked* it is: You can tell that, for all the spontaneous, *incantatory* (chantlike) quality of these lines, a poet with a remarkable ear slaved over this passage.

Look, too, at the *visual rhythm* going on. A medium line, then a line flowing out long . . . and the flow hitches up, with four of the most eloquent commas (after *day-time, gloom, torch-like*, and *points*) you'll ever read. Lengthier elements are pitched against shorter. See all that? *Feel* all that? Someone did all that on purpose. Very much so.

Much better, then, to call such muscular, winding, insistent poetry *open-form poetry* rather than the misleading *free verse*. The term *open-form poetry derives* from the theories of Black Mountain poet Charles Olson.

What open-form poetry is

Open form allows poets to do nearly anything that can be done with language. The poet has more *options* with this kind of poetry. Open forms have rhythm, music, and even some rhyme, but the poet keeps those aspects changing and changeable throughout the poem.

TECHNICAL STUFF

When writing open-form poetry, you're trying to be open to how your mind works — your special set of memories, associations, and subconscious cerebral murmurs. You're trying to pay attention, through the poem, to something you can't actually *see* directly (according to famed poetic theorist Sigmund Freud): the backstairs workings of the subconscious mind.

Poets speak of *zigs* and *zags* — sudden swings in tone, feeling, and subject. Here are a few, courtesy of U.S. poet Charles North in his poem "Shooting for Line":

> In short, we hold certain truths to be self-evident but the
> answers in code in the glove compartment,
> and they eat up the presumed distance and the leftovers
> like an unenacted crime bill or Sophocles' Oedipus at Colonus.
> It seems likely no one leaves all hope behind, a calling card
> fringed in tears and a raised border
> but the wounds are bathed in salt, also the cocker spaniel.

What do you see in this poem? The Declaration of Independence, Greek tragedy, automobile interiors, a dog. This is what people mean when they use the words *zig* and *zag* to refer to poetry — North's poem changes subject in virtually every line.

TIP

Some poets say it's not *them* doing the zigging and zagging; it's the poem, or the subconscious mind working in the poem. So, pay attention when zigs and zags beg to happen in your own poetry. If a word, image, or zig occurs to you — no matter how seemingly mundane, irrelevant, inappropriate, frightening, or contradictory it may be — consider using it. It popped up for a reason — or maybe no reason at all — but that's what makes it interesting.

TIP

Many poets speak of "trusting the poem" — being faithful to the way the poem "opens up" as you write it, not editing out things you don't like, are afraid of, or find irritating, rude, or distressing. If new pathways come up, explore them. Be not afraid.

What open-form poetry isn't

Open forms allow you to do nearly anything you can do with language. The operative word there is *nearly*. There are, in fact, things you *don't* do. Open forms, as we said earlier in this chapter, are not *closed* — meaning you don't restrict the lines to only one shape, length, or musical rule. No traditional sonnets, ballads, or rhyme schemes here. Sure, you can have a line or two of, for example, iambic verse — as long as they're there for a reason. You must decide why those lines have to be iambic. Ask yourself whether the fact that these lines are iambic contributes anything. If the answer is "no," change them.

And *it isn't prose*. It *isn't* "just saying stuff in any lines you want." It is language under pressure: In your own poetry and that of others, look for the tension, the thrust, the movement you feel in poetry. It has to be there; your job is to make it be there.

Knowing What Makes It Poetry

Open forms *are* forms. Again, when you use open forms, you start to impose on your poem — and yourself — all sorts of patterns and restrictions. You won't know what they are until you get there, however, because each poem is its own form.

Think of open-form poetry as a way of thinking — an especially intense awareness of every single aspect of the poem, from subject and tone to music and rhythm, from the physical shape of the poem to the length (in space and in time) of the lines, from grammar to parts of speech. As Charles Olson wrote for *Poetry New York* in his 1950 essay "Project Verse," the poet "has to behave, and be, instant by instant, aware."

TIP

When you write an open-form poem, try to be very conscious. Everything in the poem, every feature, every aspect, must have a reason for being there. Be conscious of the following:

- **Economy.** Cram as much energy as possible into each word. Cut everything that doesn't absolutely need to be there. Remember Ezra Pound's poetry-as-sculpture thought (see Chapter 12): You chisel off what's unneeded until all that's left is what's absolutely necessary, living, new.
- **Grammar and syntax.** Are you always using complete sentences? Fine — but you could also do it another way. Decide whether you have a *reason* to write in complete sentences for this poem. If you can come up with a reason, fine. If not, consider alternatives — bursts of words, single words, word fragments. And who says you have to use "proper" grammar? Or punctuation? Try breaking a few rules, if that improves the poem.
- **Parts of speech.** Some teachers say writers should avoid overuse of adjectives or adverbs; they should prefer nouns and verbs instead. That's an excellent starting point: Use only the words you need. If all you're doing is *prettifying* something, forget it. Use adjectives only when they're surprising ("your green voice"), contradictory ("aggressive modesty"), or give information the reader simply can't get elsewhere ("It was a Welsh stoat" — how else would we know where the stoat was from?).
- **Rhythms.** Look at the rhythms in your lines. Does the rhythm of the line contribute to its meaning? Anything sing-songy? If so, is it *good* that it's sing-songy? Often, open-form verse falls into *iambs* (a group of syllables consisting of an unstressed syllable followed by a stressed syllable, as in "alas!") and *dactyls* (one stressed syllable followed by two unstressed, as in "penetrate"). Don't let this happen unless there is a reason for it. If you see your poetry falling into repeated metrical patterns, cut and mix and stir and rejigger.
- **The physical lengths (the number of syllables and the actual length) of the lines you use.** Avoid falling into exactly the same lengths. Every line length should have a reason behind it.
- **The length (in time) it takes to read each line aloud.** If each line takes about the same number of seconds, figure out whether there's a reason for it. If not, consider other shapes and lengths.
- **Line-endings.** Poets realize that line-endings carry a certain emphasis or pressure. Your lines should end where they end for some reason. The way a line ends — where, and after what word or punctuation mark — should be the best way to end. Do you want a pause there? What's going to happen when your readers go to the next line? Something unexpected? Some surprise? Read a lot of open-form verse, and you'll notice that poets use a great deal of *enjambment,* winding the words around the ends of lines in gorgeous and meaningful ways.

As an example of a successful open-form poem, one in which each aspect of the poem is meaningful, each word bristling with energy, we offer these lines by Lorine Niedecker:

READ ALOUD

Now in one year
        a book published
                and plumbing —
took a lifetime
        to weep
            a deep
                trickle

You could read this poem literally: The main events of the year were the book I published and a plumbing job I had to get done. But you probably can feel more in there. Notice the following:

- **The echoes between *published* and *plumbing*.** The words share four sounds (*p, l,* short *u*, short *i*) and the same rhythm, a trochee (DUH-duh). With so much in common, the two get associated somehow in your brain. How are publishing and plumbing related? It may be just literal: They were the two big events of the year. Then again, what sort of plumbing is the poet talking about? Does she mean pipes and water? Or could the word *plumbing* be a metaphor for what you do when you write poetry — *plumb* (search deeply) your emotions and experience? What if the book was what took a lifetime, and the deep trickle was what became the poems? (You can come up with other possible readings as well. *Plumbing,* some may say, has overtones of sex or bodily functions.)
- **Rhyme and rhythm!** You see rhyme and rhythm both in the intriguing juxtaposition between *published* and *plumbing* and between *weep* and *deep.* And hear the rhythms, especially the last three lines:

  to weep
      a deep
          trickle

  The first two are iambs (duh-DUH), and the last one is a trochee (DUH-duh), with a very short last syllable. There's a reversal, a dwindle at the end. It even *looks* like a trickle. That. Is. *So.* Intentional.
- **The shape of the poem in space and time.** The poem gets smaller, both in terms of the number of syllables and the length of the lines (in both time and space — it takes less time to say *trickle* than it does to say *a deep*). The last three lines are two syllables, so you could say the poem trickles to its ending. Also, the poem tapers physically to an end, like a *plumb* (a lead weight attached to a line to show the vertical). Plumbs are used by architects, surveyors, construction workers, and, yes, plumbers.

If you come away with an impression of pain or perhaps sorrow, the summary of a year and also a lifetime, of long, hard work to write and to "plumb" — well, then, you have to say that this is a superb little poem.

Niedecker is conscious of every element of her poem, down to the dash in the middle: She seems as though she's about to explain what she means by *plumbing* — but doesn't really. It's a pregnant pause — maybe a misdirect, as in *You thought I'd explain . . . but I won't!* That's open-form poetry as a *way of thinking.*

Using Open Forms in Your Own Poetry

Poets have described open-form verse in various ways. In the following sections, we suggest approaches you might use when writing your own open-form poetry. These are less *definitions* than *attitudes,* ways of thinking about what you're doing.

REMEMBER

What *kind* of open-form verse you write depends on you. Practice with these different approaches. They may seem difficult or nutty at first, but after a while you'll start thinking in one of them, or in an open form all your own. You may work harder with your open-form poems than you ever thought you would. In the end, open form is both a challenge and a pleasure.

Going for the breath: Framing individual lines

As you read poetry, you become sensitive to the way you breathe. You read a group of words and then pause before reading another group of words — it's just natural. Pay attention to that when you write poetry as well. Let those natural pauses determine where lines end. The *breath,* as it's called in the poetry world, is a natural way to frame individual lines. It will be different from poem to poem, from line to line, but it can help guide both your writing and your reading.

Our guess is that Lorine Niedecker (in the poem from the earlier section, "Knowing What Makes It Poetry") is using the breath as the measure of her open-form lines. How do we know? We don't. But read the poem aloud. There seems (to us) to be a very strong pause — almost as you may have with an intake of breath — between the lines. Reading straight through seems very *un*natural — each line is roughly "equal to a breath," as some poets say.

Not all poets have the same length of breath. Some poets use a long, rolling breath, rather like a song or incantation. Beat poet Allen Ginsberg once wrote of himself, "My breath is long — that's the Measure, one physical-mental inspiration of thought contained in the elastic of a breath." One of Ginsberg's great inspirations was fellow poet Walt Whitman. You can hear the long, rolling breath in Whitman's poem, "O You Whom I Often and Silently Come":

> O you whom I often and silently come where you are that I may be with you;
> As I walk by your side or sit near, or remain in the same room with you,
> Little you know the subtle electric fire that for your sake is playing within me.

Like Ginsberg, you can regard your breath as your personal measure. Listen to your breath as a source of rhythm, pace, tone, and *inspiration* — a word based on the Latin word *inspirare*, meaning "to breathe in." Whitman's breath is different from Niedecker's, which is different from Lawrence's (earlier in this chapter). Read all three, one after the other. Feel the difference? Where?

How can you use the breath in writing open-form poetry? In revision, do the following:

- **Read aloud an open-form poem you've been working on, paying close attention to the breath as you read.** If you pause naturally in mid-line, break the line there. If you can't get a line to fit with a breath, something may be wrong with the way it's written. Revise to help the line "find" a breath-length that fits naturally.
- **Vary breath rhythms throughout the poem.** Don't keep them all the same length. Just as your body's breaths are, your breaths should be natural but varied.
- **Keep track of the interplay of breath and the sense and length of your lines.** Is your breath contributing to the sense? If not, determine why. Rework and vary the length of lines until you feel breaths and lines work together. Decide where to let breath lead and where to let sense lead. Sometimes, sense will "want" to complete a sentence, but breath "won't," and vice versa.
- **As in all open-form poetry, take special care with line endings.** Line endings generate much of the tension, much of the specialness that makes open-form verse *verse.* Slave over your line endings!

Treating the page as a field

Poets speak of the page as a *field*, a place in which each part of the poem starts to have a meaningful relation to each other part. The fun part is that you get to decide what these different relationships will mean. In the following sections, we cover three ways you can use the page as a field in your own open-form poetry.

Making the form of each line grouping meaningful

One way you can use the page as a field is to make the form of your stanza, and the movements of the lines in that form (left, right, up, down), meaningful in and of themselves. A good example of this kind of field-writing was invented by William Carlos Williams. He made up an open-form stanza that he called the *variable foot.* It plays by some interesting rules:

- **Each stanza contains three lines.**
- **Each line is indented from the previous one, moving left to right.**
- **Each indentation is *meaningful.*** It signals a shift in thought, building on what was just said or going in a new direction.
- **Each line is a *unit of sense.*** That is, each line represents a statement or an important part of a statement.
- **Each line has one *beat* (one major rhythmic stress, related to the unit of sense).**
- **Each third line propels the reader somehow into the next stanza.**

Here is the beginning of Williams's famous poem "The Descent":

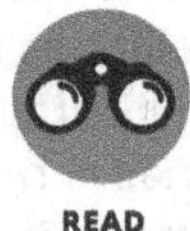
READ ALOUD

The descent beckons
as the ascent beckoned.
Memory is a kind
of accomplishment,
a sort of renewal
even
an initiation, since the spaces it opens are new places
inhabited by hordes
heretofore unrealized,
of new kinds —

Williams is saying some beautiful things here. As a reader, you don't know yet what he means by "ascent" and "descent," although they may mean something simple like "success" and "failure," or "happiness" and "sorrow."

Can you find a single, major rhythmic stress in each line? No matter how many other syllables the line may have, there's *one* syllable Williams feels is the *beat.* Each line is one unit of sense and gets one beat. So, the sixth line, *even,* gets one beat, and so does the much longer, prosy seventh line. Can you feel why? Perhaps out of sheer excitement, out of discovery. The speaker just called memory "a sort of renewal," which is easy enough to see — but then a new thought occurs — memory is *even* an initiation! Why? Maybe because memory opens new spaces for you, filled with "hordes" of new things you never knew. No memory is ever alike; as you change, memory changes and teaches you new things. So "even" deserves its beat, for sheer excitement, and the next line, which is what "even" introduces, is all one beat as well.

Visual rhythm is on display. Each third line propels you into the next stanza. The poem has both a left-to-right movement and a downward movement — a descent, as with a stairway. You can see how Williams planned his stanza out — not according to rhyme or meter, but according to the way he wanted his argument to move, *physically* as its meaning moves.

"The Descent" really makes clear how crucial variety is — in line lengths, rhythmic patterns, forward movement — in establishing and maintaining *poetic tension* (the innate excitement, the *crackle* of the poem, and the interplay of words, ideas, and images).

Managing relationships among words and syllables

A second approach to the page as a field, Olson writes, is to see it as "the place where all the syllables and all the lines must be managed in their relations to each other." All the words in a poem create a tension with one another, like the particles in an atom or the parts of a suspension bridge. The poet manages the relationships of the words and syllables, feels the tension, and orchestrates it.

Kathleen Fraser's "Vanishing Point: Third Black Quartet" is the tenth section of a beautiful poem titled "Wing." In "Vanishing Point," Fraser uses the page as a field in this way. You can almost feel the words vibrating in their tense interrelations:

X. VANISHING POINT: THIRD BLACK QUARTET

forward edge itself to be volume by necessity as if partial erase
edge itself to be volume by necessity as if partial erase other
itself to be volume by necessity as if partial erase corners
to be volume by necessity as if partial erase planes
be volume by necessity as if partial erase accumulate
volume by necessity as if partial erase depth
by necessity as if partial erase condensed
necessity as if partial erase in
as if partial erase preparation
if partial erase stagework
partial erase historic
erase tendons
of elaborate
pearly ribcage
lucent marked
decision midway
and with
little grains
tasks of
of light
pain talking
had softly
tried among
to disintegrating
lift cubes
to lift the
tried to lift falling
had tried to lift wing
pain had tried to lift will
of pain had tried to lift draw
tasks of pain had tried to lift the
little tasks of pain had tried to lift mind
and little tasks of pain had tried to lift as
decision and little tasks of pain had tried to lift a
lucent decision and little tasks of pain had tried to lift bow

itself the wing not static but frayed, layered, fettered, furling

Fraser, conscious of all the elements in this poem, created a shape that's brand-new. You can read this poem in many ways — there is literally no one "correct" order. You can start almost anywhere and get different strings of words (the exquisite "little tasks of pain" or "the falling wing will draw the mind as a bow"). The left edge appears to melt away as you read down ("as if partial erase"). You can read down from the upper right corner, or across spaces ("tendons/of/elaborate/pearly/ribcage"). You remember the title and think of the many physical "vanishing points" in the poem. And notice the shape of the white space in the center of the poem: It resembles a wing, which recalls that this is part of a work with the title "Wing."

Fraser thought it all through, created all the relations — without using a single complete sentence and only two commas! Surprising meanings erupt from the unexpected combinations of words — such is the energy she has created in this field.

REMEMBER

Fraser's poem shows you how very *formal* an open-form poem can be.

Treating white space as time (in both visual rhythm and meaning)

You may have seen poems that were groups of words scattered all over the page. One way to approach a reading of such a poem is to treat white space as time — by *pausing* before continuing to the next word you encounter. The larger the space between words, the longer the pause.

Try this principle with the following, the ninth poem in a series titled "29 Songs" by Objectivist poet Louis Zukofsky:

READ ALOUD

In Arizona
          (how many years in the mountains)
The small stumped bark of a tree
Looks up
          in the shape of an adored pup

The indians do not approach it
The round indian tents
                    remain where they are

The tanned whites
                    are never seen by it
And one can imagine its imploring eyes

You pause longer between the first and second lines than you would between the second and third lines, and even longer between the two stanzas. If you treat white space as time, you'll begin to sense a rhythm to the poem closely tied to the way the lines are laid out.

REMEMBER

Treating white space as time is one of the best methods of writing open-form poetry. Take special care with line endings: On which word will the line end? To what word will it lead? How much space or time must there be before the next word?

TIP

When writing your own open-form poetry, you can treat white space as time by doing the following:

- Vary the spatial relationships of the lines. The pauses should be a variety of lengths — all having to do with the sense and impact of the verse.
- Use enjambment to wrap the sentences around the ends of lines.
- Read your verse aloud constantly as it develops. Rearrange lines and line breaks if the reading doesn't feel right.
- Cut everything you don't absolutely need. Because pauses will be directing the reading, you may decide (as many poets do) that you don't really need punctuation (which usually directs your pauses). Let it go!

IN THIS CHAPTER

» Practicing your poetry

» Breaking logjams in your writing

» Thinking divergently, with a poet's mind

Chapter 15

Writing Exercises and Prompts for Poets

In this chapter, we give you writing exercises geared toward poets. They come from experienced teachers of creative writing — Charles Bernstein, Maxine Chernoff, Valerie Fox, Kelly Holt, Daniel J. Langton, Lynn Levin, Bernadette Mayer, Brighde Mullins, and Eileen Myles — who have designed these exercises for their students to help them:

- Get started and get their invention flowing.
- Practice writing.
- Rid themselves of habits and ruts.
- Start thinking with a poet's mind.

You don't need to try all these exercises. Simply read through, start anywhere, and try one that appeals to you.

Making Your Journal Your Office

You can write in a journal, as Walida Imarisha did here, to help improve your poetry. Here are some subjects to use as journal topics:

- Food
- Finances
- Writing ideas
- Love
- Beautiful and/or ugly things you've seen
- A daily history of your own writing life
- Reading/music/art you encounter each day
- Weather
- Descriptions of people you see
- Subway, bus, car, or other trips (for example, writing about the same bus trip you take every day)
- Pleasures and/or pains you've experienced
- Mail (sent, received, snail-mail, email, text messages, voicemail, imaginary mail, other people's mail)
- Telephone calls/answering machine messages
- The body
- Dangers

[Exercise contributed by Bernadette Mayer]

TIP

Dedicate a journal to one subject alone (for example, many poets keep *dream journals*, recording images and events in their dreams), or mix it up.

Trying a Journal Exercise

Here's a journal exercise to try. It's called the "Poetry Pentad." A *pentad* is a group of five things. This exercise applies our five major poetic principles — attentiveness, concentration (of language, insight, and emotion), originality, experimentation, and form — to seemingly mundane ideas. The pentad helps you generate material for poetry and think about what makes poetry poetic.

Here's how it works:

1. **Begin with a mundane, straightforward prose statement about the outside world.**

   You could write about a cut on your hand, a kiss, awkward silences, a cash machine that won't give you any money, the death of a loved one, the lyrics of a much-heard song you can't stand, a painful memory you avoid, a car crash, what it feels like to sit at the bottom of a pool and look up, people with nowhere to live, Leonardo Da Vinci's *Mona Lisa,* the last movie you saw . . . or a sunset. Write something as simple as, "Sure is a nice sunset."

2. **Now pay closer *attention* to the thing you just wrote about.**

   Write down what you notice. Brainstorm. List as many aspects as you can — for example, "The color of the sunset is red in some places and a flat grayish-blue in others. The sky nearer to the sun is bright and multicolored, but farther away some of it is already dark and colorless."

3. ***Concentrate* on your subject and come up with a few new ways of presenting or describing the thing your *original* statement was about.**

   Try using some metaphors, images, turns of phrase. Don't write down anything you've ever heard or read before, anything that seems familiar or secondhand. Example: "The sunset is like a bruise; it's like spilled stew on a rug; it's a molten core with a hard outer crust."

4. **Write at least two passages of poetry on this subject, *experimenting* with different *forms.***

   Choose very different forms. Here, we'll try two rhyming lines, and a passage of *open-form verse* ((the kind without a repeated rhyme scheme or set line length). Use material you generated under Step 3. For example, two rhyming lines about the sunset could be:

   > Blood-red, flat grey, the sunset colors fuse,
   > Spreading and growing dull green, like a bruise

   An open-form version might go this way:

   > The sunset spilled over the rug of the sky seeped into its fabric
   > A stain spread, a ravishing mess will leave a
   > mark no way
   >
   > I can cleanse it from my absorbent brain. It's running down
   > the corners,
   >
   > lava hardening, darkening, losing light. It's nighttime.

5. **Now rewrite one of the passages in as few words as you can.**

Go for maximum meaning and emotion. For example:

Sunset spilled on the rug, stained
What I think; can't wash it out. It's
    lava, hardening
to darkness.

We started with a pretty common subject — a sunset — and then really observed one. We brainstormed a list of interesting observations. Then we generated some widely divergent images (bruise, stew, lava) for what we saw. Then we tried a rhyming couplet and an open-form passage. We rewrote the second one, working for greater concentration.

Did we come up with Shakespeare? We didn't have to. "Sure is a pretty sunset" wasn't poetry, but in our final passage — with spills, stains, and hardening lava — we're much closer to something poetic.

TIP

Go through this process as often as you want for any one statement. If good ideas suddenly pop up, stop and work on them.

REMEMBER

The whole idea is to get used to some of the distinguishing characteristics of the poetic craft — and to generate methods you can use later in building poems. If you don't come up with anything useful in one round, don't worry — you will *always* throw more away than you use. Keep trying. See what you come up with.

Spotting and Breaking Habits

Poets need to be objective, to see their poems from outside of themselves. To find out more about what *you* do in your poems, make some analytical lists. Look for patterns and habits and think about ways to break out of them or vary them. Try sitting down with your poems and listing the following:

- **Colors that appear directly or in hints.** Compare this list to the colors you never use and look for patterns.
- **Body parts mentioned.** See if you put an emphasis on one part of the body (many poets focus on the face or the head).
- **Plants or flowers (which can be tied to the colors you use).** Again, look for patterns.

- **Animals.** Are the animals you discuss in your poems rare in your life (such as tigers) or common (such as dogs)? Are they usually alive or usually dead? Are there preferences you hadn't noticed before (insects over mammals, for instance)?

[Exercise contributed by Daniel J. Langton]

TIP

Underline every noun in your poems. Then underline every adjective. Is there a pattern in the nouns or adjectives you use? Many beginning poets have an adjective describing every noun. Is this the case in your poems? Does the last word of each line turn out to be a monosyllable? That's another common habit. Find ways to avoid or vary any pattern or habit that resembles a "rut" or has no poetic reason for existing.

Using Description

Select an object outside — a building, statue, street sign, or billboard, for example — that you pass frequently. Then describe it in the following different ways:

- Describe it in such a way that others hearing your brief account are able to draw it (an exact visual take).
- Describe it using point of view, first from far away, then from up close.
- Describe its relation to the landscape.
- Describe how it changes over time, with shifts in the weather, and at different times of day.

[Exercise contributed by Brighde Mullins]

TIP

You can also try looking in a mirror and describing what you see, without using the word *I* or any adjectives. Concentrate on nouns, verbs, and comparisons.

Unleashing Divergent Thinking

Poets find new words for new ideas and new attitudes toward their experiences — and that takes divergent thinking. Here are some exercises that encourage you to think in unaccustomed ways and create new material.

Mining descriptive texts to find your own way of writing

Reading aloud from a text full of rich description can be a great help to your own writing. The best texts for this purpose are often travel or nature writings. Take five to seven minutes to write down words, phrases, and sentences that really strike you. Steal freely. You're gathering material.

Now write a poem out of those words. Repeat, delete, or change as you please the order of the words you've harvested — but don't add anything that was not in your original list. Invent a title for the poem in your own words.

This exercise helps you see that your way of writing is exactly that — a *way* of your own. You don't even need a subject to write. When you have words, you can have your way with them. Your *way* is how you move through language and manipulate it — it's your signature. Understanding that can open a lot of doors.

[Exercise contributed by Eileen Myles]

Experimenting with different forms

Get out your trusty book of poetic forms (for example, *A Book of Forms* by Lewis Turco). Now write a poem in a different form each day for 30 days, following the order as they're covered in the book, moving from A to Z. Think of this exercise as your very own short course in poetic technique!

Starting with a prose essay

Choose a topic and write an essay in which you get your ideas about that topic as clear as possible. (This was Ben Jonson's favored method; see Chapter 1.) Keep the essay to one paragraph. Then turn that block of prose into a poem.

Rewriting well-known texts

Try selecting a well-known text, such as "The Pledge of Allegiance," and substituting each word in it with the word seven entries down in your dictionary. So the line

> I pledge allegiance to the flag

might become

> lamb Pleiades allegretto toady theater of war flagellate

REMEMBER

With exercises like these, which produce *chance poetry*, the idea is to get your invention flowing and create new resources. Nothing obliges you to use any of what you generate. But if something intrigues you, build on it, explore, see where it leads.

[Exercise contributed by Bernadette Mayer]

Pulling from a grab-bag of ideas

Here's a grab-bag of poem ideas to try. Write a poem:

- Made up entirely of the first or last lines of famous poems. (It's a *cento*! See Chapter 11.)
- Of 26 words, in which each word begins with a letter of the alphabet. (You can also scramble the order.)
- In which all the words in each line start with the same letter. This can be combined with the preceding idea.
- Consisting entirely of overheard conversation.
- That does not mention any objects.
- That contains everything you hear or that happens to you over the course of a limited amount of time (for example, 15 minutes, 1 hour, 1 day).
- Composed of everything on your text messages or voicemail over the past week.
- Composed entirely of excuses. Make the excuses relate to things you wouldn't make excuses for: "I'm sorry my nose is in the front of my head, but you see, I ____________."

[Exercise contributed by Charles Bernstein and Bernadette Mayer]

Using techniques of chance and collage

This exercise is called variously "Tzara's Hat" (named after the Dada poet Tristan Tzara, who invented it) or "Exquisite Corpse" (see Chapter 12). Cut words out of newspapers or magazines and throw them into a hat. Fish out the first 20 and arrange them — in the order in which you fished them out — into a poem. We tried this and got:

Health bullets vulnerable next covering for statistics
On hockey licensed victims' LaBella proportion stops
Cuba hits dead
Propelled family anything

Now write a response in the same number of lines, words, or syllables. One possibility is to *reverse* the words and phrases, either verbally or in some conceptual way:

Malaria wounds are invincible, the last opening; five myths
Off the unauthorized criminals of baseball. El Feo promotes lopsided
Florida, gets smacked by the inhibited corpses
Of vacuum orphans.

TIP

The point of collage exercises (like the preceding one) is to create combinations of words, phrases, and sentences that may generate new material for your poetry. Use some of what you generate, all of it, or none of it. Or, if something gives you an idea, start writing.

Mistranslating (on purpose)

Mistranslation is a technique pioneered by, among other groups, the Teacher's and Writer's Collective in New York. A similar exercise also appears in *The Oulipo Compendium*, edited by Harry Mathews.

Select a poem in a foreign language, one you can pronounce but not necessarily understand, and approximate the *sound* of the poem in English words (so, for example, the French word *blanc* becomes *blank* in English, and *toute* becomes *toot*). Here's an example of a poem to start with (Alfred De Vigny's "Les Destinées"):

Le moule de la vie étair creusé par nous.
Toutes les passions y répandaient leur lave,
Et les événements venaient s'y fondre tous.

You could use this poem to create a new one:

Lame-mule day. Larva eat air. Cruise, ape. Our new
Toot lay passion? Sí. Hear a panda on Lou. Laugh!
Hey! Lazy venom! Aunt Vinny, see fund rot, too.

Rewrite it to suit your own style.

Try picking a book at random and using its title as the key phrase for an *acrostic*, going letter-by-letter down the left edge of the page. For each letter in this key phrase, go to the corresponding page number in the book. (A = page 1, B = page 2, and so on), and copy the first line or sentence on that page as the first line of the poem. Continue through all the letters in the key, leaving stanza breaks to mark each new key word. Variations include

- » Using the author's name rather than the book title.
- » Using a friend's name — or your own.
- » Using a different book for each letter or word in the acrostic key.

[Exercise contributed by Charles Bernstein]

Thinking about transitions

Take 15 or 20 minutes to write about some transition time you've experienced today. That may include:

- » Your commute from work to school.
- » Getting from your house to the bus stop.
- » Driving.
- » Waiting in a train station.

Choose a particular moment in your chosen transit — it can be as short as the time it takes a traffic light to change. Reflect on it. Warp the speed at which it took place. Then elongate that moment into the length of a poem or paragraph.

[Exercise contributed by Kelly Holt]

Getting ideas by taking a walk

Take a walk and make a poem out of it. Walk 14 blocks and write a line for each block — a walking sonnet. Or write one poem per mile. Take notes and create a poem. Write down all the text you observe on a walk (street signs, shop names, billboards, advertisements on buses, and so on), and write a poem using *only* that material.

[Exercise contributed by Charles Bernstein and Bernadette Mayer]

Using language from one subject to write about another

Try using language from one subject area to write about another subject that is very much unrelated to it. For example, use language about roadmaking machinery to write about kissing, or the language of philosophy language to describe a shirt.

[Exercise contributed by Bernadette Mayer]

From *Poems for the Writing:* Three Prompts, Poems, and Processes

A *prompt* invites the poet to look for creative ideas in a particular direction or suggestion and generate a poem from it.

Poems for the Writing: Prompts for Poets by Valerie Fox and Lynn Levin (Norman, OK: Texture Press, 2019) is both (1) a delightful collection of prompts and (2) a pretty great anthology of poems that came out of them. *And* the poems are followed by short accounts by their writers of how they got from prompt to poem.

So, below we have three prompts, a poem in response to each, and the poet's account of the prompt-to-poem-process.

"The unanswerable letter"; Response by Karen Chase

Fox and Levin:

> Write a poem in the form of a letter to someone or something unable to reply. You might address the poem to a family member who has died, a pet, an abstract idea, a physical object. The unanswerable letter prompt could serve as theme, strategy, or both. This approach taps into the occasions of many varieties of poems. Emily Dickinson's "This is my letter to the World" (#441) is a familiar example:
>
> This is my letter to the World
> That never wrote to Me —
> The Simple News that Nature told —
> With tender Majesty

Her Message is committed
To Hands I cannot see —
For love of Her — Sweet — countrymen —
Judge tenderly — of Me

Consider using real letters or parts of real letters in your poems.

Response: "Federico Fellini's Birthday" by Karen Chase

Federico Fellini's Birthday

Today, Mom, you would have been 90 and I
Wonder what kind of old woman you
Would have become because when you died
You were young.

I never knew 'til now that
You and Fellini shared
A birthday. You'd both be surprised
How the world's changed. Dad's okay.

His wife, who is younger than me by far, is
Traveling soon to India and we, my husband
Whom you barely knew and I, will stay
With Dad while she's away.

You'd be amazed how small
The world has become. There's so much
To say — I have grandchildren — for one.

If you could see Ruby Leah,
Named after you, you'd
Die again, but this time
Of happiness.

KAREN CHASE TALKS ABOUT "FEDERICO FELLINI'S BIRTHDAY"

The first thing to tell you is I didn't write "Federico Fellini's Birthday" to a prompt — and yet the poem does what the prompt suggests, so it fits!

Basically, it was January 20, my mother's birthday, and I was thinking of her. I was reading the newspaper, and I read that it was also the birthday of Federico Fellini, the Italian director of so many good films. I had seen *La Dolce Vita*, one of his best-known movies, in college. It struck me as so strange that I'd never known such a major figure had the same birthday as my mother. It was intense.

There's a story behind that Fellini feeling. It happened one day when I was visiting the Frick Museum in Manhattan. I was young and sassy and studying Italian at Sarah Lawrence College. Remember I mentioned seeing *La Dolce Vita*? Well, I was in the Frick, I walk into a room, and only one other person was there. It was Marcello Mastroianni — this extraordinarily handsome man, the star of *La Dolce Vita*. I say, "Lei mi pare molto familiare" ["You look very familiar to me"]. And he pauses and then bellows, "Sono Marcello Mastro-*ian*ni!" It was him!

So, back to January 20: When I made that connection, it had a lot of power, and it made me write a poem. It all came as a piece, very much as a letter to my dead mother: "Both Fellini and you have been gone a long time, and the world has changed, and now your granddaughter, Ruby, is here."

"Bibliomancy"; Response by Luray Gross

Fox and Levin:

> Bibliomancy was a kind of divination based on the consultation of books, especially the Bible, or Homer's works. The practice involved locating passages for consultation.
>
> This prompt asks you to draw on quotations from books to help you create a poem. Anything goes, but works that compile aphorisms, lore, and famous quotations are good places to start. Even if your selection is based seemingly on chance, perhaps on some books you have scattered around your study, your mind will work both analytically and intuitively to connect passages, words, ideas.
>
> Here's a way to start. Make a list of quotations that you find engaging or memorable. Use the quotations as the spine or basis for your poem.

Response: "*Dolce Far Niente*," by Luray Gross*

Dolce Far Niente

Among my prayers, a long day
of sweet doing-nothing
with my heart skilled
in the works of both languages —
that of touch
and that of silence,
submitting nothing
to the tribe I left behind.

A day when weather
is my only literary speciality
and nothing discourages, not even
the pecking of a neighbor's chickens
spearing bugs among the weeds
in the kingdom of their portable yard.

It will be morning as long as I prefer
and afternoon far beyond the slanted light.
How sweet it will be to let the mind unbend,
easy as stretching out a coil of shoelace licorice,
simple as smoothing a hem
before taking up needle and thread.

The heart cannot be educated by itself,
I heard a wise man say.
Perhaps he was correct,
but I want to take my little soul
into a place never known for instruction
where wine tastes as pure as water
and poems please and last.

* The title is an Italian idiom that means "the sweetness of doing nothing."

LURAY GROSS TALKS ABOUT *"DOLCE FAR NIENTE"*

I was attracted to this prompt because it seemed like a treasure hunt. I got my *Bartlett's Quotations* and startled browsing through it, and I wrote down 23 quotations. I wrote the page numbers down but purposely did not add the authors because I didn't want them to affect me.

It was a really successful prompt because it got me started. Once I found the quotations and started the poem, I ignored the further instructions, mainly because it was just so interesting to write, now that I had the material. I just let myself use the bits that fit. The idea is to find the gems.

(That's a great way of using a prompt. You can use parts of it, as I did here. You also can ignore it completely, if it irritates you or you don't care for it. And if you're working on a prompt and something *else* wants to be written, you write *that*!)

One quote that got the whole process rolling was Mark Twain's "Weather is a literary speciality," which gave me that *dolce far niente* feeling: the "sweetness of doing nothing," and that surfaced in the second stanza (not the beginning, as you might have thought) as "A day when weather/is my only literary speciality/and nothing discourages." That feeling was strong from the beginning, and it helped the poem hold together.

Unlike many of my poems, this was an easy poem to write. Normally, I write my first drafts as freely as I can, and only later start to give some shape to them. By draft 2, though, this poem already had the first four stanzas in the same order. All I needed to do was to get rid of unnecessary words and tighten for rhythm.

Here are some of the quotes and authors. You'll see what parts I used:

- "This used to be among my prayers — a piece of land not so very large, which would contain a garden, and near the house a spring of ever-flowing water, and beyond these a bit of forest." — Horace, Satires 2
- "No poems will please for long or live that are written by water-drinkers." — Horace, Epistles 1.19
- "The touchy tribe of poets." — Horace, Epistles 2.2
- "I don't know which is more discouraging, literature or chickens" is E.B. White — and only the chickens survived!

"Fibonacci Poem": Response by Don Riggs

Fox and Levin:

> Write a poem based on the Fibonacci sequence: 0, 1, 1, 2, 3, 5, 8, 13, 21, 34, 55, 89, 144 (and so on). The sequence is formed by adding the last two terms to create each subsequent term: 0+1=1, 1+1=2, 1+2=3, 2+3=5, etc.
>
> The Fibonacci sequence, named after the most important European mathematician of the Middle Ages, Leonardo of Pisa, also known as Leonardo Fibonacci, has been called nature's numbering system. Fibonacci studied books by Indian mathematicians who were already discussing the pattern that later came to be known as the Fibonacci sequence. Fibonacci was trying, or so the story goes, to solve a problem about rabbits after a number of generations.
>
> Basing a poem on the Fibonacci sequence may lead to unexpected insights . . . . The beauty and symmetry of the series . . . may lead to beauty and symmetry in your poem.
>
> A whole group might write or, at least, begin a collaborative Fibonacci poem. One person might write the first line, another the second line that pays off from the first, and so on. Poets with an affinity for this prompt (or on counting or numbers) will find ingenious ways to craft the Fibonacci poem.

Response: "That's the Way It Goes," by Don Riggs

That's the Way It Goes

Each new year is a smaller fraction of your life.

— Mr. Gallagher, high school math teacher

First we have no age at all. Then we're one.
In another year we turn two, then three,
as our stumbling gets a bit steadier.
Suddenly, we are five, an entire hand
that we look at in wonder. Let's skip
the first few grades, because when we are eight
we have begun to discover novels
on library shelves, and not long after
we're teens. Then old enough to drink, which we
do on that first opportunity. The
hangover lasts until we're 34,
which is not quite some time for midlife crises,
though some manage. 55 is one's prime
but, we know then we'll soon be 89.

DON RIGGS TALKS ABOUT "THAT'S THE WAY IT GOES"

I'd heard of the Fibonacci series before, and when I saw "The Fibonacci Poem" prompt, I was struck by the memory of my high-school math teacher, Mr. Gallagher, who once said what you read in the epigraph: "Each year is a smaller fraction of your life."

So, I thought, "Why not apply that notion to a human life cycle?" As "we" get older, the poem stops in and looks at "us" at ages corresponding to numbers that come up in the Fibonacci sequence.

So it is, sort-of, a very abbreviated, slightly fictionalized autobiography. That business about "when we are eight/ we have begun to discover novels/on library shelves," that happened to me, only I was eleven, when I discovered J.R.R. Tolkien's *The Hobbit* at a local library. The cover was a woodcut of a lonely mountain, and the subtitle was *There and Back Again*. I was really taken by it. I checked it out, and that changed my life, it really did.

And as for "old enough to drink," I must confess that I actually had tasted alcohol before 21, but that age remains a kind of milestone, and it is true that by 34 I was no longer immersed in drinking culture. As for "midlife crises" — I've had enough of those to fill up several chapters of a book!

In the Fibonacci series, the gaps between numbers increase, so I came to the number 55 and remembered a 1953 English movie, *The Captain's Paradise*, starring Alec Guinness. There's some business there about your 50s being "the prime of life," which is not something I've ever heard someone say.

I enjoyed writing the poem a great deal. It was a challenge! I enjoyed reading other poets' responses, each taking the prompt in a different way. For me, it all started with Mr. Gallagher!

Revising Your Poetry

As we've been saying, revision is one of the most important aspects of creation. Getting some practice with it — and seeing revision from several possibly unexpected angles — is a good idea.

Hiding half of your poem from sight

Take one of your poems and fold it in half horizontally, so you can see the top half of the poem but not the bottom half. Rewrite the half you *can't* see — without

looking at the original. Compare the original to your revision. Which one is shorter, more compressed? If the new half is better, keep it. You can also pick and choose between the virtues of the two versions. As a variation, fold the poem *vertically*, and rewrite the left or right half.

[Exercise contributed by Maxine Chernoff]

Reworking poems you don't like

Select one of your poems that you're dissatisfied with. Read it through. Now put it away. Try to write the same poem again without referring to the older version. You often get a new and better poem this way.

[Exercise contributed by Maxine Chernoff]

If you've written a poem but you don't know what how to revise or improve it, take your first or second draft and put it into different poetic forms:

- Turn it into a block of prose.
- If you've used short lines, reformat them into longer lines.
- If you've used long lines, reformat them into shorter lines.
- Reformat the piece into stanzas of two lines or three lines.
- Rewrite the poem in an extremely constricting form, such as a sonnet.

The point of this exercise is to look at the poem in another way. How does each reformation change the poem? What does it add or take away? Which of the forms works best, and why? What new ideas do you get from seeing the poem anew?

[Exercise contributed by Kelly Holt]

Collaborating with Other Writers

Do some collaborative writing (see Chapter 11) with a group of other writers. (These exercises also make good party games when poets get together.) Here are some examples:

- Keep a public journal, posted on either a common online message board or a paper pinned up in a common room. Everyone can write his or her own contributions daily. As a variation, each contributor makes an entry but leaves it somehow incomplete (writing only half a phrase, leaving a word out, or asking a question). The next contributor must finish the incomplete entry and write a new incomplete entry. Or two writers can alternate days to write in the journal.

- Have 14 poets each write one line of iambic pentameter (without consulting one another). Collect the lines, throw them into a hat, and select the lines at random. Voilà! A collaborative sonnet. Try different arrangements of the lines.
- Write a verse novel together. Make up an incomplete story with three characters with names and descriptions, plus a situation, such as a kidnapping or some other mystery — but don't establish complications or resolutions. Now, each writer writes a "chapter" of no more than 30 lines, employing all the characters, in whatever form she wishes. Collect and order the chapters, read the novel, then have each person write a "final chapter" of 30 lines. Collect, read, select, and combine.
- Have everyone write on the same topic and then choose bits from everyone's poetry and combine them into one big poem.
- Have one poet write a poem, printing it out with extra space between each line. The other poets now write lines in the blank spaces.
- Have one poet write a poem. Then the other poets reverse the poem (writing the opposite of the words and statements found in the poem) or rephrase the poem using different or outlandish language (get out that thesaurus!).
- Have one person write an incomplete poem, leaving holes that other writers must fill in. As a variation, have someone select a poem and write it out — leaving out three or four words per line. Indicate the part of speech of each missing word. The other poets in the group have to come up with words to fill the blanks. Read the new version aloud.
- Have one poet bring in material from dreams and the others write poems in response.
- Take a long walk with a group of other poets. Everyone takes notes and makes the notes into poems. Mix and match, toss into "Tzara's Hat" (see Chapter 12), or play other collaborative games.

[Exercises contributed by Charles Bernstein and Bernadette Mayer]

These exercises are a tour of the many aspects of the poet's art. Moving through them will challenge various aspects of your talent, and perhaps help you identify your strengths and areas where you can improve. They're also enjoyable in and of themselves — writing poetry is one way you *can* mix work and pleasure.

IN THIS CHAPTER

» Starting a reading or writing group

» Performing at readings, open mics, or poetry slams

» Promoting your poetry in the Digital Age

» Identifying resources and community

Chapter 16 Going Public

Eventually, you may decide you're ready to take your poetry out into the world. That's an exciting decision — it can bring great changes for you and your poetry. If you do it with the right attitude, you're bound to see the poetry you read and write from a new perspective — that of your readers — which is something every poet needs to do.

In this chapter, we consider two ways to join a community of readers and writers: starting a poetry group and reading in public.

Starting a Reading or Writing Group

No one has counted, but there are possibly thousands of poetry groups in existence. From the U.S. 1 group in Northern New Jersey, to technical editors who meet on Wednesdays for poetry and pizza nights, to the lovers of Indian poetry who meet in a garage each month in a small town in Illinois, to teenagers who gather to rapping skills, poetry is everywhere.

Getting started

If you want to start a group that reads or writes poetry together, you have a few things to decide:

- **How big a group do you want?** Try a group of three to five. Some reading groups are larger, but anything larger than ten can require a lot of work. Plus, the more people, the less airtime each has.
- **How often do you want to meet?** Try meeting monthly. A once-a-month meeting gives members something to look forward to, is easier to schedule, and allows folks to get their reading done. But you can find weekly groups, as well as groups who meet once a season.
- **Where do you want to meet?** Some poetry circles meet at the same place every time; some rotate among the homes of the various members; some meet at bars, coffee shops, or bookstores that agree to host them.
- **How ambitious do you want your group to be?** In her book *How to Read a Poem . . . and Start a Poetry Circle,* Molly Peacock warns against trying to do too much. The main thing is to keep the circle from being a burden on anyone, especially yourself.
- **How do you plan to get people to join?** Chances are, you already know the folks you'd like to invite. So, invite them! And you can always advertise at your local bookstore, coffee shop, community arts center, or college or university. Consider posting on X, Instagram, TikTok, Bluesky, and similar platforms. You can also post on local online arts calendars, community or neighborhood apps like Nextdoor or GroupMe, local Facebook literary or reading groups, or even . . . what a concept . . . your local newspaper, especially arts-and-entertainment weeklies. Your local library's online site may list local literary or poetry events — if not, why not create one?

Discovering ways to spend your meetings

The nice thing about poetry circles is that they don't have to have a particular agenda — the idea is to meet to discuss poetry. Many meetings may end with a discussion of "Who should we read next?" and people will have different suggestions and agree on the next poet.

Poetry circles should be friendly, humane gatherings. So what if you cover only two poems? Or one? Or one phrase? You're doing what you like to do, which is its own reward. Relax and enjoy it.

TIP

Plan activities. Poetry need not be a passive, wholly sedentary affair. If you're looking for ways to spend your meetings, try one of the following:

- **Watch one of the Favorite Poems series, curated by Robert Pinsky, on YouTube** (`https://youtube.com/user/FavoritePoem`). This would make a great opener for any meeting. Somebody can be designated to find a poem they admire and be ready to play it when the meeting convenes.
- **Listen or watch together.** Never has the world offered so much poetry-related media. That includes
  - **Movies** such as *Stevie, Il Postino* (*The Postman*), *Barfly, Dead Poets' Society, Shakespeare in Love, Paterson, Kill Your Darlings, A Quiet Passion, Sylvia, Neruda, Set Fire to the Stars,* or *Poetry Nation.*
  - **TV or online shows** such as *Poetry in America* on PBS, which posts episodes on YouTube as well. YouTube is bulging with great poetry video. Search almost any well-known poet's name and you'll find readings, interviews, and more. Colleges and universities sometimes post poetry-related video. Possibly the greatest single trove is at the Poetry Center at San Francisco State University.
  - **Podcasts** are great fun for group listening. You can click Stop at any time to discuss/argue/titter! Many online poetry orgs list poetry podcasts. Really good poetry podcasts include *Poetry Off the Shelf,* from the Poetry Foundation; *The Poetry Magazine Podcast*; *Poetry Unbound*; *The Slowdown*; the podcast by The Poetry Society in the U.K.; *Interesting People Reading Poetry,* which really is that.
- **Attend a poetry reading together.** Dinner and a reading — sounds good!
- **Invite a local poet or writing teacher to give a workshop or read.**
- **Do some collaborative writing.** See Chapter 15 for some suggestions for ways to create poetry together in a group.
- **Create an online site on which members can post poems or write poems, singly or collaboratively.**
- **Give a group reading at either your normal meeting place or a local venue (such as a bookstore or coffee shop).**

Reading Your Poetry in Public

Performance poetry is a vigorous part of the worldwide entertainment culture. No, it's not as big as sports, Netflix, or popular music, but most major cities in the world have venues at which poets read their work in public. Many are the countries in which you can list *itinerant poet* as your occupation. In Iran, poets wander from place to place, reciting epic poetry about the exploits of, among other heroes, Alexander the Great. In India and Africa, the tradition of oral poetry is still strong as well. So, if you're considering reading your verse in public, you're in good company.

We consider three types of reading in the following sections. Each is a world unto itself, with it an etiquette and a style all its own. None should be embarked on without a little preparation.

Readings for everybody

The phrase *poetry reading* can mean almost anything. What it *usually* means is that a limited number of poets — common numbers are one, two, or three — get up and read, usually one at a time. Each poet usually reads 2 to 4 poems for around 15 to 20 minutes. The entire reading typically lasts about an hour. Then the reading breaks up and becomes an onsite party or adjourns to a local coffee shop or bar to talk poetry.

TIP

But readings can take other forms as well. They involve a certain amount of spontaneity. We've attended affairs billed as readings that involved up to 20 poets and lasted for hours and hours.

TIP

So how do you go about getting to participate in a reading? One way is to publish some poetry and get asked to read. Colleges, universities, and bookstores routinely invite prominent poets to read. Bookstores often feature readings by poets with brand-new books.

You can also set up a reading for yourself. We cover a few ways to do that in the following sections.

Holding a reading at your house

Having a reading in your home is a great way to start out, before diving into the unfamiliar terrain of a more public place (see Figure 16-1). The only disadvantage to holding a reading in your house is that your audience is made up of your friends, which means that they may be *too* nice about your poetry.

You can arrange this kind of reading as you'd arrange any party, with invitations and light refreshments. We have attended many readings in folks' living rooms and garages, and even a few in their kitchens.

FIGURE 16-1: What if they gave a birthday party and a poetry reading broke out? That very thing took place right here, even before the cake came.

Photo © John Timpane

REMEMBER

Even if your friends are not the poetry type (whatever that means), they're your friends; parties are an excuse for them to enjoy themselves. Imagine their pleasure when they discover they actually *like* hearing poetry. Also, after everyone has heard 45 to 60 minutes' worth of verse, they all have an experience in common that may furnish some great post-reading chat.

TIP

Don't be the only poet. Invite a couple other poets to read, each for 15 to 20 minutes (and adhere to this limit).

A WORD ON HOW TO READ YOUR VERSE

Poetry is meant to be read aloud. All the rules of good public speaking — don't rush; use a positive conversational tone; project — hold true when reading poetry.

You want to come across as an interesting person who writes interesting poetry. Don't whisper or appear cold and disdainful. And don't (unless you're at a slam) shout and gesticulate with wacky histrionics. (We've seen all three types, believe us.)

Practice by reading to a friend or a small group first. Then consider reading before a larger audience. When you do, *bring along an entourage!* Why do this alone? Bring friends, family, fans for moral support.

Videotape or record yourself and watch the recording. Many people find this difficult, but that's what's good about it. The videotape shows you how you sound and look as you read. Don't like what you see? Work on it!

(continued)

(continued)

Most poets — even some experienced poets — could use some work as readers. They forget that poetry isn't just print, that a certain element of *performance* is involved when they read. So, after you've selected the poems you're going to read, consider these things:

- **The volume, tone, and dynamics of your voice.** Poetry is one of the least monotonous things human beings do. Why read it in a monotone?
- **Your posture.** Don't slouch, and don't stand bolt-upright. Find a comfortable way to hold yourself.
- **The mood of your poems and how you will get that mood across.** If a poem is happy, don't make the audience sad. If it's intense, don't make the audience bored.
- **The difficult moments in your poems.** How will you bring these moments across to the audience? (Often, slowing down a little helps.)
- **How your poems come across as a group.** Are they all the same in length, subject, and tone? If so, mix them up.
- **Backstories.** If there's an interesting (and brief!) story you can tell about a poem — a personal experience, what gave you the idea, something topical, unusual, or funny — by all means tell it. It humanizes you and your work and helps connect with the audience. (*Note:* Not every poem, of course. And if such stories seem corny, forced, or inappropriate, don't!)
- **Your first and last poems.** An audience needs a few minutes to begin to follow your reading well. Warm them up with a shorter poem or two, or inject some humor or an anecdote into your opening remarks. Maintain a rhythm that keeps the audience's attention throughout, and end with a high point of concentration, mood, or significance.

There are many permutations to this kind of reading. Some (or all) of these may work for you:

- Ask friends to read your poetry for you.
- Invite them to bring their own poetry or their favorite poems to read.
- Create an open mic at home.

Reading at your local coffee shop or bookstore

Coffee shops and bookstores like it if you can bring people in who will buy coffee and books. So, get chummy with the owners of the coffee shop or bookstore. Do a little research: Have they done readings before? One day, after the purchase of a year's worth of lattes or poetry books, broach the subject. If you set up a reading, do the public relations. The coffee shop or bookstore *may* do a certain amount online and in print, but yours is the main responsibility to get the word out and get folks to come. If you draw a good crowd, it'll be that much easier to get a second reading.

Giving a reading at your local community arts center

Some centers have community readings. Subscribe to their brochures and watch for announcements. If your center doesn't do readings, suggest it or volunteer to organize one. (See Figure 16-2.)

FIGURE 16-2: Poets line up after a *Schuylkill Valley Journal* poetry reading, December 2023 at the Manayunk Arts Center, Manayunk, Pennsylvania.

Photo: © Maria-Christina Keller

Volunteering at your local arts festival

Arts festivals often feature poetry readings, open mics, or authors' tables where poets can introduce themselves and their work. If a festival is coming up, check out the schedule and see whether you can join a scheduled reading — or really amaze them and organize an open mic, reading, or slam.

Open mics

Open mics are just that: a chance for anyone to come up to the mic and read. Some open mics have admissions fees; others are free. At many open mics, there's a time-honored pass-the-hat at intervals.

If you're at an open mic and they pass the hat, *please contribute.* It's probably how the event keeps going.

Finding an open mic that's right for you

You find open mics at places such as coffee shops, bars, bookstores, colleges and universities, and community arts centers. Consult the entertainment section of your local newspaper or your community website. Some local radio stations (especially public radio and college stations) also have community events announcements that may include open mics in your area. Some places have sign-up sheets for their open mics. Some want you to sign up a few days in advance. For others, you can just walk in and sign up on the day of the event. Know the ground rules before you go.

Getting ready to read at an open mic

Visit your chosen venue before your performance — preferably at another open mic — to get a sense of the place and the poets who read there. Certain venues have their own atmosphere, and attendees may act a certain way. Knowing such things before taking the mic for the first time is a good idea.

Introduce yourself to the person(s) running the open mic. They may be connected with the sponsoring venue or may simply go around putting on open mics at different places. Either way, say hello and make friends.

Don't worry too much about the poets who read just before and after you. Audiences *do* compare readers; it comes with the territory. What you're here to do is perform and learn.

Surviving your first reading

When reading at an open mic, consider your audience. There may be five people in the place or a hundred. Either way, you have a couple of things going for you:

- They're here, and you can show them a good time.
- A good number of them like poetry and enjoy hearing it.
- Most people like performers.

Nervous? Good. For most people, nervousness goes away once they get started. If you're *really* nervous, however, concentrate on your job: to give a good reading. That means connecting with your audience. Concentrate on *being in the poem*, keeping a steady pace and making the poem accessible to the audience. Pay attention to your poetry. With experience, you'll find that at a certain point you forget you're up there. You're *into* the material, delivering it, feeling its rhythms and emotions — it's a peak experience.

TIP

For your first open mic, start small, with a poem that takes just two or three minutes to read. Come prepared; practice ahead of time. Select a poem that may touch your audience, something interesting. Avoid extremely personal poetry ("How I Broke Up with My Girlfriend," "Why I Never Have Any Money") unless you're feeling strong — you don't want to seem self-indulgent. When nerves come, welcome them and keep steady.

REMEMBER

The number-one killer of poetry readings is rushing. The number-two killer is not knowing when to stop. Go up to the mic with a cell phone or large-faced watch so that you can keep track of the time.

Read your poem, say, "Thank you," and leave the stage. We've seen some open mics at which poets read for up to half an hour, which is obnoxious and could well get you uninvited for future open mics.

Be ready for anything in terms of the audience's reaction — absolutely anything. They may do nothing at all. Or they may go crazy over your reading of the word *the*. This may be the kind of place at which it's cool to boo, or uncool to show *any* reaction, or where you're expected to offer vegetables if you like a poem. Try to learn from whatever happens. If someone approaches you after your reading and wants to talk about your work, talk. Never disparage other poets' work; instead, engage them in talk about the craft. (How did they put their poems together? What parts were especially challenging to write?)

TIP

Stick around. Don't come in, read, and bolt. If you leave right after you read, people may think you don't care about the other readers. Besides, you can learn a great deal from watching and listening to other poets read. If someone reads something you really like, find them and tell them (we say more on this in the upcoming sidebar, "How to talk to poets and editors."). It's a good way to meet other poets.

Poetry slams

Now we're into the roughest kind of public readings: poetry slams (see Figure 16-3). *Slams* are, most commonly, competitive readings at which audience reaction, or the reaction of a panel of judges, decides who "wins." You may win nothing, a free drink, or a cash prize. Poetry slams are a lot of fun to attend, and participating in them can be entertaining and useful. But it's not a world for the faint of heart.

TIP

You can find slams in all the ways — and places — you can find readings and open mics. They take place in the same kinds of places as well. Poetry slams, just like readings and open mics, have ground rules, and you need to know them. Some require a mere sign-up; others require that you submit your poetry for consideration or read in an audition beforehand. Often, there is a time limit for readings — 3 minutes and 20 seconds is a popular limit. Know the limit and prepare accordingly.

FIGURE 16-3: Performer and crowd at the 2025 Teen Poetry Slam Semi Finals, Koret Auditorium, San Francisco Public Library, March 21, 2025.

Image courtesy of YouthSpeaks.

A certain kind of poet, and a certain kind of poetry, goes over well at slams. Self-indulgence is expected. Performers will do just about anything in a poem (or a performance!) to win the audience.

What should you read at a slam? Winning poetry very often has:

- **Striking, often outrageous or violent stories (suicide, drugs, crime, childhood abuse, discrimination, poverty, sex, and mental illness) with interesting characters.**
- **A strong, assertive first-person narrator (an *I*).**
- **Immediately striking language — often ribald, vulgar, hip, or slangy.**
- **Lots of jokes and other humor.**
- **Constant allusions to contemporary popular culture (celebrity culture, TV, music), social history, politics, and poetry.**
- **An ending that leaves the audience with a concluding shock or joke.**

Slams are slams. If you're going to do them, you have to:

- **Like the rough-and-tumble of it, the theater, the crazy.**
- **Embrace the need to be a real actor, a ham if necessary.**
- **Grow the triple-thick, titanium-coated rhinoceros skin you're going to need if response to your work is less than, shall we say, wonderful.**
- **Learn to be a good sport, congratulate your conquerors, and be gracious and full of good humor if an audience or panel lets you have it. If you win, be just as gracious.**
- **Promise yourself you won't go to only one slam: experience is everything, especially in this world halfway between fine arts and World Wrestling Entertainment.**

Keep reading your poetry in public. Each chance to perform will teach you about yourself and your poetry. Many are the times that we've discovered — in mid-reading! — a flaw or problem we needed to fix. But that sort of discovery makes a reading worthwhile.

In our Cheat Sheet, we direct you to a wild, four-part online documentary about a 2000 coast-to-coast poetry slam, with poet-laden buses crisscrossing the land. It's one of those stories that gets better each time you think about it.

The human connection is what's most important when it comes to poetry readings. Folks get to hear your poetry. What could be better than that? What more direct way of sharing your poetry could there be than delivering your own words your own way? What's more, readings can be your introduction to a community of poets you may want to join. By organizing poetry circles or reading groups of your own, you can create your own community. However you go, keep your focus on poetry and on its power to touch people.

Participating in Your Local Poetry Community: Good Old Analog!

So, digital is great, very great, but, as we've been saying, poetry is a human, sociable world. Sure, you can stream, and that's fine, but it really pays to, well, *go*, be there in body as well as in signal. Want to talk to editors and publishers? Go to events where they are. Want to hear and talk to poets? Go where poets go (see Figure 16-4):

- Attend slams and open mics.
- Take courses or attend workshops.
- Go to your favorite poets' readings — and tell your friends about them.
- Become a member of a local or national poetry organization such as the American Academy of Poets or the Poetry Society of America, and enjoy their very active websites.
- Buy books of your favorite poets' work.
- Volunteer at poetry readings or festivals.
- Subscribe to poetry magazines or journals.

All of these are good ways to sharpen and widen your listening skills, your knowledge of what's happening, and your circle of friends, acquaintances, and fellow poets.

FIGURE 16-4: At Farley's Bookshop in New Hope, Pennsylvania, poets and publishers gathered for a January 21, 2024, reading at which they networked, talked shop, got snacks and beverages, and shopped for poetry books.

Photo: © Maria-Christina Keller

No one *has* to be social, of course — it's totally your call. But if you decide to attend a poetry gathering, consider talking to a poet or editor as folks mill around after the reading. Some considerations:

- **Poets are — at least this is the report we're getting — people.** Like most people, they like being treated well, as people, with interest in their work, but not fawning or exaggerated anything.
- **Practice all the common niceties of conversation.** These are just things you'd do with anyone.
- **Be pleasant and respectful.** Poetry is a beautiful thing, and it's nice when people gather with poetry in common.
- **Don't go in totally cold; have at least a little to say.** A thanks, or a question arising from their reading just now, or poetry of theirs you have read . . . congratulations on the poet's recent book or prize.
- **Set your internal social timer to a couple of minutes max.** Do not monopolize or linger. Network; don't hover or stalk.
- **Let the person talk.** If he or she is inclined to discuss, great! Listen, respond, use all applicable conversational skills.
- **Go easy on personal questions.** Sure, if it is common knowledge or arises from the subject matter of the poetry, a question about the poet's life is fine: "You were the only woman on a tuna boat? How did you survive?" "So many of your poems are about San Francisco. You lived there, right? I lived in the Castro for years."
- **If you see them again at another event, make sure to say hello.** Recall to them the last time you met. Ask them what they're working on. Be pleasant, not pushy.
- **If you liked someone's work, make it a point to tell them — and be ready with a specific instance to discuss.** This lets poets know they have connected. After having said, "I really liked the one about the Airedale," tell the poet a specific thing that reached you: "that ending, where the Airedale builds a Cessna Skyhawk and flies away — it was so heartbreaking and so funny." If you have a brief story connecting with the poems — "I grew up on Washington Island, so I've been to that old mill in your poem" — tell it.
- **If you have questions of process or craft, ask them.** "I had never heard of the 'Girdle' form in Arabic poetry. Where did you learn about it? And how did you approach writing one?"

» **Talk to publishers and editors too.** They are important people in the poetry world, interesting folks, and they like to talk about their work. Ask about their publishing house, what new titles are coming out soon, what writers they are excited about. Many editors have told us they wish they had more contact with writers!

Being an Entrepreneurial Poet

Our theme has been that the Digital Age has gathered and reorganized a great deal of disparate information and made it easy to find. That's true everywhere — but it has *revolutionized* the poetry world. Used to be, once you'd finished a poem, it was hard to find out where to submit it. Even if you published it, it was hard to let people know that had even *happened.* If you were planning a reading, it took a lot of phone calls and underbrush-beating to assemble enough of an audience to make it worthwhile. And once your reading was done? Gone, bye, see you. No one could ever look it up, enjoy your reading, compare it to others, or learn from it.

Now so, so, so much information is organized and accessible. Many poetry events now live for almost-ever on various video or audio platforms. Digital has made it a different world.

In that world, poets can now do the sweet work of making sure folks know what they're up to, where they're going, what's happening with their poems, and what events they are arranging or attending. Poets have become entrepreneurial.

In the following pages, we discuss the poet as entrepreneur.

REMEMBER

This approach is not for everyone. If you find it uncomfortable, too businesslike, mercenary, self-congratulatory, narcissistic, or *just too much work* — fine. Nobody has to do it. There are plenty of wonderful, honorable ways to be a poet, and we celebrate them all. The way we're describing, however, is by now very well-established, and is welcome throughout the world of poetry.

Eyeballs and ears

Entrepreneurs are people who run and promote their own businesses. They are self-starters. It may sound strange to speak of poetry as a "business," because, let's face it, almost no one gets rich directly from poetry. But poetry is a business in this sense: it is a marketplace, an economy of exchange, where artists present their creations and experience those of other artists. Think of the currency in this marketplace as poems and personal experience.

Since they live in the Digital Age, entrepreneurial poets are familiar with social media and are surrounded by other entrepreneurs announcing what they're doing, where they're going, when you can see them next. They let you know big achievements when they happen, and they thank the people to whom they are indebted and grateful.

Many find entrepreneurial poets *irritating*. We totally get that. Self-promotion can seem tawdry. Again: you don't have to do this. It makes sense, however, to *know* how and why it's happening.

So what, exactly, is the poet's "business?" One poet told us this: "A poet's job is to get eyeballs and ears, to attract as many readers and listeners as they can." Those words might make you reflect (because it is very true) that this is what poets have *always* done. The traveling bards of the Greek-speaking world made a living reciting the tales of Odysseus, Achilles, and Helen. Chinese poets like Li Bai and Japanese masters like Bashō traveled the land, reciting, mentoring, giving the equivalent of master classes. And if you want a world-beating poet who was also a successful businessman, go right to the top, with theater-company shareholder William Shakespeare. If it's good enough for Shakespeare — hey, if it's good enough for Taylor Swift — it's good enough for poets in the 2020s. You could argue that, as of the 21st century, the aim is the same and only the means have changed.

So, let's see the shape the poetry life can take as of the early 2000s.

Posting social media updates

One of our beloved-est poet friends is Ernest Hilbert. Here are two stanzas of his, from "We Make Mountains so We May Move Them":

> My wife dangles our baby till he squeals,
> Both nearly strangled with laughter,
> And I take off my glasses to watch them.
> He wants to fly and never be put down.
>
> We will one day be stars above a storm,
> As we were once diamonds in the ocean,
> Tiny, tough parts of the world that flicker
> And ascend and give up all our light.

This guy Hilbert is good, right? He's also a busy entrepreneurial poet. He has a great way of keeping friends and fans up to date on what's going on in the poetry world, and what's going on with his own lovely verse.

A.E. Stallings, one of the best poets ever, an old friend of Hilbert's, and also the Professor of Poetry at the University of Oxford, was coming to Philadelphia. Hilbert got busy, organizing a poetry reading at wonderful Head House Books in town and inviting two more great poets, Luke Stromberg and Nathaniel Friedman. Hilbert then asked artist Patrick McCuen to design a poster Hilbert could rocket through the digital cosmos and maybe pin to some telephone poles. McCuen did a lovely job (see Figure 16-5).

FIGURE 16-5: A great poster for "An Evening of Poetry in Philadelphia."

Reproduced with permission of artist Patrick McCuen and of Richard De Wyngaert, proprietor of Head House Books.

As for his own poetry, Hilbert is an old hand at digital newscasting (see Figure 16-6). See what's great? Hilbert tells his audience the titles of the poems and where to read them: "Click through to read!" He also thanks the journals and editors involved. (*Thank everyone*. Even Sir Paul McCartney, after a record-breaking 2010 South America concert tour, created a "Thank you Brazil & Argentina!" video on YouTube.) Build that fan base.

Boosting your posts

Remember: eyeballs and ears. Don't let your posts just sit there. You just had a poem published! Or a book! Why *wouldn't* you spread the news? It's good for your poems, for you, and for followers interested in poetry and your work.

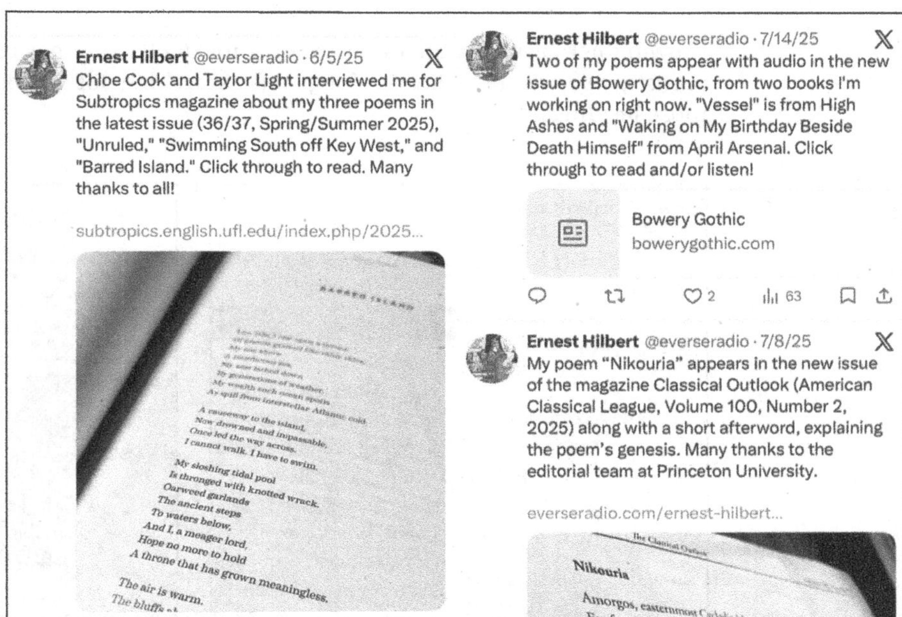

FIGURE 16-6: Two social media posts from Ernest Hilbert announcing publication of poems, June and July 2025.

There are a lot of ways to *amplify* or *boost* the reach of your posts. You can do much of that by yourself:

- Copy your posts to interested groups (on Facebook, for example) and other poetry-adjacent platforms. ***Note:*** If you begin with a Facebook post, check to see that it went through to Instagram as well.
- Post events on local events calendars, neighborhood websites, your local library's literary events listings, and/or any poetry events website you like. TikTok, too.
- This is pretty advanced, but . . . you could also *pay* an algorithm to stick the post where it will get more attention — or buy ads for your books or appearances. A few people in the poetry world do these things.

TIP

Just how entrepreneurial do you want to be? How hard do you want to work at this? Your call. The bigger the news, the more willing you might be.

Announcing appearances

Share where you're going to be, be there, and tell people where you've been. Vasiliki Katsarou is a wonderful poet and also runs a publishing house. A local arts fair was coming up, and she was going to have a friendly table all set up there, so she posted an announcement on Facebook and followed with a post showing her seated at the event (see Figure 16-7). Note her use of hashtags — *#artists*, *#poetrycommunity* — for people searching for announcements under those headings!

FIGURE 16-7: Vasiliki Katsarou takes to Facebook to announce a coming appearance.

By permission of Vasiliki Katsarou

Very graceful. Here's another graceful example. Anne Kaier had just had a meaningful moment: She saw her new poetry book in the display window of a store she had often visited back in the day. So, she posted this nice email on Nathalie F. Anderson's great [lit-philly] listserv (`lit-philly.com`), as shown in Figure 16-8.

Hilbert, Katsarou, and Kaier offer us humane, inviting news. You may even be wanting to read their poetry right now. The point is: Poets can share news of milestones, and offer their wares, without being cheap or overbearing.

The post-Pandemic poetry world

In the previous sections, we discussed the analog side of a poet's activities: where you go bodily, showing up to take part. Our point in this section is that almost all those activities also have a digital life; many of them are transmitted or stored semipermanently so the world can see. Consuming these activities, too, is the business of the Poet as Entrepreneur.

Hi All,

My new book of poems, *How Can I Say It Was Not Enough?* was featured in the front window of the famous Grolier Poetry Book Shop in Cambridge, Mass. In a blue cover, it's placed directly under the peace sign. This is a dream come true. As a grad student, I used to go into the shop, rather timidly, I fear.

FIGURE 16-8: Anne Kaier sights her new poetry book on the shelves of an old, beloved poetry shop, and she shares that sweet moment on a poetry listserv.

By permission of Anne Kaier ©.

The digitalization of the poetry world, underway for a generation already, really sped up as of the Covid Pandemic. That changed the habits of a lot of people, and poets were no exception. When bookstores, libraries, and other public venues closed up, poets were sad. How to do readings, discussions, workshops? You know the answer: Online! And poets jumped right on it. There were readings by individual poets, group readings and roundtables, discussions, reviews, slams. The world didn't stop turning; it just went virtual (see Figure 16-9).

Many poetry events took on a global flavor, with people from all over the place coming together. Many of the best-known poets in the world could be found reading online. Sure, that already had been happening for years before the Pandemic. But as Digital Age technology improved, it became easier and easier, more a matter of course. Streaming poetry readings is now pretty much what many bookstores and libraries *do* — remember that Emily Dickinson Marathon at the Library of Congress (see Chapter 1)?

Figure 16-10 shows a virtual round table on Poetry and Justice, sponsored by the Poetry Center at San Francisco State and the Poetry Coalition.

FIGURE 16-9: Poetry streaming online (Left to right): Carlos Quinteros III, Meliza Bañales, and Hilary Cruz, in a post-reading discussion at the Poetry Center, San Francisco State University, May 11, 2023.

Used by permission of the Poetry Center.

FIGURE 16-10: (Clockwise from upper left): Poet Lehua Taitano (in Santa Rosa, California), emcee Steve Dickisonand Sign Language Interpreter Odie Ashford (in California), and poets Tiffany Higgins (in Oakland, California), Ed Roberson (in Chicago), and Eli Clare (in northern Vermont) in a virtual round table.

Used by permission of the Poetry Center.

As technology improved and became more accessible, people developed new online habits. No longer was it unusual to share a screen with faces and voices from afar. And, as far as we can tell, those habits have become *permanent*. Poetry streams across the firmament, each and every day, indeed, hour. Local-access TV shows devoted to poetry are manifold (see Figure 16-11).

FIGURE 16-11: Charles A. Carr and Evan Wang discuss Evan's poetry during the Dec. 5, 2023, episode of *Philly Loves Poetry*, a regular live-streamed poetry podcast.

Used by permission of Charles A. Carr.

We don't recount this history to say something like "Poetry is cool." That's already been settled! It's to say that this *is* the poetry world, and that is where the poets are (see Figure 16-12).

FIGURE 16-12: Poet Nathalie F. Anderson hosts a live-streamed poetry reading for the Moonstone Arts Center at Fergie's Pub, July 2023, Philadelphia, PA.

Photo by Taylor Ross. Used by permission.

Finding Resources and Community

Riding the digital wave, starting around 2010, online literary communities began to emerge to help collect resources, organize them, and make them easy to access. Poets visit poetry communities, and many become members. They subscribe to newsletters on useful topics and attend online workshops and readings. It may sound like an exaggeration, but it's the unvarnished truth: Poetic communities have never before been as plentiful and interesting, with so many linked to such helpful resources.

Here are some poetry resources and communities — all types of them:

- **August Literary Hub:** This site is a place for lovers and practitioners of literary fiction and nonfiction; we include it here because it was one of the first successful online literary communities. It was started in 2015 by Morgan Entrekin of Grove Atlantic Press, Terry McDonell of the American Society of Magazine Editors, and Andy Hunter, founder of the literary magazine *Electric Literature.* It operates like a daily online magazine and is especially valuable for its wealth of literary reviews. Want to know what books are being talked about are saying? This is a good place to find out.
- **Communities associated with single writers:** You can find online communities associated with a single writer with cultlike followings, such as Rosemerry Wahtola Trommer and James Crews.
- **Local poetry groups:** You can find local poetry groups like No River Twice (`https://norivertwice.org`), "a group of poets who offer poetry readings in which audiences and poets actively interact, poem by poem, to decide the direction of the performance from beginning to end, co-creating a reading that is never the same twice." Local literary-arts communities like Philadelphia's Blue Stoop (`https://bluestoop.org`) offer everything from readings to classes to pub nights.
- **Substack:** Lots of online communities are parked at Substack. Some might look like The Poetry Salon with Tresha Fae Hefner and Friends (`https://thepoetrysalonstack.substack.com`), in which "Poet and creativity expert Tresha Faye Haefner interviews fellow poets about their writing, shares her take on their poems, and gives you honest stories about her journey towards poetry." It might also look like `Poets.org` (`https://poets.org`), famous for its much-frequented Poem-a-Day feature, publishing a brand-new poem every day.
- **WritersCafé.Org:** This online writing community offers an attractive set of possibilities for the interested writer:
  - Post your poetry, short stories, novels, scripts, and screenplays
  - Get reviews and advice from thousands of other writers

- Enter hundreds of free writing contests
- Join writing groups or start your own
- Take and subscribe to free online writing courses
- Search publishers, literary agents, and literary magazines
- Befriend and subscribe to other writers
- Save your favorite writing to your own library
- Easily share your writing with all your friends
- If you're a poet, you're thinking, "I want to find a literary magazine to submit to." Here you go. "I want to meet other poets." Well, here you go. "I want to get some feedback on my stuff." Here you go. "I was thinking of taking a writing course." Here you go. That's what we mean by *resources for poets.* Used to be it was hard to find these things. Now they have been collected and organized for you.

TAKING ONE DEEP DIVE INTO ONE ART

So, let's get deep with one of these communities and see what happens when you go to the home page and actually *hit a button.* Before getting into *ONE ART: A Journal of Poetry* (`oneartpoetry.com`), let's hang for a moment with its founder and captain, Mark Danowsky.

"The big issue for poets, as it is for a lot of people, is how can they find their tribe nowadays," Danowsky says. "Where do you find your 'beta readers?' It can be hard to break into people's social groups. Maybe that, in part, is why online communities have developed as they have."

Danowsky works with poets all the time. And when asked what poets are looking for, he says: "A community of people who will read their work in progress." He says they also want information about mentors and mentorships and submissions:

- "Where should I send my poems? Should I start with a smaller, less-known lit mag that gets fewer submissions? Or go straight to the Big Five [there aren't really five, but many lists might include *Poetry, Paris Review, The New Yorker, Virginia Quarterly Review, Granta* . . . and/or dozens of other lit mags]?"
- "Should I 'pay to play?'" [that is, pay a fee to submit to lit mags or contests? Submission fees and contest fees are more and more common in the poetry world. You probably should expect them and decide whether they're worth paying.]

(continued)

(continued)

- "What about self-publishing?" [It *is* a long-honored way for poets to get eyeballs. Walt Whitman self-published *Leaves of Grass* and snuck around and stuck copies in bookstore display windows. Don't do *that*. But many poets self-publish *chapbooks*, short selections of their work they sell for a reasonable price, online and at readings. Chapbooks function something like calling cards in the poetry world. They're neither obligatory nor to be despised.]
- And "Poets are always seeking prompts . . . there seemingly can't be enough prompt books in existence."

Asked what online communities he likes, Danowsky, a true scholar of the online poetry world, gives a list that includes, in part: ONE ART (of course), chill subs (see Chapter 11), Becky Tuch's *Lit Mag News*, `Verse-Virtual` ("which I know has a big Facebook following, and it's very community-oriented"), Michael Simms' Vox `Populi`, Ron Slate's On The `Seawall`, *Poetry Super Highway, The Poetry Salon,* and many more.

As you can see, Danowsky has thought long, hard, and with empathy (he's an accomplished poet himself) about poets and their worlds. That sensitivity to a poet's needs is all over ONE ART, in its simple, welcoming layout, its easy accessibility, and its wealth of offerings.

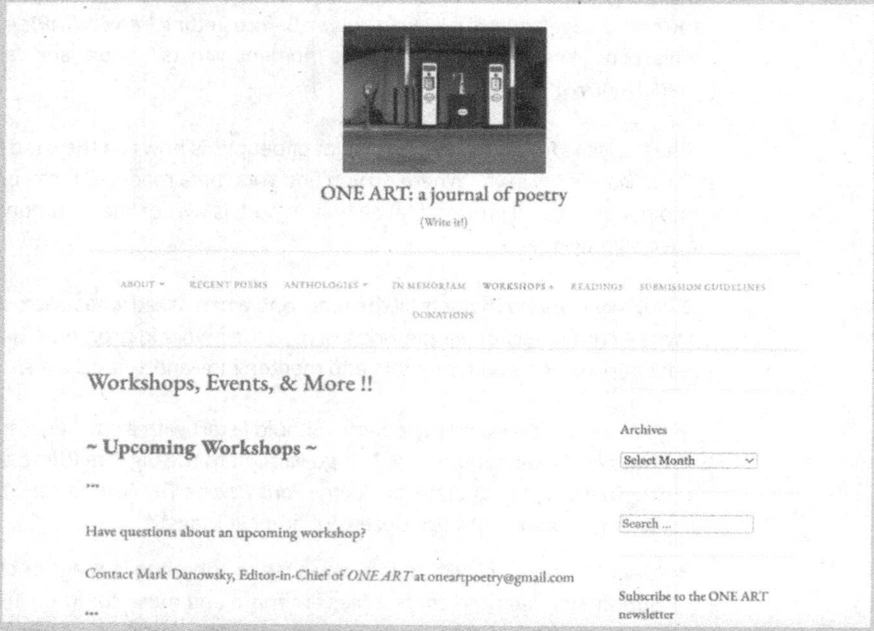

Used by permission.

IN THIS CHAPTER

» Getting ready to submit your work for publication

» Doing market research

» Sending out your poems in a methodical manner

» Self-publishing your work

Chapter 17
Getting Published

If you're an aspiring poet, you've probably looked at all the poetry you read online and in print in literary magazines — henceforward known as *lit mags* — and elsewhere, and wondered, "How can *I* get in there?" Getting published *is* an accomplishment, something to be proud of (after all, somebody read and liked your work!), and a chance to learn about your poetry through contact with editors and readers. And is it ever encouraging!

In this chapter, we offer some guidelines on publication, as well as the methods and attitudes to bring to your quest.

The advice here is a series of tips, not *commandments*. You do you: Forge your own path in the way that suits you best.

A POET BY ANY OTHER NAME?

Branding is everything! Throughout history, poets have been known to take on pseudonyms or pen names. Some poets take on shorter versions of their names, as did Dante (baptized Durante Alighieri) and Michelangelo (Michelangelo di Lodovico Buonarroti Simoni). Some Japanese poets of the classical era went by their nicknames. Basho's name means "banana plant" in Japanese (he took the name in honor of a plant near his house). The revered poet Issa's name means "bubble in a cup of tea."

(continued)

(continued)

Some women poets chose androgynous names for a variety of reasons. These include H.D. (short for Hilda Doolittle) and Ai. Some get their pen names by accident: The Irish poet George William Russell wanted to go by the name Aeon, but a typesetter got it wrong, and from then on Russell went as AE.

The modernist Portuguese poet Fernando Pessoa wrote under several names, which he devised as separate personas for himself. He even went as far as to have his different personas comment on one another's work! Other poets with more than one name include: Jack Kerouac (Jean-Louis Lebris de Kerouac), Pablo Neruda (Neftalí Ricardo Eliecer Reyes Basoalto), Claire Malroux (Claire Sara Roux), Doris Lessing (Doris May Taylor and Jane Somers), Maya Angelou (Marguerite Johnson), Anne Sexton (Anne Gray Harvey), and Sylvia Plath (Victoria Lucas).

Poets are still taking on different names. In light of the Cultural Revolution and the Tiananmen Square massacre, several Chinese poets took on pen names as a form of political comment. World-famous poet Zhao Zhenkai adopted the pen name Bei Dao, which means "Northern Island." His pseudonym is a private symbol and a reminder of the kind of poetry the Communist government dislikes. Bei Dao's name is a permanent protest against Communist oppression.

Self-renaming is especially popular in the world of performance or slam poets, who have taken names like Big Poppa E, Jennifer Blowdryer, Sapphire, and blackberry revolution. Why do poets take other names? Sometimes in imitation of others, other times to make a political statement, and, more often than not, to keep their identities as poets separate from the rest of their lives.

Submitting Your Poetry to Lit Mags

As we've been saying, poetry is a DIY marketplace. Want to get in print? Work lies ahead. Much of that work is interesting, gets you in touch with editors, publishers, and other poets, and teaches you a lot about the poetry publishing universe, which, even in its quietest state, can be as chaotic as a heifer on jimson weed.

If you're ready to show the world your verse, this section provides guidelines for putting into action your "getting published" plan.

Knowing when you're ready

Getting published feels great: You see your poetry and your name in print, it gives you something to put on your résumé, and you can send copies to friends, family, and strangers. But don't try to get published until you're ready. (You don't want to look back years later on your published work and, after reading it again, want to change your name.)

TIP

How can you tell when you're ready? You can be relatively certain you're ready for publication if you:

- **Have not just started writing but have written a fair amount and for some time.** Everyone is different, but let's call two to five years of consistent writing, revising, and producing finished poems a "fair amount" of both poetry and time.
- **Have had your poetry read by knowledgeable friends, mentors, or beta readers.** (*Beta readers* are people who will read your unpublished work and assess it from a reader's viewpoint.) The readers you choose should be able to give you frank, constructive criticism and advice about the poetry market.
- **Have done your market research.** You've gotten a general idea of the poetry marketplace, you've visited many lit mags, and you're feeling as if you know the ones to which a poet like you should send poetry like yours. You also know what journals to avoid — those that publish poetry you're not fond of, or cover topics you don't find interesting.
- **Are willing to commit yourself to being methodical about getting published.** You don't "do poetry" just now and then; you send out in a continual rhythmic fashion. You don't send your stuff out any old way, scatter-shot, here and there. Here are some best practices we've seen among poets serious about getting published:
  - You target your submissions carefully. You've done your research and found, say, five you think would welcome your poetry.
  - You have read the publication's submission guidelines and have prepared your submission package exactly as stipulated: poems, bio, and cover letter.
  - You have prepared as many poems, or as many pages, as stipulated. They are in the format requested. And you are prepared to send them in the manner requested. Does the publication require that you use a submission platform such as Submittable (used by many, if not most lit mags)? Does it require that you submit by email?
  - Your brief, personable *cover letters* (editors ask for them and read them), introduce you and your work and say, in concrete detail, why you submitted your poem to this particular venue.
  - You have a short but representative *bio* (a thumbnail sketch of your background, where you have been published, where you live, and other related details).

- You keep a *submissions journal* to track when and where you submit, and when each poem is either accepted (yay) or not (waaah). In that journal, you never have just one target venue; for every poem you're trying to get published, make sure to identify at least five target homes. That commits you to repeated tries: When a poem is not accepted, you can prepare a new submission package to suit the next place down the list and kick it out the door.

» **Have a realistic attitude.** You know publication of poetry is extremely competitive, response often slow or nonexistent, and you usually get paid only with a copy of the issue your poem appears in, if that. Rejection does not mean you're a bad poet and worthless human being; it can actually be a chance to learn something about your poetry. Acceptance, although wonderful, does not confer sainthood on you. You still have to get up in the morning and pour your own cornflakes. You're not putting all your hopes and dreams in one single attempt; you'll be sending your work around a lot. And once you send out your poems, you *are not waiting around*. You are continuing to write and revise your work, sending other poems out to other places, *and* doing things poets do in their communities.

If you're wondering where you should you start, we've got you covered. The next section provides an action plan for poetry market research.

Following the *Poetry For Dummies* action plan for poetry market research

As a poet, you need to be just as market-savvy as any other entrepreneur. You need to survey your territory and identify target publications. This is *market research*, poetry friends. It is absolutely essential. Make it a central part of your poetry-writing life. You are literally learning as much as you can about the market (the world of poetry venues) into which you are sending your products (poems). Market research involves:

» Looking at a lot of lit mags, online or in print.

» Reading lit mags that seem attractive and getting to know them.

» Asking the right questions and knowing where to find the answers.

We suggest you visit lit mags in the categories described in the following sections. The order of the sections does *not*, please know, reflect a ladder of importance or excellence. Each list represents a different sector, a different slice of the cheese-jalapeño-prune tort, a different tilt of the Klieg light. Skip among them. Dabble. Loll. Visit widely within each of these sometimes overlapping lists.

Note: We tried hard to ascertain and double-check the information in the lists and tables below. Lit mags come, go, blink on, blink off, change names, and change mission: We apologize if any information below is no longer so.

The Big Five

Starting in 2006, a hardworking and knowledgeable man named Clifford Garstang started running a yearly ranking of lit mags, including poetry publications. He based his rankings solely on how many Pushcart Prizes (big deals in the poetry cosmos) and Pushcart Special Mentions each mag has received in the last 10 years.

To see his list, go to `https://cliffordgarstang.com`, then click on Blog, then to Literary Magazine Rankings, then to the poetry rankings for the most recent year. Know what's cool? You can click on the name of almost any ranked magazine and be linked right there! Market research rocketized!

Garstang's top 10 currently looks like this:

1. *Poetry* — `https://poetryfoundation.org`
2. *American Poetry Review* — `https://aprweb.org`
3. *Kenyon Review* — `https://kenyonreview.org`
4. *New England Review* — `https://nereview.com`
5. *Poem a Day* — `https://poets.org/poem-a-day`
6. *Threepenny Review* — `https://threepennyreview.com`
7. *Yale Review* — `https://yalereview.org`
8. *Adroit Journal* — `https://theadroitjournal.org`
9. *Southern Review* — `https://thesouthernreview.org`
10. *Paris Review* — `https://theparisreview.org`

REMEMBER

Our main point is that the lit mags poets call The Big Five are on this list *somewhere* . . . in different orders, depending on who is speaker. In getting used to reading lit mags, then, it makes sense to look into all these ten, *just to get a sense of what people see as the top of the mountain, where they are pointing their aspirations.* Anybody who at least tries to get a sense of these 21 mags is going to get a strong helicopter view of the entire field — not every mountain, but a few of the sharpest peaks. You'll see some of the most prominent poets at work, and the kind of work they're doing. This is essential groundwork for any poet's market research. Who knows? Maybe someday you'll submit to one of them.

Uni's

Universities and colleges, taken together, have done a remarkable job in sustaining the cause of poetry for everyone. Perusing the Top 21, you may have seen the *Georgia Review*, the *Iowa Review*, *Ploughshares*, *New Ohio Review*, and others. Your market research may include them and several other fine, first-line publications put out by institutes of higher learning in the United States:

- *The Antioch Review* (Antioch University) — `https://antiochcollege.edu/antioch-review`
- *The Beloit Poetry Journal* (Beloit College) — `https://bpj.org`
- *The Colorado Review* (University of Colorado) — `https://coloradoreview.colostate.edu`
- *Cottonwood* (University of Kansas) — `https://english.ku.edu/cottonwood`
- *The Harvard Review* (Harvard University) — `https://harvardreview.org`
- *The Massachusetts Review* (University of Massachusetts) — `https://massreview.org`
- *The Michigan Quarterly Review* (University of Michigan) — `https://sites.lsa.umich.edu/mqr`
- *Raritan: A Quarterly Review* (Rutgers University) — `https://raritanquarterly.rutgers.edu`
- *Salmagundi* (Skidmore College) — `https://salmagundi.skidmore.edu`
- *The Southwest Review* (Southern Methodist University) — `https://southwestreview.com`
- *TriQuarterly* (Northwestern University) — `https://triquarterly.org`
- *The Western Humanities Review* (University of Utah) — `https://westernhumanitiesreview.com`

Indies

Colleges and universities aren't the only places that put out excellent poetry journals. *American Poetry Review* (`https://aprweb.org`), a tabloid published in Philadelphia, is one of the most widely-read of all poetry journals. So is *The Poetry Project Newsletter* (`https://poetryproject.org`), published in New York City. *Poetry* (`https://poetryfoundation.org/poetrymagazine`) is one of the longest continually-publishing poetry journals in the United States. And several leading magazines — including *Atlantic Monthly*, *The New Yorker*, *The New Criterion*, and *The Nation* — publish poems with each issue.

Other journals are published independently by folks who love good writing. These include:

- *Conjunctions* — https://conjunctions.com
- *The Greenfield Review* — https://greenfieldreview.com
- *Hambone* — https://hambonejournal.com
- *The Hudson Review* — https://hudsonreview.com
- *New American Writing* — https://newamericanwriting.com
- *Tikkun* — https://tikkun.org

Lit mags at smaller colleges and universities

One of the most deserving, and least sung (or is it most unsung?) sectors of the poetry world are the great folks who work on the lit mags of our small colleges, smaller universities, and community colleges. A glorious army of hundreds, most are unpaid, doing it for the experience and the love. We see you. We love you.

Many, perhaps most of these lit mags are for the students and staff of their institutions, a wonderful thing. But many also throw wide the net to all who wish to submit. These are among our favorite lit mags. We encourage you to consider them for your work. Here's a dozen. Read!

These are not, we hasten to clarify, "starter" mags, in the sense of "elementary" or "easy" or "low-bar." Some of these are among the best, and all are good places to submit. Here, you have an excellent chance of being attentively read and responded to, and if you are accepted, these publications also tend to be well curated and beautiful.

REMEMBER

Do your market research: read a few issues and read the Submission Guidelines closely. If you love the work you read, you know what to do.

- *Apricity Magazine* — University of Texas at Austin
  https://apricitymagazine.com
- *The Dodge* — College of Wooster (Ohio)
  https://thedodgemag.com
- *The Kelsey Review* — Mercer County College (West Windsor, NJ)
  https://kelseyreview.com
- *Lumière* — MassBay Community College (MA)
  https://www.lumiere.litmag.com

» *The MacGuffin* — Schoolcraft College (Livonia, MI)
`https://schoolcraft.edu/macguffin`

» *The Mid-American Review* — Bowling Green State University (Ohio)
`https://casit.bgsu.edu/midamericanreview`

» *MUSE* — Riverside Community College (CA)
`www.rcc.edu/community/publications/muse.html`

» *Prism* — University of La Verne (CA)
`artsci.laverne.edu/prism/`

» *Santa Fe Literary Review* — Santa Fe Community College (NM)
`www.sfcc.edu/santa-fe-literary-review`

» *Southampton Review* — SUNY Stony Brook
`https://thesouthamptonreview.com`

» *Stonecrop* — College of Western Idaho
`https://stonecropmag.com`

» *Tampa Review* — University of Tampa (FL)
`https://tampareview.org`

The *Poetry For Dummies* 14 suggested places to send first submissions

Don't call them "starter lit mags." Call them *good first submission targets.* Our main questions were: Where are first-time submitters likely to have a good, useful experience? Where will they find it easy to submit? Where will they actually be read, and be most likely to get a timely, substantial response?

Table 17-1 details the *Poetry For Dummies* 14 suggested places to send first submissions. We've mixed up some of the best with some of the smaller mags, some of the most famous with some of the ones that, well, IYKYK. In the row with each lit mag, you'll find some excellent-to-know information:

» **Email address:** Important contact information.

» **P/O:** Whether the lit mag is online only (O), print (P), or both (B).

» **What to send:** How many poems can you send? Should you send a cover letter and bio? (Actually, just go ahead and always send those last two things.)

» **S/C/O:** Will this pub consider any of the following:

- *Sim subs:* Simultaneous submissions; poems you have submitted simultaneously here and to other lit mags.

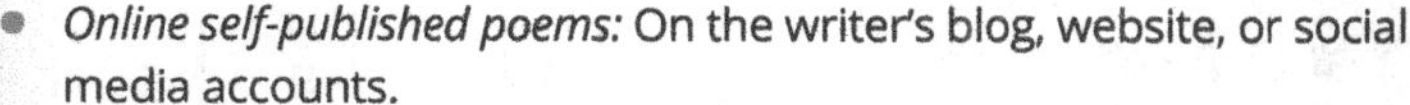

- *Curated poems:* Already edited and published by someone else.
- *Online self-published poems:* On the writer's blog, website, or social media accounts.

TIP

A common answer is Y/N/Y: Yes on sim subs, no on curated (few places do), and yes on online self-pubs. But lit mags have different standards; read up.

» **Reading period(s):** Times during the year when the lit mag accepts poetry submissions.

» **Response time:** How long it normally/aspirationally takes for the lit mag to let you know the verdict.

» **Fee:** Whether this lit mag charges you for your submission.

» **Pay:** Whether this lit mag pays you if your work is accepted.

Note: Table 17-1 is for general information only. Some information may have changed. For up-to-date, accurate facts and figures, please read the Submission Guidelines page of your target lit mags.

Asking the right questions when you visit a target lit mag

Okay, so, you're visiting *Jeannie and Al's Do-It-Ourselves Poetry Mag and Grill.* What now? How best to determine whether *JaADIOPMaG* is the home for your poems?

Your main guides as your read through lit mags, online or print, should be your own tastes and interests. You want your poems to appear amid writing you admire. So, imagine your poetry in the pages of the lit mag in front of you. If you read poems and like them, read more and decide whether this is the environment for your work, too.

REMEMBER

Although hundreds and hundreds of places in the world publish poetry, *hundreds*, editors often have quite different tastes and interests. Some lit mags may accept poetry:

» **Only from people who live in a certain area.** For example, don't send to *ZYZZYVA* unless you live in the West.

» **Only about certain subjects.** If your poem is about plants, don't bother sending it to a journal that wants only poems about dogs. Don't send a poem on bowel surgery to *Cowboy Poets Today.*

TABLE 17-1 Fourteen Places to Send First Submissions

Name	Online/ Print/Both?	What to Send	S/C/O?[1]	Reading Period(s)[2]	Response Time	Fee?[3]	Pays?[4]
32 Poems 32poems.com	Both	Up to 5 poems or 32 total lines max	N/N/N	2/1–4/30; 8/1–9/30	Within 3 weeks	$3	$25/poem + 2 copies
Baltimore Review baltimorereview.org	Both	3 poem + bio, cover letter	Y/N/N	2/1–6/31; 8/1–11/30	4 months	No	$50
Bayou Magazine bayoumagazine.org	Both	Up to 5 poems	Y/N/N	9/15–12/15	5 months	No	One copy
Black Horse Review www.blackhorsereview.com	Online	Up to 3 poems	N/N/N	Rolling[5]	6 months	$4.95	No
Cleaver cleavermagazine.com	Online	Up to 5 poems + bio, cover letter	Y/N/Y	Rolling	2–12 months	$5	$0.16 per word
Ghost City ghostcitypress.com	Online	3 poems + bio, cover letter	Y/N/Y	Rolling	2–4 months	No	No
Kenyon Review kenyonreview.org	Both	Up to 6 poems	Y/N/N	9/1–9/30	6 months	No	No
Lily Poetry Review lilypoetryreview.blog	Online	5 poems	Y/N/N	Rolling	3–6 months	No	No
LitMag litmag.com	Both	Up to 3 poems	Y/N/N	2/1–6/31	ASAP . . . "We try" . . .	$5	$100 online/ $125 print
New Delta Review ndrmag.org	Online	5 poems max	Y/N/N	1/1 to early March; 10/1 to mid-November	180+ days	$3	No

Name	Online/ Print/Both?	What to Send	S/C/O?[1]	Reading Period(s)[2]	Response Time	Fee?[3]	Pays?[4]
North Dakota Quarterly `ndquarterly.org`	Both	3–5 pages of poetry	N/N/N	3/1–6/1; 8/1–12/1	60–131 days	No	$100
ONE ART `oneartpoetry.com`	Online	1–5 poems, 7 pages max + bio	Rather not/N/N	Rolling	3 hours to 1 week	No — there is a Tip Jar!	No
Only Poems `onlypoems.com`	Online	Up to 10 pages of poetry max + bio, cover letter	Y/N/Y	Rolling, especially 1/15–31 and 7/15–31	2 weeks	No	$77
Rattle Poetry `rattle.com`	Both	Up to 4 poems	Y/N/Y	Rolling	Variable but "within a normal range"	No	$200 print/ $100 online

[1] *S/C/O stands for* ***S****imultaneous/*__*C*__*urated/*__*O*__*nline Self-Published. Does this lit mag accept "Sim subs," simultaneous submissions, poems you sent to other lit mags at the same time as you sent them to this one? Curated publications, selected and edited by someone else? Online Self-Published poems, poetry you have posted on personal blogs or other social media? Y/N/Y in this row would mean the lit mag in question does accept sim subs, does not accept curated pubs, and does accept online self-publications.*

[2] *Reading periods change frequently. Read those Submission Guidelines!*

[3] *Does this lit mag charge you a submission fee? Fees are variable; consult the Submission Guidelines page. Note: Lit mags that do not charge such fees may charge for contests, printed collections, or other special circumstances. Some lit mags also offer higher, "expedited" fees for quicker review of your submission.*

[4] *Does this lit mag pay you if they accept your poem(s)? Payment in copies is most common.*

[5] *The term* ***Rolling*** *under Reading Period(s) is a very nice thing. It means this lit mag considers submissions year-round!*

» **Only in certain forms or genres.** Don't send an epic poem to a journal named *Haiku. The New Formalist* is looking for poems in traditional forms, so a sprawling open-form poem isn't going to fly. Is *Hellhound* the right place for you? Not unless you write horror. *Nowruz Journal* specializes in the beautiful Persian culture — so maybe send that baseball poem elsewhere? *The Southern Review* has published leading poems in the great American tradition for generations — but its vision is very different from the viewpoint you may encounter in, say, *sprout.*

REMEMBER

Now for the all-important specifics: Read 5-10 poems at random, to get a sense of the tastes of that particular lit mag. Then seek and read, very carefully, two specific pages (if they exist) at the sites you visit: the About and Submission Guidelines pages.

The About page may discuss the history of the venue, maybe the reasons it was started, and what the editor(s) hope(d) to accomplish.

The Submission Guidelines page is, as we've mentioned, Solid. Gold. Here is where editors explain what they are looking for and *not* looking for. They tell you:

» **Their reading period(s)** ("We read poems all year except for May 15–September 15" or "Our reading periods are October through November for the Spring issue and April through June for our Winter issue.").

» **How many poems to send** (usually 3–5 poems), **whether there is a specific length limit** (many venues have them), **such total number of pages** ("no more than 10 pages," for example). This last one is to make sure you don't abuse the system and send 5 poems of 75 lines apiece.

» **How to format your poems on the page.** This is crucial. Mess Up and Go Home. Specifications may include file formats (`.doc`, `.docx`, `.htm`, `.pdf`, `.rtf`, or `.txt`), fonts, or spacing ("Poems should be single-spaced, unless the poem is meant to be double-spaced, using 12-point, regular-face Times New Roman"), plus issues specific to poetry ("If you are writing in stanzas, do not run stanzas over the page break; begin new stanzas on a new page"). Carefully follow instructions about where your name, email address, and other identifiers go.

» **What they don't like so don't even bother.** Everybody has stuff they can't stand, and many mags will let you know. Read such statements attentively and with respect. Don't bother to send anybody stuff they hate.

» **What to include with the submission** (usually, a cover letter and bio).

» **How long it generally takes them to read submitted work** ("We take from 24 hours to six weeks to read your poems"). If sending again after a waiting period, don't send the same batch as the first time, at least not in Batch Two; send a new batch and send Batch One elsewhere.

» **How long to wait, if your poems are rejected, to send new ones** ("If your poems are not accepted, please wait at least six weeks/six months/37 years before sending us a new batch").

» **S/C/O?** Whether they do or do not accept (1) "Sim subs," (2) Curated publications, and/or (3) Online self-published poems.

» **Fees for submissions.** An increasing number of poetry venues request a reading fee. It's usually not much, often $3–$5 or something thereunto adjacent.

Writing contests have charged entry fees for a long time. It's reasonable to pay $20 or so to have your work read in a contest; reading fees often make up the prize money, and the reader(s) get a little something.

But fees for getting published are not traditional. Much has changed, however, in the poetry world. It was never easy to run a poetry magazine or website; now it's even less easy. Many of the granting agencies that used to support small publications have gone away or in other directions. And many poets don't mind supporting poetry venues they like. It feels like donating to a good cause (because that's what it is).

Expect some places, then, to ask for small fees for reading your work. If the fee goes much beyond $1 a poem or $1 a page, though, we wouldn't blame anyone for saying, "Forget it. Yes, I'm a quadrillionaire, but . . ."

TIP

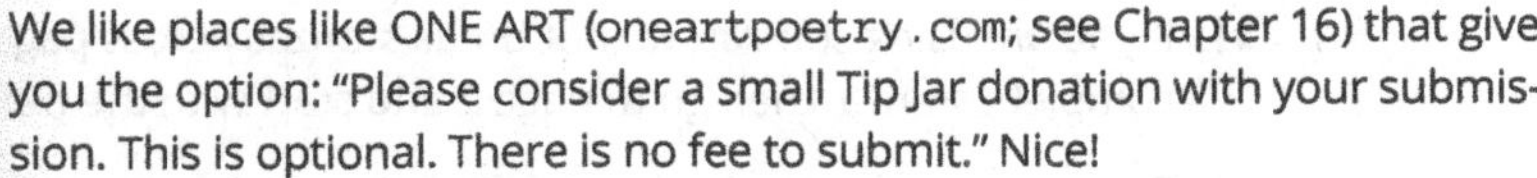

We like places like ONE ART (`oneartpoetry.com`; see Chapter 16) that give you the option: "Please consider a small Tip Jar donation with your submission. This is optional. There is no fee to submit." Nice!

» **Find out what other people think about this lit mag's tastes and methods.** Consult online sites such as Duotrope (`https://duotrope.com`) or chill subs (`www.chillsubs.com`) that describe and evaluate your target(s).

Submitting your poetry

When you send your submission, you send the poems, a cover letter, and a short (50 words is a common length) bio. The following sections show how to prepare each of these three items.

Preparing a text of your poems

How many poems? Consult your target lit mag's Submission Guidelines page and do exactly as bidden. Usually, you'll be invited to send something like 3–5 poems and/or around 10–12 pages max. Do not fudge or exceed the limit. That is a good way to get ignored.

Whether you create a digital document by inputting it into a device like a laptop, a tablet, or something similar, or type the poems in the analog, Classic Mail fashion, *be methodical.* Follow this checklist:

- » If inputting, make sure you are using an accepted document format and size and font of type.
- » No such specifications? Fine. Your default should be a commonly used format and an 11- or 12-point typeface in a font fairly free of serifs and other adornment. You want as clean, neutral, and legible a look as possible. Garamond? Too warm. Helvetica? Much more like it.
- » Center your poem titles two spaces above the first line, unbolded and unitalicized, without quotation marks, in the same type as the body of the poem. Use initial capitals as if the title were a headline.
- » If you are typing, find a typewriter with a neutral, unfussy typeface. Type neatly. Type on only one side of the page.
- » *Your poems should appear exactly as you want each poem to appear if it is published.* No page should have more than one poem on it. Don't double-space a poem unless you want it to be published double-spaced.
- » If you are *not* using stanzas or other kinds of spaced breaks, it is usually fine to go to the end of the page and, if the poem continues, pick up again on page 2.
- » If you *are* using stanzas, do not break stanzas across pages. End page 1 with a complete stanza, then go to page 2 and start with the next stanza.
- » Proofread and spell-check everything. A typo in a poem is like a bad note in a symphony.

Preparing a cover letter

Cover letters are nice. They are polite. They are professional. They also are a chance to make a moment's connection with the person(s) who will read your submission. Many editors appreciate them (see the later section, "An Editor's POV: Diane Lockward of Terrapin Books"). Editors want to feel a human connection, too.

Keep cover letters brief, graceful, and simple. We recommend that you use the cover-letter template provided on the submissions page of the ONE ART website (`https://oneartpoetry.com/submissions`).

Here are the important bits:

- **»** Standard, polite opening salutation to the editor(s).
- **»** Polite request for consideration and the names of the poems you are submitting.
- **»** [Optional but appreciated] If this is your first time and you want to say so, you can. Many editors like to know that new poets are sending in their poems.
- **»** [Optional but appreciated] A very short reason you are sending your submission to this particular venue. Refer to something you especially liked. For example, "I admired the emphasis on experimental poetry in your Winter issue" or "I have enjoyed your journal's emphasis on working life and everyday experience."

WARNING

Don't overdo it. We hereby abjure and condemn fawning and cringing. A thoughtful, informed comment will show the editor you know something about the lit mag and are not picking it at random; they also engage editors on a subject they care about: choosing good poetry.

- **»** A courtesy-thanks.
- **»** Name, complimentary close ("Sincerely"), and email.

Digital submissions pages usually give you a space to fill out for your cover letter. If you want to find out how you may send submissions the analog way, see the "Sending submissions by classical mail" section, later in this chapter.

WARNING

Do *not* include the following in your cover letter:

- **» Your assessment of your own work.** Offering your self-estimate ("I believe these poems are timely and eloquent") may do nothing but annoy your editor. Let the editors decide for themselves whether they like your work.
- **» Explanations of the themes, meanings, or forms of the poems.** Saying something like, "'Your Second Dance' is about the fears and frustrations of doing something a second time when the first time wasn't so good" or "'Exploding Horses' is a triple dizaine in acephalic anapestic heptameter" is only stating the obvious. Editors can figure these things out for themselves.
- **» Explanations of your motives for seeking publication.** A line like "I've been writing a long time, and it's really time for me to get my poems out there" serves little purpose and can only irritate.

Preparing a bio

Bio is short for *biography,* and that's what a bio is: a short, really short literary biography. It is suggestive, not exhaustive. It gives the reader a taste, but modestly. Often, if your poem is submitted, your bio will run with those of other contributors somewhere in the lit mag. So, imagine your three lines. What will they say? Here's a possible template:

> X's poems have appeared in X, X, X, X, and X. X is also the author of X (X Press). X lives and writes in [name of place].

Filled out, it could read this way:

> Chris Doe's poetry has appeared in, among other places, *Locomotive, Sequoia Bole, American Review of Iconoclastic Verse,* and *Transatlantique*. His latest collection is titled *Bellicose Pencil* (Notwithstanding Press). He lives and writes in Anytown, California.

All in only 35 words! The "lives and writes part" is optional; if uncomfortable with publicizing where you live, don't. We're down to 28 words!

Sending your submission

Most lit mags use some sort of submissions manager — a platform with fields you fill out or upload documents to, everything from *author's name* to *fee* (if any). Find which one your target lit mag uses, learn how to work it, and work it. All your stuff is prepared, right? So, all you'll need to do is cut and paste.

The most commonly used such platform is called Submittable. One guess is that about 85 percent of all U.S. lit mags use it. Several short YouTube tutorials are available to guide you on how to use it. Here's one by poet Dimitri Reyes: `https://youtube.com/watch?v=HKGUUHzKyzo`.

Other places have on-site platforms. Read those submission guidelines and go forward!

Sending submissions by classic mail

If your target lit mag accepts submissions by classic mail, you'll still prepare your poems pretty much as we've been describing. One question is: should you put your name on the poems someplace? There's really no non-awkward way to do it, especially since most editors require that submissions remain anonymous until a decision is made. So, include the titles of your poems in your cover letter. You may wish to use something closer to a standard business letter form, something like the letter shown in Figure 17-1. The bio will appear beneath your closing signature and info.

Patricia DeNeve
Editor
XYZ Poetry Journal
100 Main Street
Anytown, NY 10012

February 32, 2222

Dear [Editor(s) or Patricia DeNeve]:

Please consider the enclosed poems — "Your Second Dance," "November 1992," "Exploding Horses," "For Lena," and "Chortle" — for publication in XYZ Poetry Journal. This is my first time submitting my work to your journal. [Or if applicable:] My work has not previously been published.] I am submitting to *XYZ Poetry Journal* because I like your selection of poems that are written in traditional forms but concern contemporary problems and viewpoints.

A short bio appears below. Thank you for reading my work.

Sincerely,

Chris Doe

Chris Doe
123 Elm Street
Anytown, CA 90210
(555) 555-1212
cdoe8.&@aol.com

Chris Doe's poetry has appeared in, among other places, *Locomotive, Sequoia Bole, American Review of Iconoclastic Verse,* and *Transatlantique*. His latest collection is entitled *Bellicose Pencil* (Notwithstanding Press). He lives and writes in Anytown, California.

FIGURE 17-1: A sample hand-typed cover letter. The body of the letter and the bio at the bottom are pretty much the same as you'd send digitally.

Okay. You have cover letter, bio, and poems all typed out and longing for the road. Take one manila envelope, address it to yourself, and put appropriate postage on it. That's your Self-Addressed Stamped Envelope (SASE). If your poems are not accepted, they will come back to you in the SASE. Address another envelope to the lit mag and put the postage on. Make sure each envelope has a return address. Fold the one addressed to you (leave it unsealed!) and slip it into the envelope addressed to the lit mag.

Gather your poems. Assemble them with their cover letter and bio, *sign* the cover letter, affix a paper clip to the upper-left-hand corner, slip everything into the envelope, lick, close, kiss the whole package, and stick it in a mailbox. Done.

TIP

We've known poets who have groups of poems in stacks on one side, envelopes on another side. As the SASEs come back with rejections, these poets simply create new cover letters, assemble the submission, and ship the rejected stuff out to the next lit mag, like clockwork. They *make* themselves do it as a point of professional discipline.

Keeping a submissions journal

Digital, classic, it doesn't matter: well-organized and methodical poets will keep some kind of submissions journal. What's important is to keep track of where everything is: what has gone out, when, to whom, when it came back, when it landed. You could imagine a fairly commonsense table with columns titled Poem, Submitted, Result, and Notes. In the Submitted and Result columns, you would record dates and places. The Notes column could include emails or phone numbers, communications with or from editors, fees, payments, scheduled publication dates, and any other circumstances. Many lit mags, for example, encourage you to drop them an email if it has taken unusually long for them to respond; *take advantage of the invitation.* When you do, note when and the outcome in the Notes column.

Digital has advantages over paper for a submissions journal. It's easier digitally to track both submitted *groups* of poems and *individual poems*, cross-referencing to see how variously composed groups fared. And if you were a glittering digital edgelord, you could create repeated Submitted/Result/Notes cycles beneath the same poem.

TIP

A submissions journal is a good place to amass the email addresses and phone numbers of your submissions-related contacts: editors you've met, friends who have landed or not landed at lit mags X or Y, and admired poets who have appeared in lit mags you like. ONE ART lists poets who have published there recently (`https://oneartpoetry.com/poems`) and "representative poets," poets ONE ART admires (on their submissions page, `https://oneartpoetry.com/submissions`)!

Submissions journals come in handiest at three points in the process: when you send out a poem, and after it has returned five times:

- **When you send the poem out,** the journal becomes your timer, recording when the process began. Tracking your poems helps the whole process seem less chaotic, helps you maintain a sense that, if not in control, you at least know where everything *is.*
- **When the poem comes back,** you can consult your journal to help decide where it goes next. It can help assure you don't send the same thing twice in a row. It can ping you when it's okay to submit something new to that lit mag that rejected you last year — or to remind you it's time to try that lit mag you've been thinking about but have not yet approached.
- **If a poem comes back more than five times,** maybe it's time to consider it again, determine whether any changes need making. Main question: Do *you* feel the same about this poem? How have your feelings changed?

IF YOU GET REJECTED

Most editors do not have the time or the staff to send personalized notes to every poet whose work they reject. So, you may receive form rejections or very brief notes ("Respectfully, no").

If an editor takes the time to write a substantive, personalized rejection note, *feel very, very good.* It means you came close. The editor liked your work enough to encourage you and tell you why you didn't make it this time. Pay close attention to such notes; they could help you get published in the future — not that they will guarantee getting published (they surely don't), but that they will help you focus on your poems and possibly help you produce better versions.

If you get a personal rejection note, wait a few weeks, send out a new batch of poems to the same editors, and in your cover letter, include some words of thanks to the editors, reminding them of the kindness of the rejection note. This constitutes a contact. Do not instantly flood responsive editors with huge gobs of new material, and do not send the same poems you just sent (only tweaked to reflect the editors' suggestions).

We can't promise you'll never get an ill-mannered or cranky rejection note, but honestly, this is rare. If it happens, put it — and that editor — out of your mind.

Take initiative. After you send out your poems, start planning where to send this same group of poems if they return rejected. And start on the next batch.

Pursuing Other Kinds of Publication

Getting your poetry curated and published in a lit mag is, let's just say, a journey. Thousands of poets, only dozens of spaces. The following sections cover other ways to get your poems before eyes and ears.

REMEMBER

To publish is to send your words out into the world. It's an exciting endeavor, and sometimes you hit the jackpot: useful responses from readers. Don't rush into publication, but when you feel ready, be professional and patient about the quest, and you'll discover a great deal about yourself, the poetry world, and your own verse.

Collections and contests

It's totally arbitrary and insanely variable, but for here and now, we'll define a *collection* of poems as being 51 or more pages long. A number of presses put out periodic calls for longer manuscripts of poetry. These "reading periods" are either contests or function something like a contest. They are likely to publish only a couple of these manuscripts, maybe even only one. Keep patrolling your favorite poetry site — chill subs, `Poetry.org`, `Litmag.org`, any online community that runs the news — and you'll see announcements of such reading periods.

Diane Lockward's Terrapin Press is a nice example of a press that does reading periods. She gives her view of things later in this chapter, in the section "An Editor's POV: Diane Lockward of Terrapin Books."

TIP

These reading periods are very competitive. A few thoughts:

- (Exactly as with lit mags!) Learn and closely observe the Submission Guidelines the press gives for manuscripts, especially regarding *length*.
- Contests and reading periods *do* tend to charge reading fees, with \$20-\$25 being currently a common range.
- A collection needs to have a shape. This can be a theme that helps your group of poems cohere, a point of view, even a story or place functioning as a central point of cohesion. It shouldn't be just an unsorted bunch of poems on all sorts of stuff. Collections are thoughtful gatherings. Take time to read through your work; create groups that bring readers on a journey, a progression. You could also have a trusted friend or fellow poet help you.
- Some of the most famous collections are also beautifully cohesive, fine examples of what good poets can do as arrangers of their own works. Check out *North of Boston* by Robert Frost, *Cathay* by Ezra Pound, *The Tower* by William Butler Yeats, *V* by Tony Harrison, *The Wild Iris* by Louise Glück, *Stay, Illusion* by Lucie Brock-Broido, *Citizen* by Claudia Rankine, *American Sonnets for My Past and Future Assassin* by Terrance Hayes, or *Buffalo Girl* by Jessica Q. Stark. Or visit your local bookstore or library and peruse the individual collections on their shelves!

Chapbooks, pamphlets, and broadsides

These generally are shorter than 51 pages. For the sake of just stipulating something, we'll say a chapbook is a small collection of up to 50 pages, often between 35-50. *Pamphlets* could be anything of any length, but generally also fall into this range. *Broadsides* are very short publications of 1-10 poems or fewer.

This is the golden era of the chapbook, and local, smaller presses have reading periods for them. There are also chapbook contests in which winners get published. Here's a shout-out to the wondrous and amazing Moonstone Press in Philadelphia, which has been doing this for a long time and is the happy heart of the Philly poetry community. We could name several other such presses around the county.

Self-publishing in print

Many poets post their poems online. Many also publish themselves in print. These days, self-publication of short collections (*not* full-length books; don't do it, they're seldom worth it) is relatively easy, not cripplingly expensive, and the results, as they say, "look great."

Keep the following considerations in mind when deciding whether you should publish your own chapbook:

- **Know what you are doing.** You are paying to create 50-200 (agree with your printer/publisher!) copies of your little chapbook. Hurray! Here they are at your door. Uh-oh . . . *now what?* If you're very, very lucky, your publisher may help out a little with distribution and P.R. But guess who gets to do the bulk of it!
- **Do it for the right reasons.** The two main wrong reasons? Vanity and greed. By vanity we mean that you love yourself more than the poetry and are doing this not for the poetry but rather for yourself. Always, self-publish not to rattle your train but instead to offer your works to readers and hearers. Greed is greed, and poetry pays mostly in human connections, so . . . greed is silly.
- **Be willing to work.** Self-publishing means self-publicizing, self-selling, self-stocking, and self-driving to local bookstores. It means self-advertising on your personal website and elsewhere online. (Your printer/publisher may offer you OK rates on ads. Consider buying some.) It means gracefully self-mentioning your chapbook amid poets. It means self-scheduling readings *and* self-staffing the merch table after readings. Distributing your book, even in your locale, much less far and wide, requires a lot of time and effort. But it has its rewards.

TECHNICAL STUFF

Self-publishing has a long and glorious history. (In the days before printing, self-publishing *was* publishing.) The Beat poets of the 1950s used to hand out mimeographed poems as the "daily news for the masses." Julia Vinograd, the "Bubble Lady" of Telegraph Avenue in Berkeley, California, self-published her little books for years and even made it into anthologies published by others.

Self-publication often is *part* of the life of a poet. Self-published chapbooks and other collections can be calling cards to give to fellow poets, distribute or sell at personal readings, open mics, and slams, or send to poets, readers, publishers, or editors you admire. Some poets have established presses of their own, assembling mailing lists, creating websites, and reaching an appreciative audience. Several poets — including a favorite of ours, Kathy Acker — easily and happily did both, back and forth between self-publishing and conventional publishing.

From 1970 to 2019, famed publisher David R. Godine ran his own publishing house, called simply Godine, driving boxes of books his press published from bookstore to bookstore, day after day. He solicited manuscripts, selected and edited them, and worked hard on everything from fonts to covers. A veritable one-man band of publication, he upheld the highest standards. And it showed: his books were beautiful, publication at Godine was prestigious, and writers he published included two Nobelists, one National Book Award winner, and a Pulitzer finalist.

REMEMBER

Poets self-publish because they have become part of a mutually supportive circle of other poets and want to join the conversation about poetry here and now. Publishing your own short collections or starting your own poetry press lets you be a part of that conversation. When you publish yourself or other poets, you are in effect saying, "This poetry is worth your attention. What do you think?"

AN EDITOR'S POV: DIANE LOCKWARD OF TERRAPIN BOOKS

Photo used by permission of Diane Lockward.

Diane Lockward is a poet, educator, and publisher with an admirable career. Her poetry books include *The Uneaten Carrots of Atonement* (2016), *Temptation by Water* (2010), *What Feeds Us* (2006), and *Eve's Red Dress* (2003), all from Wind Publications, and two chapbooks, *Eve Argues Against Perfection* (1997) and *Greatest Hits: 1997-2010* (2012). She is also the author/editor of four poetry craft books: *The Crafty Poet: A Portable Workshop* (revised edition, Terrapin

Books, 2016), *The Crafty Poet II: A Portable Workshop* (Terrapin Books, 2016), *The Practicing Poet: Writing Beyond the Basics* (Terrapin Books, 2018), and *The Strategic Poet: Honing the Craft* (Terrapin Books, 2021). She is also the editor of *What the House Knows* (Terrapin Books, 2025), an anthology of 116 poets around the theme of houses and their places in life and imagination.
We might add that Lockward is also the Poet Laureate of West Caldwell, New Jersey!

Notice "Terrapin Books" in the paragraph above? That is Lockward's very own press; she began it in 2015. She speaks with us about why she started it, how the press operates, and the editor's point of view regarding poets and publishing.

What led you to start your own press?

I had published *The Crafty Poet* with Wind Publications, and I had a second manuscript all ready — but then Wind went out of business! I didn't want to spend two years trying to find another publisher — and besides, for a while I'd been giving some thought to starting a small press. It seemed to be as good a time as any.

Was starting Terrapin a very involved process?

Less than you might have thought. I didn't find it that difficult. I already knew how to make a book; I'd done it several times already. I wasn't going to do my own printing, though, so the main thing was to find a reliable and accessible company that would. I decided it made sense to use Ingram Publishers House. If you take care of producing the book, they are easy to work with, easy to get started with, and easy to order from.

Terrapin books are beautiful objects, lovely homes for the poetry inside. So . . . are you swamped with manuscripts? How do you stay fresh as a reader?

I limit it to two open reading periods a year; I take three to four manuscripts every six months. So, the average is about six accepted manuscripts a year. This way, I'm not getting thousands of submissions. I get a couple hundred, and that feels about right.

So many poets feel that, very often, you just send your work out into the void and wait; there's no human presence on the other side. But you are that living, breathing person on the receiving end. Poets would probably appreciate knowing how things look from your side. So, let's start by asking: What are your tastes in poetry?

I publish mostly lyric poetry. I like formal poetry as well as free verse — I'm perfectly happy publishing books that have a combination of the two.

(continued)

(continued)

I appreciate your Guidelines page, especially the FAQs. You're delightfully direct about your tastes and requirements. For example, you say you have grown tired of "poems about poems." You also don't want all one kind of poem (e.g., all sonnets), translations, or collaborations. How about the plus side? What do you really appreciate when you find it?

I like good evidence of craft: I like to read work that shows intelligent and moving command of the work of making poems.

What should poets know about publication from the editor's or publisher's viewpoint? What missteps should they avoid?

They should know the publications they're submitting to — not just take some wild shot at a journal they don't know anything about or aren't ready for. Same thing if you are looking for a press to publish your book. I like it when poets show they know Terrapin and the kinds of work Terrapin has published. That's vital homework all poets should do before they submit.

Do you value cover letters?

Oh, yes. I really like a professional tone in a cover letter, a sense that the poet is prepared. I like to know something about the poet, get a little acquainted: where they've been published, what they're working on. And again, I like it when the poet tells me who they are, who we are, how they've been doing, and why their work is a good fit.

Let's say you accept a manuscript. What happens then? What do you expect of the poet?

I expect the poet to take a very active role in publicizing the book. I like to know that the poet is going to support that book and commit themselves to putting it in readers' hands. It's essential that they'll seek out readings and do them and be willing to travel. For Terrapin it's essential that you are willing to get out there, willing to do the work of being a poet.

Which is?

Poetry is first and foremost an aural and oral art. People need to hear your poems, ideally in your voice, in person. Doing readings is important. If you have a new book out, you get out there and read for people. Online readings are great, too: they became especially popular during COVID, and now they are very well established. You make sure you publicize your readings, and you read your work to audiences. With online readings, I hope the poet will do all the little things that make the most of the personal connection. If you're doing a Zoom reading, for example, you should always make sure to answer the chat room posts afterward. I've been doing readings for *What the House*

Knows, and it's been nice to have so many of the poets on hand to join in, and of course wonderful to see the audiences responding.

You require poets to have and use a Facebook account and a personal website. As you say, "Social media matters." Do you work with poets on marketing and audience-building?

One request I make is that the poet create an extensive email list, start building it, in fact, well before publication: your neighbors, your schoolmates, family members, colleagues at work, other poets and writers, not just a few people, into the hundreds if you can, anybody you know who might be interested. Because you never know! I ask poets to do an email blitz when the book is accepted, to build up enthusiasm; another when it's available for preorders, and another when it's actually published. People appreciate reminders. These techniques aren't limited to email, of course; I hope the poet will amplify all book-related announcements in *all* the media they are using, Instagram, Bluesky, and so on.

As editor, do you really edit? When and if you do, how do poets react?

In the FAQS on my Guidelines page, I say, "If you are unwilling to accept editorial input, this is probably not the press for you. All accepted manuscripts are edited." Most poets are fine, and some are even eager, for it: many of us are hungry to hear ideas about our work. But some poets resist that input, whether it's individual poems or the organization of the book. That's disappointing. If they were going to be that way, they really should have self-published the book. It's very rare, though, that I've had to part over things like that. When it has happened, it has been over editorial input or cover design.

Ah, covers. I love creating covers. Can you talk about that?

Looks matter. I work hard to create an attractive book, and I'm always interested in the poet's input. At the earliest stage of design, I ask about their expectations as far as the layout of the poems, the font, and so on. As for cover art, I really appreciate it if the poet has ideas for an artist or particular art for the cover design. If they're promising ideas, then I won't have to go through dozens of possibilities on my own. I like that teamwork aspect, and I especially like it when the poet's ideas work out.

Just now, you were saying that, regarding people who find various routes to buying your book, "You never know." What's a good example of a surprising customer?

How about my mailman? No joke. My mailman bought my book on Amazon.

Diane Lockward's website is `https://dianelockward.com`*, and Terrapin Books is at* `https://terrapinbooks.com`.

4

The Part of Tens

IN THIS PART . . .

Read ten poems worth knowing by heart and memorize the ones you like.

Enjoy ten poems about various aspects of love, from many times, places, and people.

IN THIS CHAPTER

» Stretching your mind by memorizing poetry

» Challenging your family and friends in a poetry-memorizing competition

Chapter 18 Ten Poems Worth Memorizing

In this chapter, we give you 10 poems worth permanently installing in your brain. Practice reading them aloud. Have memorization parties. Give prizes to those who can memorize "Kubla Khan," the longest poem here. Give a grand prize to anyone who can memorize the whole list.

Sonnet 73 by William Shakespeare (1564–1616)

That time of year thou mayst in me behold
When yellow leaves, or none, or few, do hang
Upon those boughs which shake against the cold,
Bare ruined choirs, where late the sweet birds sang.
In me thou see'st the twilight of such day
As after sunset fadeth in the west;
Which by and by black night doth take away,
Death's second self that seals up all in rest.
In me thou see'st the glowing of such fire,
That on the ashes of his youth doth lie,
As the deathbed whereon it must expire,

Consumed with that which it was nourished by.
This thou perceiv'st, which makes thy love more strong,
To love that well which thou must leave ere long.

Psalm 23 (King James Version, 1611)

The Lord is my shepherd;
I shall not want.
He maketh me to lie down in green pastures;
He leadeth me beside still waters;
He restoreth my soul.
He leadeth me in paths of righteousness
For his name's sake.
Yea, though I walk in the valley of the shadow of death,
I fear no evil,
For thou art with me;
Thy rod and thy staff,
They comfort me.
Thou preparest a table before me
In the presence of my enemies.
Thou anointest my head with oil;
My cup runneth over.
Surely goodness and kindness shall follow me
All the days of my life,
And I shall dwell in the house of the Lord
Forever.

Love (III) by George Herbert (1593–1633)

Love bade me welcome: yet my soul drew back,
Guilty of dust and sin.
But quick-eyed Love, observing me grow slack
From my first entrance in,
Drew nearer to me, sweetly questioning
If I lacked anything.
"A guest," I answered, "worthy to be here."
Love said, "You shall be he."
"I, the unkind, the ungrateful? Ah, my dear,
I cannot look on thee."

Love took my hand, and smiling did reply,
    "Who made the eyes but I?"
"Truth, Lord; but I have marred them; let my shame
    Go where it doth deserve."
"And know you not," says Love, "who bore the blame?"
    "My dear, then I will serve."
"You must sit down," says Love, "and taste my meat."
    So I did sit and eat.

Three Haiku by Kaga no Chiyo (1703–1775)

After a long winter, giving
each other nothing, we collide
with blossoms in our hands.

Don't dress for it.
The moon will transfigure —
those darling rags.

Once my parents were older
than I, still children,
same cicadas.

"The Tyger" by William Blake (1757–1828)

Tyger, Tyger, burning bright,
In the forests of the night,
What immortal hand or eye
Could frame thy fearful symmetry?

In what distant deeps or skies
Burnt the fire of thine eyes?
On what wings dare he aspire?
What the hand dare seize the fire?

And what shoulder, & what art
Could twist the sinews of thy heart?
And when thy heart began to beat,
What dread hand? & what dread feet?

What the hammer? what the chain?
In what furnace was thy brain?
What the anvil? What dread grasp
Dare its deadly terrors clasp?

When the stars threw down their spears
And watered heaven with their tears,
Did he smile his work to see?
Did he who made the Lamb make thee?

Tyger, Tyger, burning bright,
In the forests of the night,
What immortal hand or eye
Dare frame thy fearful symmetry?

"Kubla Khan" by Samuel Taylor Coleridge (1772–1834)

In Xanadu did Kubla Khan
A stately pleasure dome decree:
Where Alph, the sacred river, ran
Through caverns measureless to man
    Down to a sunless sea.
So twice five miles of fertile ground
With walls and towers were girdled round:
And there were gardens bright with sinuous rills,
Where blossomed many an incense-bearing tree;
And here were forests ancient as the hills,
Enfolding sunny spots of greenery.
But oh! that deep romantic chasm which slanted
Down the green hill athwart a cedarn cover!
A savage place! as holy and enchanted
As e'er beneath a waning moon was haunted
By woman wailing for her demon lover!
And from this chasm, with ceaseless turmoil seething,
As if this earth in fast thick pants were breathing,
A mighty fountain momently was forced:
Amid whose swift half-intermitted burst

Huge fragments vaulted like rebounding hail,
Or chaffy grain beneath the thresher's flail:
And 'mid these dancing rocks at once and ever
It flung up momently the sacred river.
Five miles meandering with a mazy motion
Through wood and dale the sacred river ran,
Then reached the caverns measureless to man,
And sank in tumult to a lifeless ocean:
And 'mid this tumult Kubla heard from far
Ancestral voices prophesying war!
    The shadow of the dome of pleasure
    Floated midway on the waves;
    When was heard the mingled measure
    From the fountain and the caves.
It was a miracle of rare device,
A sunny pleasure dome with caves of ice!
    A damsel with a dulcimer
    In a vision once I saw:
    It was an Abyssinian maid,
    And on her dulcimer she played,
    Singing of Mount Abora.
Could I revive within me
Her symphony and song,
To such deep delight 'twould win me,
That with music loud and long,
I would build that dome in air,
That sunny dome! those caves of ice!
And all who heard should see them there,
And all should cry, Beware! Beware!
His flashing eyes, his floating hair!
Weave a circle round him thrice,
And close your eyes with holy dread,
For he on honeydew hath fed,
And drunk the milk of Paradise.

"Spring and Fall" by Gerard Manley Hopkins (1844–1889)

To a Young Child

Márgarét, áre you gríeving
Over Goldengrove unleaving?
Leáves, líke the things of man, you
With your fresh thoughts care for, can you?
Áh! ás the heart grows older
It will come to such sights colder
By and by, nor spare a sigh
Though worlds of wanwood leafmeal lie;
And yet you *will* weep and know why.
Now no matter, child, the name:
Sórrow's spríngs áre the same.
Nor mouth had, no nor mind, expressed
What heart heard of, ghost guessed:
It ís the blight man was born for,
It is Margaret you mourn for.

"If — " by Rudyard Kipling (1865–1936)

If you can keep your head when all about you
  Are losing theirs and blaming it on you;
If you can trust yourself when all men doubt you
  Yet make allowance for their doubting too:
If you can wait, and not be tired by waiting,
  Or being lied about, don't deal in lies,
Or being hated don't give way to hating,
  And yet don't look too good, nor talk too wise;

If you can dream — and not make dreams your master;
  If you can think — and not make thoughts your aim,
If you can look on Triumph and Disaster
  And treat those two imposters just the same:
If you can bear to hear the truth you've spoken
  Twisted by knaves to make a trap for fools,
Or watch the things you give your life to, broken,
  And stoop and build them up with worn-out tools;

If you can make a heap of all your winnings
    And risk it on one turn of pitch-and-toss,
And lose, and start again at your beginnings,
    And never breathe a word about your loss:
If you can force your heart and nerve and sinew
    To serve your turn long after they are gone,
And so hold on when there is nothing in you
    Except the will which says to them: 'Hold on!'

If you can talk with crowds and keep your virtue,
    Or walk with Kings — nor lose the common touch,
If neither foes nor loving friends can hurt you,
    If all men count with you, but none too much:
If you can fill the unforgiving minute
    With sixty seconds' worth of distance run,
Yours is the world and everything that's in it,
    And — which is more — you'll be a Man, my son!

"Sea Rose" by H.D. (1886–1961)

Rose, harsh rose,
marred and with stint of petals,
meagre flower, thin,
sparse of leaf,

more precious
than a wet rose,
single on a stem —
you are caught in the drift.

Stunted, with small leaf,
you are flung on the sand,
you are lifted
in the crisp sand
that drives in the wind.

Can the spice-rose
drip such acrid fragrance
hardened in a leaf?

"One Art" by Elizabeth Bishop (1911–1979)

The art of losing isn't hard to master;
so many things seem filled with the intent
to be lost that their loss is no disaster.

Lose something every day. Accept the fluster
of lost door keys, the hour badly spent.
The art of losing isn't hard to master.

Then practice losing farther, losing faster:
places, and names, and where it was you meant
to travel. None of these will bring disaster.

I lost my mother's watch. And look! my last, or
next-to-last, of three loved houses went.
The art of losing isn't hard to master.

I lost two cities, lovely ones. And, vaster,
some realms I owned, two rivers, a continent.
I miss them, but it wasn't a disaster.

— Even losing you (the joking voice, a gesture
I love), I shan't have lied. It's evident
the art of losing's not too hard to master
though it may look like (*Write* it!) like disaster.

IN THIS CHAPTER

» Finding fantastic love poems worth knowing

» Inspiring your one true love with poetry

Chapter 19
Ten Love Poems

As long as poetry has existed, poets have explored the passions, urges, surprises, and complications of this exalted feeling. Readers have turned to love poems for solace, a touch of beauty, or better understanding of their own situations. Below are ten love poems. Written by men and women from many different times and places (archaic Greece, 10th-century Japan, 20th-century Chile, 21st-century New Jersey) and points of view, they explore all aspects of love, from lust to devotion to loving others to loving yourself. These are great poems to memorize, to send to significant others, or simply to contemplate as examples of what the meeting of great passion and great art can accomplish.

"Seems to me godlike" by Sappho (about 630–570 BC)

Seems to me godlike, that man
who sits near you, and you
close, speaking sweetly — he
listens intently —

and you laughing, charming,
truly compel my heart to
quake in my chest
for whenever, even

a moment, I glimpse you, no
words, my tongue has broken,
lightning has run beneath my
skin, I see nothing

rushing takes my ears, I run
with sweat, trembling
seizes all me, I am
greener than grass

and to myself little
short of dying
I seem

"If Someone Would Come" by Lady Izumi Shikibu (970–1030)

If someone would come,
I could show, and have him listen —
evening light shining
    on bush clover in full bloom
        as crickets bring on the night.

"Western Wind" by Anonymous (About the 15th Century)

Western wind, when wilt thou blow?
The small rain down can rain.
Christ, that my love were in my arms,
And I in my bed again.

"As Long as Eyes Can Cry" by Louise Labé (1522–1566)

As long as eyes can cry as all eyes should,
Regretting my time with you is in the past,
And voice resists my groans, and I at last
Can make myself a little understood,

As long as hand makes tender strings ring true
And gentle lute can help me sing your grace,
And spirit is content to find a place
In nothing more than understanding you,

I'll be content and not yet wish to die –
But when I feel my gritty, drying eye,
My shattered voice, my paralytic hand,

And if my spirit, in its mortal way
Can show no sign of love, I'll understand
And pray that death benights my brightest day.

"When I Heard at the Close of the Day" by Walt Whitman (1819–1892)

When I heard at the close of the day how my name had been receiv'd with plaudits in the capitol, still it was not a happy night for me that follow'd,

And else when I carous'd, or when my plans were accomplish'd, still I was not happy,

But the day when I rose at dawn from the bed of perfect health, refresh'd, singing, inhaling the ripe breath of autumn,

When I saw the full moon in the west grow pale and disappear in the morning light,

When I wander'd alone over the beach, and undressing bathed, laughing with the cool waters, and saw the sun rise,

And when I thought how my dear friend my lover was on his way coming, O then I was happy,

O then each breath tasted sweeter, and all that day my food nourish'd me more, and the beautiful day pass'd well,

And the next came with equal joy, and with the next at evening came my friend,

And that night while all was still I heard the waters roll slowly continually up the shores,

I heard the hissing rustle of the liquid and sands as directed to me whispering to congratulate me,

For the one I love most lay sleeping by me under the same cover in the cool night,

In the stillness in the autumn moonbeams his face was inclined toward me,

And his arm lay lightly around my breast — and that night I was happy.

Poem 640 by Emily Dickinson (1830–1886)

I cannot live with You —
It would be Life —
And Life is over there —
Behind the Shelf

The Sexton keeps the Key to —
Putting up
Our Life — His Porcelain —
Like a Cup —

Discarded of the Housewife —
Quaint — or Broke —
A newer Sevres pleases —
Old Ones crack —

I could not die — with You —
For One must wait
To shut the Other's Gaze down —
You — could not —

And I — Could I stand by
And see You — freeze —
Without my Right of Frost —
Death's privilege?

Nor could I rise — with You —
Because Your Face —
Would put out Jesus' —
That New Grace

Grow plain — and foreign
On my homesick Eye —
Except that You than He
Shone closer by —

They'd judge Us — How —
For You — served Heaven — You know,
Or sought to —
I could not —

Because You saturated Sight —
And I had no more Eyes
For sordid excellence
As Paradise

And were You lost, I would be —
Though My Name
Rang loudest
On the Heavenly fame —

And were You — saved —
And I — condemned to be
Where You were not —
That self — were Hell to Me —

So We must meet apart —
You there — I — here —
With just the Door ajar
That Oceans are — and Prayer —
And that White Sustenance —
Despair —

"A Negro Love Song" by Paul Laurence Dunbar (1872–1906)

Seen my lady home las' night,
Jump back, honey, jump back.
Hel' huh han' an' sque'z it tight,
Jump back, honey, jump back.
Hyeahd huh sigh a little sigh,
Seen a light gleam f'om huh eye,
An' a smile go flittin' by —
Jump back, honey, jump back.

Hyeahd de win' blow thoo de pine,
Jump back, honey, jump back.
Mockin'-bird was singin' fine,
Jump back, honey, jump back.
An' my hea't was beatin' so,
When I reached my lady's do',
Dat I could n't ba' to go —
Jump back, honey, jump back.

Put my ahm aroun' huh wais',
Jump back, honey, jump back.
Raised huh lips an' took a tase,
Jump back, honey, jump back.
Love me, honey, love me true?
Love me well ez I love you?
An' she answe'd, " 'Cose I do" —
Jump back, honey, jump back.

"Leaning Into the Afternoons" by Pablo Neruda (1904–1973)

Leaning into the afternoons I cast my sad nets
towards your oceanic eyes.

There in the highest blaze my solitude lengthens and flames,
its arms turning like a drowning man's.

I send out red signals across your absent eyes
that move like the sea near a lighthouse.

You keep only darkness, my distant female,
from your regard sometimes the coast of dread emerges.

Leaning into the afternoons I fling my sad nets
to that sea that beats on your marine eyes.

The birds of night peck at the first stars
That flash like my soul when I love you.

The night gallops on its shadowy mare
shedding blue tassels over the land.

"The Business" by Robert Creeley (1926–2005)

To be in love is like going out-
side to see what kind of day

it is. Do not
mistake me. If you love

her how prove she
loves also, except that it

occurs, a remote chance on
which you stake

yourself?
But barter for
the Indian was a means of sustenance.

"the cubist," by Lauren Fedorko (1988 –)

I hang onto you like you'll leave me if I blink
I secretly want you to touch me
in public, preferably — a bookstore, a museum
on the streets, in front of passersby
as if I could feel your love in sharp pieces
as if time were approaching death
as if I had a choice in our certain fate
I don't want to miss
your inside-out feelings
put together on your skin
a regurgitated array of storm clouds
the cubist would say
I could rearrange you the way I'd like
or that I could look at you unassembled
either way

I like you dismantled and in the dark —
a hundred thousand pieces
on their backs
lying in a peculiar angle
you'd still carry a sense of conviction
although estranged
I know you even when I try to forget

I know you even when you're in pieces
and
the more things change
the more they stay the same
the sum of your parts
out of order: familiar but new
remind me of my place in your world — :
a mustard stain on your favorite pair of slacks.

5
Appendixes

IN THIS PART . . .

Find quick and clear explanations of essential terminology.

Choose poems to read from each era covered in *Poetry For Dummies,* 2nd Edition.

Appendix A
Glossary

accent: See *stress.*

allegory: A story in which all the characters and events symbolize truths about human life. Allegories make sense on at least two levels: a literal level and a symbolic level (which may be very different from the literal level).

alliteration: Repeated sounds in a passage of verse. The word *alliteration* often means repeated consonant sounds at the beginning of neighboring words (as in *doggy diner*). It also is used to mean the general repetition of a consonant sound, as in the repeated *m* sounds in Tennyson's famous lines from "Come Down, O Maid":

> The moan of doves in immemorial elms,
>
> And murmuring of innumerable bees.

allusion: A reference to something — a person, place, or historical event — outside the poem, usually as an illustration of the poet's point or as a metaphor.

anapest: See *meter.*

apostrophe: Direct address to something you wouldn't ordinarily address, such as an abstraction ("Oh, love!") or an object in nature ("Oh, trees! Oh, rocks!"). Apostrophe is often a way to bring new life to things with which we are normally silent. It's a way to quickly become intimate with unexpected things.

Archaic Period or Era: What's older than Classical? Archaic! This term refers to the period, in what became Europe, between about 800 BC (when alphabets started to arise) to about the beginnings of democracy in the city-state of Athens (about 508 to 507 BC) The "next" period is called *Classical.* Standout poets in the Archaic Period include Homer, Hesiod, and Sappho.

assonance: Repetition of a sound; usually used to denote repetition or abundance of vowel sounds.

automatic writing: A practice in which the poet attempts to write but without conscious control. The aim is to give the subconscious freer rein, to loosen up the way the poet normally writes, producing (everyone hopes) new associations and new, unpredictable situations. Automatic writing is a practice central to the poetry of many Surrealist, Symbolist, and chance poets.

ballad: One of the most enduring forms of lyric poetry. Ballads are short, narrative songs, often with refrains. *Folk ballads* are anonymous ballads passed on orally. *Art ballads* are written by contemporary poets in imitation or reminiscence of the folk ballad.

blank verse: Poetry in iambic pentameter (see *meter*) that does not rhyme. (It isn't the same as *open-form poetry*, which isn't supposed to be written in any meter at all.) A good example of blank verse is "Ulysses" by Alfred, Lord Tennyson.

caesura: The heaviest pause in a line of verse.

canon: The established or accepted list of the "best" pieces of art, painting, or poetry. Who establishes them? Well, lots of people — mainly scholars in the universities. Canons can help guide you to what's good, and they're a good way to introduce yourself to excellent poetry. But the other nice thing about them is that you can ignore them and make up your own personal canon — the pieces of art *you* think are best.

cento: A poem made up of quotations from other poems. Centos come in all sorts of forms. Some may be *only* the first lines of other poems. Others may use only the last lines. Still others may run together parts of quotations, as in

> Something there is that does not love
> a pair of ragged claws scuttling across the floors of silent
> subways of cement he calls his home.

This passage stitches together moments from poems by Robert Frost, T.S. Eliot, and Elizabeth Bishop.

chapbook: A small book of poems, often published by a small press or self-published by the poet.

Classical poetry: This term can refer to Greek or Roman poetry written between 508 BC and AD 200 (or later; plenty of people disagree); poetry written in imitation of those writers; or any very famous or exemplary poetry. Many other cultures have "classical" periods. For example, Chinese poetry of the T'ang Dynasty, or other dynasties famous for the excellence of their verse, is known as *classical*.

concrete poetry: Poetry written to resemble the physical shape of its subject, as in a Coke-bottle-shaped poem about a Coke bottle.

convention: A widespread general agreement on how to do something. Poetry is full of such things. You could call rhyme a convention.

couplet: A pair of lines. Usually, but not always, a pair of lines written in the same form. Rhymed iambic pentameter couplets are called *heroic couplets*.

dactyl: See *meter.*

Digital Age. A literary or socio-historical period beginning around 2000, characterized by the rise and spread of new forms of communication enabled by digital technology and media. The Digital Age is just starting, and it has already revolutionized the poetry world.

dissonance: A combination of sounds that is gruff or discordant. It can be either displeasing to the ear or surprisingly pleasing even though harsh.

distich. A self-contained unit of two lines of verse. See *Psalm.*

dramatic monologue: A passage of verse written as if meant to be spoken by a single speaker on a stage. During a dramatic monologue, speakers usually narrates events in their real or psychic lives, thereby implying or revealing secrets about their viewpoints or psychological makeups. Also called *soliloquy.*

dramatic poetry: Poetry that's either meant to be put on as a play with actors, or poetry that could potentially be performed that way. Dramatic poetry has all the hallmarks of the drama, including plot, setting, character, and dialogue.

end rhyme: See *rhyme.*

enjambment: The practice of running a phrase or sentence over the end of one line and into the next without a punctuated pause.

> She vacuums his moaning
> bedroom with a scowl as
> dusty as he wouldn't want
> to dream of, not leaving
> anything clean.

Such twisting and turning can create opportunities for line endings that lead the reader around the end of the line into . . . all sorts of surprises.

Enlightenment: A period of European art and history (about 1660–1798) characterized by a renewed interest in human reason (alongside or instead of such institutions as tradition or religion), clarity of thought and statement, and proportion.

entrepreneurial poets: Poets who use all the tools of the digital and communications age to let people know about their activities, publications, and participation at poetry-related events. Poets, believe us, have *always* been entrepreneurs, but the rise of new tools in the *Global* and *Digital* Ages, plus the COVID-19 Pandemic of 2020-2023, changed a lot of people's habits and attitudes, and as of 2026, the entrepreneurial poet is a common figure on the poetry scene.

epic poetry: Traditionally, poetry on a grand scale, which tells the story of the establishment of a nation or community, with an epic hero who carries that community's values into battle against anything that threatens it. The hero may descend into hell, battle monsters, or contend with evil forces.

exact rhyme: See *rhyme.*

figure of speech: Any special use of language, including metaphor, simile, analogy, or pun. Figures of speech usually are not meant to be taken literally but imply more and other than what they say on the surface.

foot: A single rhythmical unit. See also *meter.*

free verse: We very much prefer and suggest the term *open-form poetry.*

genre: A kind of artwork or poetry, as in comedy, lyric, tragedy, satire, and so forth.

ghazal: A verse form practiced in Arabic and Persian poetry, as well as poetry in several of the languages of India. Ghazals became popular in English-language poetry in the late 1960s.

Global Period: A period of literature and culture. The Global Period began around 1989, with the fall of communism in Europe, and ended around the year 2000.

haiku: A traditional verse form originally practiced in Japan and China. It was brought into American and European poetry in the 20th century and now is one of the most familiar of verse forms. As it is usually taught and practiced in the Western world, a haiku is composed of three lines, the first having five syllables, the second having seven, and the third having five. Haiku traditionally begin with a natural scene tied to a season.

Harlem Renaissance: An African American art and literary movement that flourished in the 1920s.

hero: The central figure in an epic, tragedy, or other tale. The hero usually undergoes or performs most of the important events in the tale. Heroes cause the big changes that drive the story; their accomplishments have far-reaching meanings for the surrounding cast of characters. Not all heroes are successful or even clearly good. Heroes who don't act the way you'd expect heroes to act are often called antiheroes.

iamb: See *meter.*

image: Either (a) a vivid picture evoked through language, or (b) a particularly vivid evocation of the senses, especially sight.

internal rhyme: See *rhyme.*

inversion: In poetry, inversion is the practice of writing phrases or sentences out of their normal syntactical order. Compare "He isn't Leonardo DiCaprio" to "Leonardo DiCaprio he isn't." The second sentence is an inversion. Older poetry accepted inversion as a normal part of poetic expression. More recent poets use inversions for the sake of emphasis and surprise.

irony: Two kinds of irony are referred to most often. *Verbal irony* is the practice of saying one thing when you mean another. Such forms of irony include understatement, overstatement, *litotes* (created by negating a negative), and sarcasm. A second kind of irony is *situational irony,* which refers to events that happen at variance with or contrary to your expectations.

Late Antiquity: A period of European history and culture extending from the fall of Rome in AD 476 to around AD 1000.

light verse: Poetry that is playful or humorous and usually rhymed. Ogden Nash and Dorothy Parker are two poets who wrote excellent light verse.

line: A row of words considered as a unit in poetry.

lit mag: Widespread term meaning *literary magazine,* either printed or online.

litotes: See *irony.*

low diction: See *diction.*

lyric poetry: Short, usually songlike or personal poetry, as contrasted with the longer, communal poetry of the epic.

lyrics: The words to a song. Song lyrics have been one of the major sources of world poetry.

metaphor: An implicit comparison between two things, as in "My love is a red, red rose" (as opposed to the comparison in Robert Burns's line, "O my love's like a red, red rose," in which the comparison is a simile because it uses *like* to make the comparison *explicit*). Metaphors are more intimate and more ambiguous than similes. Poets often speak of A in terms of B; it's one of the driving engines of all poetry — encouraging readers to think of familiar things in new and unfamiliar ways.

meter: The patterned repetition of strong and weak stresses in a line of verse. Much of English poetry is written in lines that string together one or more *feet* (individual rhythmical units). Feet are the individual building blocks of meter. Here are the most common feet, the rhythms they represent, and an example of that rhythm.

- anapest: duh-duh-DUH, as in, *Get away!*
- dactyl: DUH-duh-duh, as in, honestly
- iamb: duh-DUH, as in *alas!*
- trochee: DUH-duh, as in *pizza*

To build a line of verse, as mentioned, poets can string together repetitions of one of these feet. Such repetitions are named as follows:

- one foot: monometer
- two feet: dimeter
- three feet: trimeter
- four feet: tetrameter
- five feet: pentameter
- six feet: hexameter

Thus, *iambic pentameter* is a string of five iambs, as in Christopher Marlowe's line from *Dr. Faustus:*

> Was this the face that launched a thousand ships
>
> Duh-DUH-duh-DUH-duh-DUH-duh-DUH-duh-DUH

Middle Ages: The historical period in Europe coming between the Dark Ages and the Renaissance, from about 1000 to about 1450.

Modern Period: The Modern Period in literature began roughly around 1910, when George V became King of England, and ended when the atomic bomb fell on Hiroshima and Nagasaki in 1945.

Modernism was a movement, characteristic of the *Modern Period,* that sought to renew and re-invigorate poetry. Faced with what many poets saw as the chaos and depersonalization of the world, they sought to break away from older forms of writing. Their poetry focused on concrete, precise imagery, sometimes difficult or alienating language, and startling, disorienting effects that included fragmentation, *Surrealism,* and *open-form poetry.* Searching for ways to "make it new," some modernist poets rediscovered the poetry of Japan or ancient Greece.

music: A catch-all term to cover the sum of all the sounds and rhythms in a piece of poetry; everything in a poem that strikes the ears.

myth: A story (fictional or true) told to set forth or explain the universe, history, or some enduring truth about human experience.

narrative poetry: Poetry that tells a story.

Old English: The earliest kind of English, spoken from at least AD 600 until about AD 1066.

onomatopoeia: The naming of a thing by imitating a sound associated with that thing. Onomatopoeic words include *moo, splash, blurt, zoom,* and *bang.*

open-form poetry: Poetry in which the poet avoids repetition of the same line length, meter, or rhyme scheme from line to line. Individual lines, or short passages, may have these features, but the poem as a whole is constructed to avoid them. See also *blank verse.* If you think of poems that are metered or rhymed as *closed* forms, you may call poems that reject those kinds of organization *open.* In open poetry (including chance poetry, Surrealism, and free verse), any of a wide variety of experimental techniques are used to blast open the possibilities of words on the printed page. The term also refers to the open use of language, theme, or subject.

oral poetry: Poetry that is primarily spoken rather than written. Also, poetry that is written but meant to recall the informality, rhythms, and surprises of oral verse.

paradox: An apparently contradictory state that is nevertheless true to life. When the Roman poet Gaius Valerius Catullus writes, "I hate and yet I love," it seems contradictory, yet few of us will accuse him of lying.

periods: Spans of time in literary history. Scholars speak of periods as having characteristics that make them easy to group together. You may say, for example, that the *Medieval Period* (about 1000–1450) is characterized by religious belief, whereas the *Postmodern Period* (1945 to the present) is less so. Why do people make these distinctions? To help them make sense of the poetry and history of the past. Although they are arbitrary, periods can be very helpful in giving you a context for the poetry you read.

persona: (a) The identity assumed by a writer in a literary work; (b) a word sometimes used as a synonym for *speaker;* (c) a speaker with an especially complicated or involved personality or mental state. See also *speaker.*

personification: The act of treating a nonhuman entity as though it were human. You can personify concrete things (such as your car), natural events (such as the weather), or abstractions (such as love). When poets personify, they are creating a metaphor, a comparison between the thing personified (a car) and various human characteristics (the propensity to break down or disappoint).

Postmodern Period: A period beginning in 1945 and extending until about 1989 and the fall of communism in Europe. The word *postmodern* also denotes a kind of attitude toward art and history, one that seeks to create new, open ways of writing and thinking.

Pre-Homeric Period: The time preceding the Homeric era, reckoned to have begun about 1000 BC That's a long time, covering the very earliest existing poetry (about 3500-3000 BC) and much of the poetry of the Egyptians.

prose poetry: Prose written employing the musical, rhythmic, and symbolic resources of poetry.

Psalm: A form of verse best known from the Book of Psalms in the Bible. Psalms are written in units of two lines; these units are known as *distichs*. The first line makes a statement that the second may echo, amplify, undermine, reverse or take into a whole new direction.

renaissance: Any vigorous rebirth of learning or artistic activity.

Renaissance Period: A literary and historic period extending from about 1450 to 1680. The Renaissance began and ended at different times in different European countries.

rhyme: The repetition of like sounds in a passage of poetry. The most familiar kind of rhyme is *end rhyme,* the repetition of the same (or nearly the same) sound at the end of consecutive lines, but there are several other varieties of rhyme, including

- internal rhyme: Rhyme that occurs within lines, as in this line from William Blake's "The Tyger": "Did he who made the Lamb make thee?"
- sight rhyme: Rhyme based on words that look as though they should rhyme perfectly, but in fact do not, as in

  the turkey bone
  says the turkey's gone

- slant, squint, or virtual rhyme: Various names for rhymes that are inexact or distant.
- vowel rhyme: Repetition of sounds based only on the vowel sounds in the rhyming words.

rhythm: The naturally occurring patterns of stressed and unstressed syllables in a passage of poetry. Different from *meter,* which is a repeated pattern of stresses.

romance: A genre of literature in which the characters and events are extremely fanciful or far from reality. Medieval romances may concern the activities of knights and dragons, whereas Shakespeare's romances, such as *The Tempest,* concern magic and the marvelous.

romantic: (a) Any aspect of literature having to do with the genre of *romance*; (b) any aspect having to do with love or amorous activity.

Romantic Period: A literary period (about 1798–1832) that saw an explosion of poetic activity across Europe. The Romantic Period was associated with an often revolutionary outlook, emphasizing the importance of personal emotions, the inspiration of the artist, innovation in ideas and the arts, and unity with nature. Some of these developments emerged as a reaction to the Industrial Revolution.

sarcasm: See *irony.*

satire: A genre in which a social behavior, whether of individuals or groups, is held up to public ridicule in an attempt to correct that behavior.

setting: The time, place, and physical environment in which a story takes place.

sight rhyme: See *rhyme.*

simile: An explicit comparison of two things, often using the words *like* or *as.* See also *metaphor.*

situation: (a) The circumstances or state of affairs at a given moment in a poem or story; (b) the circumstances a character finds himself in at a given moment.

slant rhyme: See *rhyme.*

soliloquy: See *dramatic monologue.*

sonnet: A poem of 14 lines, usually in iambic pentameter and usually rhymed. The two most familiar kinds of sonnet are the Italian (or Petrarchan) and the English (or Shakespearean).

speaker: The imaginary person who "speaks" the words in a poem. Some poems feature speakers as full-fledged characters with names and histories. But for the sake of discussion, people imagine all poems as having speakers. See also *persona.*

spondee: A metrical foot in which both syllables are long, as in "charmed lives."

squint rhyme: See *rhyme.*

stanza: A group of poetic lines that seem to belong together. In most traditional, rhymed verse, all stanzas have a predictable or regular form. In free verse, any sequential group of lines that appear to stand together may be considered a stanza.

stress: The emphasis or push given to a syllable in a word or a word in a line.

Surrealism: A movement in the arts, arising from the trauma of the First World War, that seeks to harness the unconscious as the source of creativity. Surreal poetry is characterized by dreamlike language and landscapes, fragmentation (broken or incomplete phrases, images, actions, even words), bizarre images and events, super-intense incursions of the uncanny, and the putting together of objects, words, or ideas in ways that may seem illogical, startling, hallucinatory, or frightening. Surrealism connected with several other tendencies in 20th- and 21st-century verse, especially with *modernism, postmodernism*, and *open-form poetry.*

symbol: Something that stands for something else, which in turn brings with it an intense world of meaning. In Christian religious symbolism, for example, the cross stands for the death of Jesus, an intensely meaningful event.

symbolism: The sum total of a poem's symbols and their meanings; the way a particular symbol is connected to its meaning.

Symbolism: A poetic movement that began in France and Germany in the late 19th century and spread later to England, the United States, and beyond. Many Symbolist poets stepped away from realistic, descriptive poetry about the real world, favoring the world of dreams and emotions. Some poets sought to create entire poems out of symbols, where new kinds of meanings and emotions might be generated. Symbolism, still vigorous today, fed into later movements that include *Surrealism, Modernism,* and *Postmdernism.*

tanka: A classical Japanese poetic form. As practiced by English-language poets, the tanka is a syllabic stanza with 5 lines, with syllable counts of 5-7-5-7-7. Many poets think of the tanka as a haiku (5-7-5) with two added 7-syllable lines.

tone: This word usually refers to the attitude of the speaker or the poet toward the subject of the poem. Thus, a poem's tone may be sincere, angry, ironic, jubilant, doubtful, or sad. *Tone* is also used to mean the attitude of the speaker or the poet toward the *audience*, or the general emotional weather of the poem.

tragedy: A genre in which an admirable person is undone. Most tragedies contain the following characteristics:

- A tragic protagonist or tragic hero to whom most of the important events of the tragedy occur.
- A calamitous fall from good fortune by the tragic protagonist, usually ending in his or her destruction. Usually this fall is brought about by an error in the protagonist's judgment or character (called the *hamartia* or *tragic flaw*). This hamartia is
  - An ending in which the protagonist's entire family line or nation is destroyed, to be succeeded by others who have learned from the protagonist's fall.

- Usually related to the protagonist's *hubris* or excessive pride.
- Usually (and ironically) the best and most admirable thing about the protagonist.

tragic flaw: See *tragedy.*

trochee: See *meter.*

verse: (a) A line of poetry; (b) poetry in general. See also *light verse.*

Victorian Period: The historic and literary period occurring during the same time as the reign of Queen Victoria of England (1837–1901).

virtual rhyme: See *rhyme.*

visual rhythm: (a) The effect produced by the alternation of lines of varying length; (b) the total effect of the shape of a poem.

voice: The impression of a personality behind a piece of writing. Although the term *voice* is often used as synonymous with the word *style,* it's actually the impression that style leaves of the stylist's character.

vowel rhyme: See *rhyme.*

Appendix **B**

The *Poetry For Dummies* Reading List

This bonus chapter contains the *Poetry For Dummies*, 2nd Edition, supplemental reading list. The works listed here provide a springboard for exploring the eras we cover in the book. Dip in, and enjoy all that these volumes have to offer!

TIP

You often can find poems by searching on the following websites:

- Poem-a-Day (`https://poets.org/poem-a-day`), a daily offering of new poems by the American Academy of Poets
- Poetry Foundation (`https://www.poetryfoundation.org/poems`), an enormous trove of all kinds of poetry, good for searching, even better for reading
- Poetry Daily (`https://poems.com`), more than 9500 poems, plus a daily poem, news, features, and a vast archive
- Poetry Society of America (`https://poetrysociety.org`), with plenty of poems to read, plus news, interviews, essays, programs, and events
- The Poetry Archive (`https://poetrysociety.org`), a wonderful collection of recordings of poets reading their work
- AllPoetry (`https://allpoetry.com`), which bills itself as "the world's largest poetry site," with poems to read, writing groups, poetry communities, and more

The Pre-Homeric Period

If you're interested in reading poetry from the pre-Homeric period, check out the following:

- *The Bhagavad-Gita*, translated by Juan Mascaró
- *Gilgamesh: A New Rendering in English Verse*, translated by David Ferry
- *Gilgamesh: A Verse Narrative*, by Herbert Mason
- *Love Poetry and Songs from the Ancient Egyptians*, compiled by Gilbert Moore
- *The Ramayana: A New Retelling of Valmiki's Ancient Epic — Complete and Comprehensive*, by Linda Egenes and Kumuda Reddy

The Biblical Period

If you're interested in reading more poetry from this era, check out the following books:

- The authorized King James Bible is the traditional source for the poetry of the Old Testament. Try to find an edition that renders the poetry in lines.
- *The Iliad,* by Homer, translated by Emily Wilson.
- *The Odyssey,* by Homer, translated by Emily Wilson.
- *The Psalms,* translated by Robert Alter.

The Archaic and Classical Periods

These eras embrace the high points of Greek and Latin poetry. The story of these two great languages and cultures makes up a golden six centuries of recorded history.

Check out the following books to read more from these periods:

- *7 Greeks,* translated by Guy Davenport
- *The Aeneid,* by Virgil, translated by Shadi Bartsch
- *The Erotic Poems,* by Ovid, translated by Peter Green

- *The Essential Horace: Odes, Epodes, Satires, and Epistles*, translated by Burton Raffel
- *If Not, Winter: Fragments of Sappho*, translated by Anne Carson
- *Metamorphoses*, by Ovid, translated by David R. Slavitt
- *The Nature of Things*, by Lucretius, translated by A.E. Stallings
- *The Penguin Book of Greek and Latin Verse*, translated by Christopher Childers
- *The Poems of Catullus*, translated by Peter Whigham
- *Seven Famous Greek Plays*, edited by Whitney J. Oates and Eugene O'Neill, Jr.

Late Antiquity and Golden Ages

If you're interested in reading more poetry from Late Antiquity and the Golden Ages (the classical era of poetry in Arabic, the T'ang Dynasty in China), check out any of the following:

- *Beowulf*, translated by Seamus Heaney
- *Beowulf and Other Old English Poems*, translated by Constance B. Hieatt
- *Classical Arabic Poetry*, translated by Charles Greville Tuetey
- *Classical Chinese Poetry*, translated by David Hinton
- *Ten Thousand Leaves: Love Poems from the Manyoshu*, translated by Harold Wright
- *Three Chinese Poets: Translations of Poems* by Wang Wei, Li Bai, and Du Fu; translated by Vikram Seth

The Middle Ages

The Middle Ages were anything but middling, as you can see from the poetry of the time:

- *The Canterbury Tales*, by Geoffrey Chaucer, translated by Nevill Coghill
- *Gold* and *Water*, by Rūmī, translated by Haleh Liza Gafori

- *The Inferno of Dante: A New Verse Translation,* translated by Robert Pinsky
- *Lyrics of the Troubadours and Trouvères: An Anthology and a History,* translated by Frederick Goldin
- *The Nibelungenlied,* translated by A.T. Hatto
- *The Rubaiyat,* by Omar Khayyam, translated by Edward FitzGerald
- *Selections from the Canzoniere and Other Works,* by Francesco Petrarca, translated by Mark Musa
- *The Song of Roland,* translated by Patricia Terry
- *The Tale of Genji,* by Murasaki Shikibu, translated by Royall Tyler; check out `genjipoems.org`.
- *Tristan,* by Gottfried von Strassburg, translated by A.T. Hatto

The Renaissance

To read poetry from the Renaissance, check out the following books:

- *Elizabethan Drama: Eight Plays,* edited by John Gassner and William Green
- *English Renaissance Poetry: A Collection of Shorter Poems from Skelton to Jonson,* edited by John Williams
- *Le Cid,* by Pierre Corneille, translated by Vincent Cheng
- *Life Is a Dream and Other Spanish Classics,* edited by Eric Bentley, translated by Roy Campbell
- *Phaedra: Tragedy in Five Acts, 1677,* by Jean Racine, translated by Richard Wilbur
- *The Portable Milton,* edited by Douglas Bush
- *The Riverside Shakespeare,* 2nd Edition, edited by G. Blakemore Evans
- *The Sonnets,* by William Shakespeare
- *Tartuffe: Comedy in Five Acts, 1669,* by Molière, translated by Richard Wilbur

The Enlightenment and the Eighteenth Century

For poems from the Enlightenment, check out the following books:

- *The Norton Anthology of English Literature, Volume 1,* edited by M.H. Abrams
- *The Essential Haiku: Versions of Basho, Buson, and Issa,* translated by Robert Hass

Romantic Poetry, the Victorian Period, Symbolism, and Whitman and Dickinson

The 19th century was a worldwide explosion of poetries. Here are some things to read to get a taste.

Romantics:

- *Don Juan,* by George Gordon, Lord Byron, edited by Leslie A. Marchand
- *Eugene Onegin: A Novel in Verse,* by Alexander Pushkin, translated by James E. Falen. (You can find a recording of Stephen Fry reading *Eugene Onegin* aloud by searching on SoundCloud or YouTube.)
- *Faust: A Tragedy,* by Johann Wolfgang von Goethe, translated by Walter Arndt, edited by Cyrus Hamlin. Readings and performances of this play exist on YouTube and elsewhere — it's a lot, but it's the Romantic era concentrated in one drama.
- *Poets of the English Language, Volume 3: Romantic Poets,* edited by W.H. Auden and Norman Holmes Pearson
- *Selected Poems,* by William Wordsworth
- *Women Romantic Poets: 1785–1832: An Anthology,* edited by Jennifer Breen

The Symbolists:

- *The Flowers of Evil,* by Charles Baudelaire, edited by James. N, McGowan
- *French Symbolist Poetry,* edited by C.F. MacIntyre

Walt and Emily:

- *Leaves of Grass*, by Walt Whitman. Edited by Michael Moon
- *The Poems of Emily Dickinson: Reading Edition*, edited by R.W. Franklin

Masoaka Shiki and New Style haiku:

Haiku Master Shiki, translated by Earl Trotter

The Modern Era

These anthologies contain poems of the Modern Era:

- *The Norton Anthology of Modern and Contemporary Poetry,* 3rd Edition, edited by Jahan Ramazani, Richard Ellmann, and Robert O'Clair
- *Poems for the Millennium,* Volume 1, edited by Jerome Rothenberg and Pierre Joris

Postmodernism

Here are some anthologies of postmodern poetry to check out:

- *The Harvard Book of Contemporary American Poetry,* edited by Helen Vendler
- *The New American Poetry: 1945–1960,* edited by Donald M. Allen
- *The Norton Anthology of Modern Poetry,* edited by Richard Ellmann and Robert O'Clair
- *The Pittsburgh Book of Contemporary American Poetry,* edited by Ed Ochester and Peter Oresick
- *Postmodern American Poetry: A Norton Anthology,* edited by Paul Hoover
- *The Postmoderns: The New American Poetry Revised,* edited by Donald M. Allen
- *The Vintage Book of Contemporary World Poetry,* edited by J.D. McClatchy

The Global Era

Check out any of the following to get an idea of the kinds of poetry being written in the Global Period:

- *Aloud! Voices from the Nuyorican Poets Café,* edited by Bob Holman and Miguel Algarín
- *An Anthology of New (American) Poets,* edited by Chris Stroffolino, Lisa Garnat, and Leonard Schwartz
- *The Anthology of Rap,* edited by Adam Bradley and Andrew DuBois
- "Lyric Legend – 90s Rap and Hip-Hop." Public Playlist. Spotify.
- *Moving Borders: Three Decades of Innovative Writing by Women,* edited by Mary Margaret Sloan
- *Poems for the Millennium, Volume 2,* edited by Jerome Rothenberg and Pierre Joris

The Digital Era

Here are some great examples of poetry based on other kinds of art:

- Danez Smith writes his poem "Dinosaurs in the Hood" while thinking about the movie Jurassic Park.
- In his 2016 poem "Book of Statues," Richie Hofmann goes from looking at pictures of statues to considering some of the era's worst crimes against human rights.
- In his 2019 poem "My Life in Brutalist Architecture #1," John Gallaher thinks aloud about living among buildings, people . . . and squirrels!
- In her 2021 poem "Macabre Dance", Fiona Sze-Lorrain hears "the spirit/ in three-four beat" and is carried into a surreal world.
- And, always, music: Ocean Vuong's "Aubade with Burning City" laces together parts of the Irving Berlin song "White Christmas" with images of refugees in wartime.

Modern and Contemporary Poetry

Take a look-in to Modern and Contemporary Poetry at ModPo (`https://modpo.org`). Easily the largest modern poetry course in the world, ModPo has more than 43,000 participants at any one time; it's estimated that more than 900,000 people have visited since it began. Run by Professor Al Filreis and the Kelly Writers House at the University of Pennsylvania, it's all discussion, all the time. You can choose and cruise, make your own way, listen to other folks, use this amazing course as your wondrous heart desires. A splendid time is guaranteed for all.

Listen to Al Filreis talk about ModPo and his book about it, *The Classroom and the Crowd*, on the Musical Innertube podcast: `https://youtu.be/IfyK6fiQRhQ`.

Many practitioners of other arts (Michelangelo, Leonardo, Picasso, and others) also have written poetry. One of these was Frida Kahlo, probably the most famous female painter, in fact the most famous Surrealist painter, in the world. Easily. She also was an enthusiastic, longtime journal-keeper! In that journal she wrote poetry that was, by turns, passionate, Surrealist, witty, and painful ("I am not sick. I am broken. But I am happy to be alive as long as I can paint.") And many Frida Kahlo exhibits have made her poetry part of the exhibit. A great example was *Viva Frida Kahlo*, an immersive installation that surrounded audiences with her art — through which laced her strongly-voiced, musical verse, either as writing or as reading. The exhibit began in Mexico City and traveled throughout the world.

Permissions

Abû-l-`Alâ' al-Ma'arrî. *See* Timpane, John.

Adonis (Ali Ahmad Sa'id). *See* Hibbard, Allen and Osama Isber.

Antin, David. Translation of "A Man and Woman Absolutely White" by André Breton. Reprinted by permission of David Antin.

Barnstone, Willis. Translation of "Mother's Song" ("If snow falls"). Reprinted with permission of Willis Barnstone. Excerpted from *A Book of Women Poets from Antiquity to Now: Selections from the World Over*, edited by Aliki Barnstone and Willis Barnstone. New York: Schocken, 1992.

Bei Dao. *See* Finkel, Donald.

Bernstein, Charles. Writing exercises from `http://epc.buffalo.edu/authors/bernstein`. Reprinted by permission of Charles Bernstein.

Bishop, Elizabeth. "One Art," from *The Complete Poems 1927–1979* by Elizabeth Bishop. Copyright 1979, 1983 by Alice Helen Methfessel. Reprinted by permission of Farrar, Straus and Giroux LLC.

Breton, André. *See* Antin, David.

Carter, Steven D. Translation of Lady Izumi Shikibu, "If someone would come." Reprinted from *Traditional Japanese Poetry: An Anthology*. Translated, with an Introduction, by Stephen D. Carter. Reprinted with permission of the publishers, Stanford University Press. Copyright © 1991 by the Board of Trustees of the Leland Stanford Junior University.

Césaire, Aimé. *See* Davis, Gregson.

Chase, Karen. "Federico Fellini's Letter" and narration of its composition. By permission of Karen Chase.

Chernoff, Maxine. Writing exercises. Reprinted by permission of Maxine Chernoff.

Chilam Balam. *See* Sawyer-Laucanno, Christopher.

Chiyo. *See* Ray, David.

Corbett, William. "Vermont Apollinaire." Copyright © 1995 by William Corbett, from *New & Selected Poems.* Zoland Books, Cambridge, Massachusetts.

Creeley, Robert. "The Business." From *Collected Poems of Robert Creeley, 1945–1975.* Copyright © 1983 The Regents of the University of California. Reprinted by permission of University of California Press on behalf of the author.

Cummings, E.E. "in Just-." Copyright 1923, 1951, © 1991 by the Trustees for the E.E. Cummings Trust. Copyright © 1976 by George James Firmage, from *Complete Poems: 1904–1962* by E.E. Cummings, edited by George J. Firmage. Used by permission of Liveright Publishing Corporation.

Davis, Gregson. Lines from "Since Akad, Since Elam, Since Sumer" by Aimé Césaire. Excerpted from *Non-Vicious Circle: Twenty Poems of Aimé Césaire*, translated, with an introduction and commentary, by Gregson Davis. Reprinted by the permission of the publishers, Stanford University Press. © 1984 by the Board of Trustees of the Leland Stanford Junior University.

Dickinson, Emily. Lines from Poems 214, 440, 621, 640, and 1732. Reprinted by permission of the publishers and The Trustees of Amherst College from *The Poems of Emily Dickinson*, Thomas H. Johnson, ed., Cambridge, Mass.: The Belknap Press of Harvard University Press, Copyright © 1951, 1955, 1979 by the President and Fellows of Harvard College.

Eliot, T.S. Excerpt from *The Waste Land* from *Collected Poems, 1909–1962*, copyright 1930 and renewed 1958 by T.S. Eliot, reprinted by permission of Faber and Faber Ltd.

Enheduanna. *See* Hallo, William W. and J.J.A. van Dijk.

Feinstein, Elaine. Excerpts from translation of Marina Tsvetayeva, "Poem of the End." From *Selected Poems.* Reprinted by permission of Carcanet Press Limited.

Fedorko, Lauren. "the cubist." By permission of Lauren Fedorko.

Ferlinghetti, Lawrence. Excerpt from "Constantly Risking Absurdity" (*Coney Island of the Mind*, #15) from *A Coney Island of the Mind.* Copyright © 1958 by Lawrence Ferlinghetti. Reprinted by New Directions Publishing Corp.

Finkel, Donald. Excerpts from translations of Bei Dao, "Answer," from *A Splintered Mirror: Chinese Poetry from the Democracy Movement*, translated by Donald Finkel. Translations copyright © 1991 by Donald Finkel. Reprinted by permission of North Point Press, a division of Farrar Straus & Giroux, LLC.

Fox, Valerie and Lynn Levin. Poetry prompts from *Poems for the Writing: Prompts for Poets*. 2nd ed. By permission of Valerie Fox and Lynn Levin.

Francis, Robert. "Silent Poem." From *Collected Poems* by Robert Francis. Copyright © 1976 by Robert Francis. Reprinted by permission of University of Massachusetts Press.

Fraser, Kathleen. "Vanishing Point: Third Black Quartet" from "Wing." From *il cuore: the heart* © 1997 by Kathleen Fraser, Wesleyan University Press. Reprinted by permission of University Press of New England.

Frost, Robert. "Nothing Gold Can Stay." From *The Poetry of Robert Frost*, Edited by Edward Connery Lathem. Copyright 1916, 1923, © 1969 by Henry Holt and Co., copyright 1944, 1951 by Robert Frost. Reprinted by permission of Henry Holt and Company, LLC.

Gafori, Liza Haleh. Translation of "You Found Me Again." Used by permission of Liza Haleh Gafori.

Glück, Robert. Translation of "Departure" by Pierre Reverdy. Reprinted by permission of Robert Glück.

Graham, Jorie, Lines from "In What Manner the Body Is United with the Soule," from *Erosion* by Jorie Graham. Copyright © 1983 by Princeton University Press. Reprinted by permission of the publisher.

Gross, Luray. *"Dolce Far Niente"* and narration of its composition. With permission of Luray Gross.

Guest, Barbara. Lines from "Red Lilies." Reprinted by permission of Barbara Guest.

Hallo, William W. and J.J.A. van Dijk. Translation of *The Exaltation of Inanna*, "Antiphonal Hymn in Praise of Inanna" by Enheduanna. Reprinted by permission of Yale University Press.

H.D. (Hilda Doolittle). "Oread" and "Sea Rose." From *Collected Poems, 1912–1944*. Copyright © 1982 by The Estate of Hilda Doolittle. Reprinted by permission of New Directions Publishing Corp. and Carcanet Press Limited.

Hibbard, Allen and Osama Isber, excerpt from translation of Adonis (Ali Ahmad Sa'id), "A Desire Moving Through the Maps of the Material." Reprinted by permission of Allen Hibbard and Osama Isber.

Hilbert, Ernest. Excerpt from "We Make Mountains so We May Move Them" and two posts on X. Used by permission of Ernest Hilbert.

Hoffman, Roald. Excerpt from "Deceptively Like a Solid." Reprinted with permission of David Moore, Managing Editor, Society of Glass Technology.

Holt, Kelly. Writing exercises. Reprinted by permission of Kelly Holt.

Homer. *See* Timpane, John.

Howe, Fanny. "About Face." Reprinted by permission of Fanny Howe.

Imr El-Qais. *See* Timpane, John.

Issa, Kobayashi. *See* Timpane, John.

Jarrell, Randall. "The Death of the Ball Turret Gunner," from *The Complete Poems* by Randall Jarrell. Copyright © 1969, renewed 1997 by Mary von S. Jarrell. Reprinted by permission of Farrar, Straus and Giroux LLC and Faber and Faber Ltd.

Keats, John. Excerpt from "The Eve of St. Agnes." Reprinted by permission of the publisher from *John Keats: Complete Poems*, edited by Jack Stillinger. Cambridge, Mass.: Harvard University Press. Copyright © 1978, 1982 by the President and Fellows of Harvard College.

Langton, Daniel J. Writing exercise. Reprinted by permission of Daniel J. Langton.

Laozi. *See* Timpane, John.

Lawrence, D.H. "Bavarian Gentians" by D.H. Lawrence, from The Complete Poems of D.H. Lawrence by D.H. Lawrence, edited by V. de Sola Pinto & F.W. Roberts, copyright © 1964, 1971 by Angelo Ravagli and C.M. Weekley, Executors of the Estate of Frieda Lawrence Ravagli. Used by permission of Viking Penguin, a division of Penguin Putnam Inc., and by permission of Laurence Pollinger Limited and the Estate of Frieda Lawrence Ravagli.

Li Bai. *See* Timpane, John.

Liu Zongyuan. *See* Timpane, John.

Lorde, Audre. Lines from "Coal." From *Chosen Poems: Old and New* by Audre Lorde. Reprinted by permission of W.W. Norton, Inc.

Mac Low, Jackson. Excerpt from "Antic Quatrains," from *Bloomsday*, Copyright © 1984 by Jackson Mac Low. Published by permission of Station Hill Press, Inc. in Barrytown, N.Y.

Mayer, Bernadette. Writing exercises. Printed by permission of Bernadette Mayer.

McCuen Pat. "HALLOWEEN HEAD HOUSE BOOKS." Poster reproduced by permission of artist Pat McCuen and of Richard DeWyngaert, proprietor of Head House Books.

Merwin, W.S. Excerpt from "Leviathan." Copyright © 1956 by W.S. Merwin. Reprinted by permission of the Wylie Agency. Translations of Pablo Neruda, "Leaning into the Afternoons" and "Walking Around," from *Selected Poems* by Pablo Neruda, translated by W.S. Merwin, edited by Nathaniel Tarn. Published by Jonathan Cape. Used by permission of the Random House Group Limited.

Milton, John. Excerpts from "L'Allegro" and *Paradise Lost*. Reprinted by permission of Random House, Inc.

Moore, Marianne. Except from "The Monkeys." Reprinted with permission of Faber and Faber Ltd and Scribner, a Division of Simon & Schuster, from *The Collected Poems of Marianne Moore*. Copyright 1935 by Marianne Moore. Copyright renewed © 1963 by Marianne Moore and T.S. Eliot.=

Moriarty, Laura. "The Mouth." Reprinted by permission of Laura Moriarty.

"Mother's Song" ("If snow falls"). *See* Barnstone, Willis.

Mullins, Brighde. Writing exercises. Reprinted by permission of Brighde Mullins.

Myles, Eileen. "The Honey Bear." Copyright © 1995 by Eileen Myles. From *Maxfield Parrish: Early & New Poems*. Reprinted with permission of Black Sparrow Press. Writing exercise. Reprinted by permission of Eileen Myles.

Neruda, Pablo. *See* Merwin, W.S.

Niedecker, Lorine. "Now in one year." Reprinted by permission of Cid Corman, literary executor of The Lorine Niedecker Estate, 2000 A.D.

North, Charles. Excerpt from "Shooting for Line," pages 168–175 in *New and Selected Poems*. Copyright © 1999 by Charles North (Los Angeles: Sun & Moon Press, 1999). Reprinted by permission of the publisher.

Oppen, George. Excerpt from "Psalm." From *Collected Poems*, Copyright © 1975 by George Oppen. Reprinted by permission of New Directions Publishing Corp.

Parker, Dorothy. "Résumé." Copyright 1926, 1928, renewed 1954, © 1956 by Dorothy Parker. From *The Portable Dorothy Parker* by Dorothy Parker. Used by permission of Viking Penguin, a division of Penguin Putnam Inc., and Gerald Duckworth & Co. Ltd.

Perelman, Bob. ("The speakers vibrate through the entire house"), excerpt from *a.k.a.* First published by *The Figures.* Reprinted by permission of Geoffrey Young, editor/publisher of *The Figures*.

Pound, Ezra. "In a Station of the Metro." From *Personae*, Copyright © 1926 by Ezra Pound. Reprinted by permission of New Directions Publishing Corp and Faber and Faber Ltd.

Ray, David. Translation of lines from Chiyo. Reprinted by permission of Willis Barnstone.

Reverdy, Pierre. *See* Glück, Robert.

Riggs, Don. "That's the Way It Goes" and narration of its composition. By permission of Don Riggs.

Rimbaud, Arthur. *See* Timpane, John.

Rumi, "You Found Me Once Again," translated by Haleh Liza Gafori. From *Gold,* published by NYRB Classics, 2022. Translation copyright (c) 2022 by Haleh Liza Gafori.

Sappho. *See* Timpane, John.

Saunier, Hayden. "City Bus," first and second drafts, and narration of revision. Used by permission of Hayden Saunier.

Sawyer-Laucanno, Christopher. Excerpt from translation of Chilam Balam, "Flight of the Itzás," from *The Destruction of the Jaguar: Poems from the Books of Chilam Balam*. Copyright © 1987 by Christopher Sawyer-Laucanno. Reprinted by permission of City Lights Books.

Shikibu, Lady Izumi. *See* Carter, Steven. D.

Spicer, Jack. Lines from "Imaginary Elegies, Parts I–III." Copyright © 1975 by The Estate of Jack Spicer. Reprinted from *The Collected Books of Jack Spicer* with the permission of Black Sparrow Press.

Stewart, Susan. "The Knot." From *Cinder: New and Selected Poems.* Copyright © 2017. Reprinted by permission of Graywolf Press.

Timpane, John. Translations of the *Bhagavad-Gita,* excerpt from Canto 11 ("Arjuna said"), Dante ("In the midst of the road"), *Beowulf* ("soon he saw"), Homer ("Then wide-ruling Agamemnon," "Infinite terror," "war spears"), Labé ("As long as eyes"), Machado ("Traveler, Your Footsteps"), Rimbaud, "Bateau Ivre" ("If I desire") and "Memory" ("Longing for young arms"), the *Rig-Veda* ("There were no things"), Salinas ("From *The Voice Due to You*"), and Sappho ("Rainbow-throned, deathless Aphrodite," "The moon has set," "Seems to me godlike, that man"); versions of Abû-l-`Alâ' al-Ma'arrî ("Friend, this world"), anonymous Egyptian poem ("Only one, matchless sister"), Bashō ("beneath a warrior's"), Imr El-Qais ("Here was the place I watched her"), Issa ("morning"), Laozi ("Rule a large nation"), Li Bai ("Moonlight pools"), Liu Zongyuan ("From one thousand mountains"), Murasaki Shikibu ("Dew on the Wings," "In my heart, as if," "You love the beauty"), and Ono no Komachi ("They say autumn nights"). Printed by permission of John Timpane.

Tomlinson, Charles. Lines from "Mr. Brodsky." From *American Scenes* by Charles Tomlinson. Copyright © 1966. Reprinted by permission of Carcanet Press Limited.

Trinidad, David. "Monster Mash." From *Plasticville* by David Trinidad. Reprinted by permission of Turtle Point Press, 2000.

Tsvetayeva, Marina. *See* Feinstein, Elaine.Waldman, Anne. Excerpt from "Iovis XIX." Reprinted with permission of Coffee House Press.

Weldon-Soiset, Melanie. "A Lullaby Patchwork Quilt" from *Welcome Calm, Silence Tyrants: Adult Lullabies.* Copyright © 2025 Melanie Weldon-Soiset. Reprinted with permission, Shanti Arts LLC.

Williams, William Carlos. Excerpt from "The Descent." From *Collected Poems 1939–1962, Volume II.* Copyright © 1953 by William Carlos Williams. Reprinted by permission of New Directions Publishing Corp. and Carcanet Press Limited.

Yeats, William Butler. "The Second Coming," reprinted with the permission of Scribner, a Division of Simon & Schuster from *The Collected Poems of W.B. Yeats.* Revised Second Edition edited by Richard J. Finneran. Copyright 1924 by Macmillan Publishing Company, renewed 1952 by Bertha Georgie Yeats and A P Watt, Ltd.

Zukofsky, Louis. "In Arizona" from "29 Songs," from *Complete Short Poetry.* p. 45. Reprinted with permission of The Johns Hopkins University Press.

Index

J

K

L

M

N

O

P

Q

R

S

T

About the Author

John Timpane was the Commentary Page Editor, Theater Critic, and Books Editor of *The Philadelphia Inquirer* from 1997 to 2019. How'd he get there — and how'd he get from there to *Poetry For Dummies?* To answer the question, we'll report that John got an email and phone call one day from Marina Watts (see below), asking if he'd be interested in helping write *Poetry For Dummies,* and it turned out he would be. John has written poetry since he was very small, works at the craft, and is very much involved in the poetry scene. He was graduated from Stanford University with an M.A. and Ph.D. in English and the Humanities in 1980. John won the Academy of American Poets Prize at Stanford in 1980 and, while teaching at Rutgers University, was a Fulbright Scholar in 1983–1984. Pre-*Inquirer*, John taught English in colleges and universities for 20 years; wrote books on composition and poetry; published articles on Shakespeare, Spenser, Ntozake Shange, Tennessee Williams, August Wilson, and other great writers; and, on the side, did (and still does) a nifty little freelance writing gig, everything from scientific writing and film scripts to journalism and ghost-writing. Poetry, with its demand for clarity of vision, concentration of feeling in a small space, and richness of language, helps John be a better editor and writer. The eldest of nine children, he is married to Maria-Christina Keller, Copy Director at *Scientific American* and a beautiful writer. Perhaps inevitably, their daughter Pilar and son Conor are thoroughly poetic spirits. John also musicks about as a flutist and bassist in the virtual band Car Radio Dog. You can e-mail him at `jtimpane652@aol.com`.

The Poetry Center & American Poetry Archives at San Francisco State University was founded in 1954 on the basis of a gift by W.H. Auden. The Poetry Center is one of the most long-lived, prestigious, and nationally renowned literary arts institutions in the United States. For almost 50 years, since Ruth Witt-Diamant, with esteemed poets Robert Duncan and Josephine Miles, initiated the Poetry Center's pioneering reading series, the Center has presented readings by poets, novelists, and other writers, in accord with the highest standards of literary excellence. The Poetry Center presents readings over two seasons annually, both on- and off-campus, open to the public.

The Poetry Center today operates under the aegis of San Francisco State University's Creative Writing Department, the largest in the country, and represents an irreplaceable collective record of the past half-century of American literary accomplishment. The Poetry Center's American Poetry Archives is a collection of over 2,000 original recordings of poets and writers reading from their work, recorded since the 1950s at Poetry Center readings. The collection includes rare readings by Allen Ginsberg, William Burroughs, Langston Hughes, William Carlos Williams, Marianne Moore, Alice Walker, Anne Sexton, Frank O'Hara, and many other great writers of the past 50 years.

Marina Watts graduated from the University of California San Diego with a B.A. in Communications/Writing and started her career in book publishing as a receptionist at a small publishing company in Berkeley, California. From there, she entered the world of book publicity, marketing, sales, and licensing and became a literary agent. The idea for *Poetry For Dummies* came to her while she was driving across the San Francisco Bay Bridge on a bright day in March. A long-time poetry activist, she was on the board of several non-profit literary arts organizations in the San Francisco Bay Area, including Small Press Traffic Literary Arts Center in the Mission District of San Francisco in the 1990s. She attributes her love for poetry to growing up in the Midwest, spending time in nature, and keeping a poetry journal that has kept her sane since adolescence. She hopes others who read *Poetry For Dummies* might also find inspiration in reading and writing poetry.

Marina was in the graduate writing program at Portland State University and studied intellectual property through Golden Gate School of Law in San Francisco. When publishing went digital in the early 2000s, she became a literary rights agent working for various start-ups in nontraditional digital book formats. She worked remotely as a licensing agent and lived outside Guadalajara, Mexico, for several years and traveled around Mexico. In 2016 she became a mortgage broker in Santa Cruz, California. Marina lives in the Monterey Bay area and spends her free time swimming, traveling, and writing.

Dedication

To our families and to everyone — from Enheduanna to the pair of eyes on these very words — who loves reading and writing poetry. Let *Poetry For Dummies* declare our lifelong thanks.

Author's Acknowledgments

Twenty-five years between editions have brought many changes, both for *Poetry For Dummies* and the world it seeks to capture. We are delighted to re-thank all the people we thanked in the First Edition; they all are still deeply reflected in this new one. Renewed, loving thanks to Marina Watts, whose early initiative was crucial in restarting this school bus. We are especially thrilled that writer, teacher, translator, and poet Andrew Joron of the Department of Creative Writing at San Francisco State University was our liaison this time around with the Poetry Center at SFSU. Andrew led us to a wealth of resources, especially the treasures of the American Poetry Archives at the Poetry Center. He was also a sharp-eyed, insightful reader, editor, and contributor as the school bus rounded the bend. Thanks and thanks again to Carmen Krikorian, Shannon Kucaj, Kristie Pyles, Alicia Sparrow, and Colleen Diamond at Wiley Publishers, especially Colleen, who took the brunt of having to work most closely with John; the book shows the happy results. As any authors do, we owe a particular debt of thanks to our book designers. We are beyond thrilled to thank so many new people for their contributions to *Poetry For Dummies*, 2nd Edition. First shouts go out to poets Mark Danowsky of ONE ART, Benjamin Davis of chill subs, and Diane Lockward, proprietor of Terrapin Press, for graciously sitting for interviews. Poets and teachers Valerie Fox and Lynn Levin, authors of *Poems for the Writing: Prompts for Poets*, opened up their brilliant prompts and explanations to our readers. Karen Chase, Luray Gross, and Don Riggs let us use their poems and told us about their creative processes. Melanie Soiset-Weldon was truly kind and patient in helping us present an excerpt from her marvelous cento "A Lullaby Patchwork Quilt," and Haleh Liza Gafori helped us present her sparkling translation of "You found me once again" by Rūmī. A very special individual thanks to Hayden Saunier for so kindly sharing her *draft* titled "City Bus," her published *result* titled "City Bus," and her invaluable discussions of her method and choices in getting from one to the next. More special thanks goes to J. Keith Vincent, Associate Professor in the Department of World Languages and Literatures at Boston University, for his encouragement and help with our feature on `genjipoems.org`. Three-way gratitude goes to poet Ernest Hilbert, artist Patrick McCuen, and Richard De Wyngaert, for helping us reproduce a wondrous poster advertising a singular, memorable night of poetry. Among the many poets who happily shared their work and workings were Charles Carr, Joseph Chelius, Lauren Fedorko, Ross Gay, Ernest Hilbert again, Anne Kaier, Vasiliki Katsarou, Susan Stewart, and Evan Wang. Maria-Christina Keller, Peter Krok, Joanne Leva, and Taylor Ross contributed photographic resources and good cheer. The Poetry Center at San Francisco State was, of course, our major collaborator in getting *PFD2* all the way to school, but many other organizations and venues also deserve thanks, including Barnes and Noble Princeton, Farley's Bookstore, Fergie's Pub, Head House Books, Labyrinth Books of Princeton, the Library of Congress, the Manayunk Arts Center, Moonstone Publishing, No River Twice, Shanti Arts LLC, the U.S. National Parks Service, the U.S. Navy, the Volta Center of Writing Arts at Bucks County Community College, and YouthSpeaks. All those named here, along with many others, have shown us time and again that poets are often wonderful people and that poetry is for everyone.

Acknowledgments for the first edition:

Creating *Poetry For Dummies* has taught us that collaboration is the best part of writing. We'd be amiss not to thank all who helped us nose this project over the finish line.

First, thanks go to the Poetry Center at San Francisco State University. Frances Phillips and Professor Robert Glück, board members at the Poetry Center, played instrumental roles in getting this book written, commenting on the manuscript, suggesting poems, and, in many cases, rewriting things until they worked. Special thanks go to Robert Glück for his hard work, particularly with the section titled "Experimental poetry" in Chapter 7, and to Steve Dickison, executive director, and the staff at the Poetry Center, who opened the Center's resources to us. Special thanks go to Dr. Robert A. Corrigan, President of San Francisco State University, and Maxine Chernoff, chair of the Creative Writing Department at SFSU.

Our friends and editors at Hungry Minds, Inc., saved our necks at many a parlous turn. Elizabeth Kuball, our faithful and brilliant editor, teamed with Kathy Cox, Karen Young, Joyce Pepple, Roxane Cerda, Carmen Krikorian, and Susan Decker kept us on track all the way. Kathy Welton and Hollie McGuire first said "yes" and remained steadfast and enthusiastic from the very beginning. Our technical editor was Paul Hoover of Columbia College Chicago; his kind and patient comments made this a much better book.

Thanks also to Willis Barnstone, Damion Searls, Jerome Rothenberg, Pierre Joris, Dana Gioia, Laura Moriarty, and Chris Satullo for generous and indispensable assistance; Lawrence Ferlinghetti, Ed Taylor, and Michael Warr, for reading the manuscript; the Amherst College Archives and Special Collections; the Allen Ginsberg Trust; the National Poetry Association; Scott Tambert of PD Images.com; David Huang, Rob Lee, Chris Felver, and Emily Grossman for their photographs; Richard Linker, Brian Rowling, Marjorie Rauen; and Roberta Greifer and Lea Rude, librarians at the Noe Valley Library for their research assistance; and Charles Bernstein, Maxine Chernoff, Kelly Holt, Daniel J. Langton, Bernadette Mayer, Brighde Mullins, and Eileen Myles for their permission to use their writing exercises. Watts thanks Timpane, and Timpane thanks Watts.

Special thanks goes to Elizabeth Vahlsing and Tom Southern of Boaz Press, who let Timpane out of his cage long enough to type up the book, and to Chris Van Buren and Nancy Webb for special guidance and never-ending support.

Publisher's Acknowledgments

Associate Acquisitions Editor: Alica Sparrow
Development Editor: Colleen Diamond
Copy Editor: Colleen Diamond
Editorial Assistant: Shannon Kucaj
Senior Managing Editor: Kristie Pyles
Production Editor: Athiyappan Lalith Kumar
Cover Image: © mizar_21984/stock.adobe.com